LAND OF THE
RADIOACTIVE MIDNIGHT SUN

SEAN MICHAEL FLYNN

LAND OF THE
RADIOACTIVE MIDNIGHT SUN

A Cheechako's First Year in Alaska

THOMAS DUNNE BOOKS
St. Martin's Press ⚚ New York

THOMAS DUNNE BOOKS.
An imprint of St. Martin's Press.

www.stmartins.com

Design by Kathryn Parise

Library of Congress Cataloging-in-Publication Data
Flynn, Sean Michael.
    Land of the radioactive midnight sun : a Cheechako's first year in Alaska /
Sean Michael Flynn.—1st ed.
        p.   cm.
    ISBN 0-312-28554-X
    1. Flynn, Sean Michael.   2. Fairbanks Region (Alaska)—Biography.
3. Fairbanks Region (Alaska)—Description and travel.   4. Fairbanks
Region (Alaska)—Social life and customs.   5. Bush pilots—Alaska—Fairbanks
Region—Biography.   6. United States, Air Force—Biography.   7. Alaska—
Description and travel.   8. Alaska—Social life and customs.
    I. Title.

F914.F16F58 2003
979.8'6—dc21

                                                                                2003046876

First Edition: November 2003

10   9   8   7   6   5   4   3   2   1

For Lori Ann

CONTENTS

☼ Contents

LAND OF THE
RADIOACTIVE MIDNIGHT SUN

☼ ☼ ☼ ☼ ☼ ☼ ☼ ☼ ☼ ☼ ☼ ☼

INTRODUCTION
Buying Chicken Nuggets with Gold Nuggets

Somewhere, thousands of miles from your house, is Alaska. On a TV weather map, if it's there at all, Alaska is usually floating somewhere below California and New Mexico—just to the right of Hawaii. It's an altogether different kind of place: a wild place of never-ending nights, of subzero cold, of icy rivers, and of grizzly bears. A place populated by Eskimos and icebergs and roughnecks and oil wells. A place crossed by dogsleds in the winter and kayaks in the summer. Only the roughest of the rough and the toughest of the tough can survive that kind of place.

It's big, too. I mean *really* big—it is almost one-fifth the size of the continental United States. If it were superimposed on a map of the continent, the Alaska land mass would stretch from New York to Los Angeles. Yet most of the state is virgin wilderness. Alaska has 34,000 miles of shoreline—more than the combined coasts of the rest of the country. It has 17 of the nation's 20 highest peaks and 65 mountains taller than 10,000 feet. There are 3,000 rivers in Alaska, and the Yukon is the third longest in America. Glaciers, an estimated 100,000 of them, cover one-fifth of the state. More than 70 active volcanoes fume on her land.

There's something primordial in the word "Alaska," something Darwinistic. The simple idea (and we know this from watching movies) that death lurks behind every snowy pass makes the blood run cold. Those who have gone there and returned alive become deities in the eyes and minds of the men and women around them. "It was nothing," he shrugs. "You'd have done the same thing if a grizzly stole your Mets hat." Of course, nobody can challenge his story, because so few of us have actually been to Alaska. He's like the eight-year-old boy who lectured the other kids about sex because he was the only one with a *Playboy.*

Even though we haven't been to the place the Natives call the "Great Land," we know all about the extreme cold, the savage wolves, the Kodiak bears, the king salmon, the glaciers, the permafrost, and the pipeline. We know all about it from Jack London books and the Discovery Channel and John Wayne's *North to Alaska* and that cool show *Northern Exposure* with the cranky Jewish doctor and philosophical disc jockey. We're not exactly sure how or when Alaska became a state, but we know that the highest point in North America is in Alaska—Mt. McKinley. We had to memorize that in junior high. We enjoy watching coverage from the Iditarod dogsled race every spring on ESPN. Of course, we all have an Uncle Frank and Aunt Mary who went to Alaska on a cruise a couple of years ago. They loved it.

Alaska: It captivates our minds like no other state in America. Indeed, it is all that we have imagined, but at the same time, it is also so much *less.* Jack London lived in Alaska and the Yukon for less than a year. *North to Alaska* was filmed in California, and *Northern Exposure* was shot somewhere near Seattle.

Beyond the films and the books, beyond the fancy travel ads made by the tourism industry, and beyond the hype—there is Alaska. It is a land of unending beauty and uncompromising weather, of hardy souls scraping a living against Mother Nature's wrath, of adventure and frontier spirit—all serviced by dozens of fast food chains, gourmet coffee shops, used car dealerships, department stores, and bars. Alaska: Where else can you mush your dog team through a McDonald's drive-through window?

One Who Licks Cold Metal Objects

I arrived in Alaska in typical American fashion—stridently confident, but exceptionally unprepared. It was December. I didn't own a jacket, the warmest pants I had were a pair of ripped blue jeans, and I hadn't yet installed the hardware that would prevent my vehicle's engine from freezing solid at temperatures colder than 10 or 20 degrees below zero. It was already much colder. Longtime Alaskans could peg me for a cheechako easier than they could identify their own mothers.

In New York City, a cheechako (chee-CHA-ko) would be the kid who just fell off the turnip truck: no street smarts, a pink windbreaker, a subway map sticking from his back pocket, and some guy running away with his brand-new camera. In Alaska, a cheechako is even easier to spot. He's the guy with his tongue stuck to a metal pole, a tenderfoot, a greenhorn. The word "cheechako" finds its roots in the Alaskan gold rush. Back then, a new guy would remain a cheechako until he survived his first year—or died trying. If he lived, he could then boast that he was finally an Alaskan. If he died, his frozen corpse would be preserved forever in the permafrost, sort of like being buried in concrete under Giants Stadium.

Despite the proliferation of modern conveniences on the Last Frontier, cheechakos like me still have a lot to worry about. Every year scores of newcomers fall victim to animal attacks, car wrecks, hiking accidents, and just plain stupidity. After one week in Alaska I hoped I wouldn't be next. I wanted to graduate from the status of cheechako to that of Alaskan overnight, but the half million or so people who currently held the title "Alaskan" were not likely to bestow the honor upon me for just showing up. Tradition demanded that I spend twelve months on probation, and even then it wasn't a lock. There are some who survive a year but are never accepted among Alaskans as peers. They become outcasts, city slickers on an extended vacation. I, on the other hand, was intent on making it. Only I didn't know how to hunt. I didn't like the taste of fish. I couldn't grow any facial hair. I didn't really know how to fix things. I had a major aversion to outhouses. And I had a suntan. Worst of all, I was from New York, a place so far from Alaska in both geography and culture that a common language couldn't begin to bridge the gap. Time would have to tell.

DECEMBER

Rednecks, Roughnecks, and a Guy
Named Catfish

Things to Do When it's 30 Degrees Below Zero

Fairbanks in December is miserable. It's too cold to ski, not that there are any real hills to do it on anyway. It's too cold to make a snowman or a snowball or a snow fort. Snow angels are out of the question. It's too cold to go out to dinner, even if you could get your car started. It's too cold to kiss or rub noses or hold mittens. It's too cold to wear anything from the L. L. Bean winter catalog. It's dark, too, virtually around the clock. When it's not dark, a thick fog made of frozen auto and power plant emissions lowers visibility to a couple of yards. Fairbanks in December is too cold and too dark to do just about anything except lie under the covers with a flask of whiskey and dream about hell.

Of course, all of that assumes the people of Fairbanks are sane. They are not. For starters, normal people don't live in a place where you have to plug your car in when you get home at night so it will start again in the morning. They don't live in a place where outhouses outnumber convenience stores. They don't live in a place where the equivalent of softball in the park is a leisurely rugby game played in temperatures colder than 30 below zero on a frozen river that doubles as a highway for most of the year.

These were my thoughts as I drove into town around noon on December 10, my first Saturday in Alaska. That morning the temperature had gone up from 40 below zero to 30 below, yet the heater in my truck still failed to keep me warm. It was just starting to get light outside when I hit the Fairbanks town line. This was one of my first real looks at Alaska. For a guy who knew the state from documentaries on the Discovery Channel, the vista was pretty lame.

No giant mountains, no streams or rivers, no picturesque cabins, no grizzly—there was just a straight, flat road cut through a wilderness of spruce trees. I assumed they were spruce, but the thin trees actually looked more like bottle washers. The woods broke as I crossed the flood plain for the Tanana River. The clearing provided a hint of the *other* Alaska; a row of barely visible mountain peaks rose from the south. After a few more miles, the main feature of the drive presented itself. It was the village of North Pole, where a fifty-foot Santa Claus beckoned me to go Christmas shopping. As I approached Fairbanks, more houses appeared. I expected solid structures that could ward off the cold and heavy snow, but the houses seemed little different from shacks I had seen in small towns in the Lower 48. Then there was the junk. Broken-down cars and appliances and other industrial equipment was peeking out from the blanket of snow on the road-side. Fast food wrappers cluttered the shoulders. As I approached Fairbanks, the road began to buckle under my tires. Frost heaves. The frozen ground under the highway had thawed in some places, causing the road to ripple like a washboard. I exited for the Mitchell Expressway. Fairbanks lay sprawled out to my right. Instead of seeing some arctic village of log cabins, I saw an industrial-looking town that could have been in Ohio: parking lots with trucks, small bars with neon signs, a half dozen strip malls, traffic clogging the streets, and auto exhaust misting the air.

I didn't go into the town center that day. My destination was a restaurant on the outskirts of Fairbanks, near the airport. Pike's Landing stood on the edge of the Chena River, and it was the meeting point for the big rugby game. Eager to experience

Alaska, I had told a couple of guys I met the night before that I would play.

It's always tense entering a strange bar in a strange land alone. When you open the door, you expect the piano player to stop the music and a wild man with an unkempt beard to spit tobacco at your feet. Fortunately, I figured, there wouldn't be a large bar crowd around noon. I was wrong. The place was packed to the gills with giant men and women sporting Kmart-style flannel and well-worn Carhartts. Most of them were well past their first round. As far as I could tell, I was the only one who showed up looking for a rugby game. Everyone else appeared to be there for an Elks Club meeting or a cockfight.

Several people looked at me when I walked in. Satisfied I wasn't the game warden, they immediately turned back to their drinks. I casually walked up to the bar as if I had been there a hundred times before. I wanted to order a hard drink to fit in with the gun club atmosphere, but since I was expecting to play rugby, I ordered a Coke. Maybe everyone would think there was rum in it. I tried not to stare around the place but couldn't resist looking at the collection of dead animals on the walls. There was a giant moose head, grizzly furs, ram and caribou heads, some birds, some fish, and some other creatures I didn't recognize.

The guy on my right was staring at me through a set of deeply sunken eyes. Even though he was seated, I could tell he was a monster, probably responsible for a couple of the grizzly furs on the walls. He looked to be in his forties—but then again, so do a lot of Alaskan high school students. His shoulders and thick beard suggested he might be a lumberjack. He held a full pint of beer in his hand. There were several empty pint glasses in front of him and what appeared to be a well-used knife on his belt. He seemed like the kind of guy who was raised by a woman with an eye patch and a bad limp, the kind of guy who would be barred from the White House tour just for the way he looked. He was, in short, one of the most intimidating men I had ever seen. I avoided his stare the best I could. As I looked down at my shrinking manhood, I saw a rugby bag next to his feet on the floor.

"You here for the game?" he asked.

Please, please, please don't be a rugby player. "Which game is that?"

"The rugby game. We should be getting started in a bit."

Okay, stay calm. There's an airport close by. You could head for the door and book the next flight back to someplace warm, someplace without chandeliers made from antlers. It's not like you have to play the game. The worst thing that will happen to you is that someone might call you a girly man. So what if word gets around that you really don't have the stuff. Better to quit now and run away and live to play some other day—in some other state with a lot of midgets. Right? Or you could stop being a wimp and just play. You said you wanted to experience Alaska. Well, here's your chance, bub. Whatever happens, happens. If it gets real bad, you can always fake an injury.

"So what do you say?"

"Yes. Yes, I am. I am here for the rugby game. The rugby game on the ice. Outside where it's thirty below."

"Hey, it might warm up some. Might get up to twenty-five below."

His name was J. D. Williams, and he was a longtime Fairbanks rugby player—as were most of the hard-drinking frontiersmen in the bar. I chatted with him for several minutes while waiting for the guys whom I had met earlier in the week. They were Air Force officers like me and easy to spot because they were the only ones in the place without beards or large scars caused by industrial equipment.

Kevin Groff was the first to arrive. He was a little more at home at Pike's than I was. In addition to having been in Fairbanks for a year, Groff bonded with the Alaskan rugby players, who were similar in many ways to the people from his hometown in the remote reaches of Virginia—a place where kissing your sister after a couple of drinks doesn't seem like that bad an idea. Groff was a tobacco-chewin', God-fearin', squirrel-shootin', monster-truck-drivin', go-to-Florida-on-your-honeymoon kind of guy. Despite a keen lack of social grace and a flagrant disregard for any sort of political correctness, Groff is the kind of person you keep around if you never learned to change your car's oil, fix your plumbing, or just plain build shit. I had met him on the night I arrived in Fairbanks three days before.

"Welcome to Alaska," Groff said. "I heard you play rugby. That's good. We have a team here in Fairbanks. I also heard you haven't winterized your car yet. That's bad. Go buy a block heater and have someone put that in. I will put everything else in for you." Since it was clear to Groff that I had never done anything that required a pipe wrench or plumb bob, he immediately took me on as a charity case.

Doug Nikolai arrived a bit later. Nikolai, call sign "Stoli," was an F-16 pilot. He had been in Alaska for a couple of years and was a veteran ice rugby player. It was obvious to me early on that Stoli had gone native. Not only did he drink like an Alaskan, he dressed like one. Let's contrast Stoli's ice rugby gear with mine. I wore a pair of regular long johns, another pair of insulated polypropylene, and a pair of sweatpants. On top, I had a similar arrangement with a rugby shirt over everything else. I wore a wool cap pulled low over my head and a pair of mittens that made it virtually impossible to carry the ball. Stoli wore shorts and a rugby shirt. Did I mention that it was 30 below and that the game was on the ice?

Of course, my attire was much more appropriate than Stoli's. I would be warmer. My skin would be more protected. It was less likely that I would get hurt. It was the sane thing to do. This was Fairbanks in December, though, and sanity goes out the window. Far from being committed, Stoli was praised for his "toughness." He wasn't just another wimpy Air Force guy in town for a year. He had become an Alaskan, tougher than the next guy, independent, afraid of nothing. Stoli did it by wearing only shorts, but other Alaskans were praised that day for having a bigger truck than the next guy, for drinking more beer than anyone else on the planet, or for having a thicker beard than Santa Claus. By the end of the day, I began to sense that my manhood was on trial every minute—and that I was failing miserably.

The game started an hour late. The group of twenty-five players crowding the bar was divided into two teams: the Sundawgs and the Wild Hares. Everyone had consumed several drinks at the bar by the time we headed for the ice—everyone except me, which basically made me look more like a wimp. However, these guys weren't just drinking for the taste of it; they were premedicating themselves for a level of pain I was not accustomed to.

Getting tackled on the snow and ice in 30-below temperatures hurts, but breathing the arctic air is like swallowing lye; it was impossible to catch your breath. I couldn't talk or breathe normally for more than a week after the game. I had played sports in the cold during New York winters; after you moved around for a little, you tended to warm up. In Fairbanks in December, you never get warm.

The first half ended when we paused to let several trucks pass over the frozen river. At halftime, both teams made it back inside the bar for more warming liquor. This time I had no reservations. Despite a couple of drinks, however, the second half of the game was as painful as the first, and I thanked God as the daylight faded so we couldn't play anymore. Stoli, the Air Force pilot turned Alaskan, was the big hero of the day. Despite his frozen, bloody legs, he had managed to score three trys (a touchdown in rugby), leading the Sundawgs to victory. There was much celebration, but to be honest, I didn't really care. I only wanted to get warm, which seemed the sane—albeit wimpy—thing to do.

Staking Claim to the Northern Lights

Obsession with the extreme cold is common among newcomers who first reach Alaska in the winter. The cold cuts through layers, and the air seems unfit for breathing, causing a reaction that can only be described as "cold shock" for newcomers as they first step outside at Fairbanks Airport. Many people gag on the temperature as if they are suffocating and immediately retreat to the comfort of the airport lobby. It wouldn't matter if you were driving by a burning building or a dozen nude cheerleaders. Nothing can take away from the feeling of cold and the small voice in the back of your head that wonders if you can survive in this place at all.

Then one day, Stoli advised, you finally get over the shock. *It's bone-chilling cold here, and there's nothing I can do about it.* That same day, an entire new Alaska opens up before your eyes, an arctic Eden that is both forbidding and inviting at the same time. I thought that moment *almost* came for me on my drive home from the rugby game.

Since arriving in country that week, I had been pining to see the aurora borealis. The aurora, or northern lights, occurs when the solar wind blows across Earth's magnetic field, generating electrical energy in the form of charged particles in the atmosphere about sixty miles above the surface. When these particles strike molecules in the atmosphere, the air glows, creating an awesome show for anyone in the northern reaches of the planet. Famed Alaskan poet Robert Service described the aurora in his *Ballad of the Northern Lights:* "They danced a cotillion in the sky; they were rose and silver shod/ It was not good for the eyes of man—'twas a sight for the eyes of God." However it's described, one thing is certain: The aurora is truly divine.

One minute, the sky showed only stars. Moments later, a glow caught my eye, and there, encroaching from the north toward me, was the aurora. Even though I had seen pictures of the lights, I was unprepared for their rhythmic beauty. Two contrails of blue-green light originated at the far north horizon and danced their way ever closer until they commanded the night sky. The colors were celestial, more brilliant than any pattern ever seen on the ground—something from *Fantasia,* perhaps: animation added to a normal night sky, a painter splashing the colors on with a brush in a long arc that extended beyond the horizon.

I had to pull the truck over and gawk at the lights. Opening the window, I no longer felt the cold and pain that had consumed me only minutes before. My chest welled up, and I lamented that not everyone in the world could be there with me admiring this newfound beauty of Alaska. Even as I mused, though, other cars flew by me, seemingly oblivious to the sight I was watching. A disturbing thought hit me. *Will I become immune to this beauty? Will I be like those people just driving by? Maybe I'm like the tourists who marvel at the skyscrapers in Manhattan on their first visit while the New Yorkers impatiently push their way by. Do real Alaskans ever stop to look at the aurora? Or is it just another tall building?*

Back in the Heart of Dixie

You should never eat two Big Macs and supersize fries before flying into a hurricane. Of course, nobody mentioned that to me before I strapped myself into the cargo-net seat of a WC-130 airplane headed for a massive storm that swirled somewhere over the Gulf of Mexico. The plane belonged to the 53rd Weather Reconnaissance Squadron of the 403rd Air Reserve Wing—Mississippi's famous Hurricane Hunters. Their job was to fly in and out and up and down through a hurricane, taking measurements of the storm along the way and making the guy in the back with special sauce on his fingers sick. The mission was twelve hours long, and I thought it would be fun to go along. In retrospect, it was a lot like drinking tequila. It seems like a good idea at the time, but . . .

Drinking was exactly what the first Hurricane Hunters were doing in 1944 when they dared each other to fly through a tropical storm in their AT-6 Texans. Having made two successful flights through the storm, somebody with a sick sense of humor decided it should be a regular thing. The first Hurricane Hunters flew out of Newfoundland in search of perfect storms over the Atlantic. After years of moving and name changes, the unit ultimately found itself at Keesler Air Force Base in Biloxi, Mississippi, the site of Hurricane Camille in 1969, one of the most damaging hurricanes ever to come on land.

I was a public affairs officer at Keesler, and my job during the flight was to escort news crews as they got pictures of the storm from the front lines and interviewed the brave pilots, asking them the right way to hold a barf bag. It was my first flight with the legendary outfit, and I was nervous. Just a few weeks earlier, another public affairs officer was on board when his plane was struck by lightning. Still, I had to go. As a new second lieutenant, I had no "war" stories and desperately needed something to tell the nurse trainees at the base medical center.

The Hurricane Hunters had been dispatched to determine the precise location, motion, strength, and size of a storm that seemed headed toward New Orleans. Flying between 500 and 1,500 feet above the Gulf of Mexico, the news crew was able to get great shots of merchant ships being hammered by the high seas, but the crew's euphoria didn't last. Gaining altitude, we flew directly into the face of the storm and began a crisscross pattern that would have been boring if it hadn't felt like we were being thrown around by the Jolly Green Giant. The only respite occurred when we passed through the eerie calm of the eye.

Aim high! said the man with the blue hat. *It's not just a job, it's an adventure!* There are dozens of moments during military service when you look around at the bizarre or amazing situation you're in and find an inner feeling of satisfaction that you are doing something your buddies at home could never imagine and would never have the opportunity to do. Then again, there are times—like when you're flying through a hurricane and burping up pieces of your lunch—when you come to the profound conclusion that being in the military sucks more than anything else in the world. That's when you ask the age-old question, *Why in God's name did I pass up law school to do this?*

Serving in the military as an officer was something I always wanted to do. Since the Civil War, it seemed, everyone in my family had done it, but mostly I was sold by the Rambo movies in the 1980s. I wanted to lead men in combat, rescue prisoners from far-away jungles, and sit on the beach with nurses somewhere in the South Pacific. There were no wars raging when I entered the University of Maryland, but I made it a point to visit the officer candidate recruiters right away. The Army and Marines certainly looked Rambo-esque. However, the women in the Air Force were much more attractive, a fact I could not simply ignore. Although part of me still wanted to storm the compound with guns blazing, my choice of military service pretty much guaranteed I'd be more of a lover than a fighter. (Actually, the Marines just call me a wimp.) My eyes were too weak for flying, so the Air Force ultimately matched my journalism degree with the service's need for a public affairs officer in Mississippi—a career choice that would have been the equivalent of castration for John Rambo.

Keesler Air Force Base was far from the exotic locations I had requested while an ROTC cadet, but it was far enough from my native New York to be considered an alien culture. My supervisor, Don Wylie, tried to prepare me with a letter.

"Mississippi, for some folks, appears to be at the end of the world, but I am a native New Yorker who came here forty years ago, and I wouldn't live anywhere else," he wrote. "To some it is a culture shock, but I can assure you that you will get to know a bunch of great people who live along the Gulf Coast."

If only they could read. Mississippi's public schools are perennially ranked last or second-to-last in the nation. "Dixie" is every school's fight song, and "Respect for the Confederate Battle Flag 101" is a required course for all white Christians. Perhaps I should have been more prepared. Before I departed from my parents' home in New York, Don called me.

"Are you a Catholic?" he asked, pronouncing it Cath-oh-lick.

"Why, yes. Is that a problem?"

"Oh, no. Just tell your mama that the KKK hasn't been a problem here for years."

In his letter, Don mentioned the culture shock. He was right, but Biloxi was growing up. A few years earlier, the town had been given the okay to build casinos, and gaming was changing the culture of the Gulf Coast at a rapid rate. Better education would have helped, too, but the city of Biloxi was spending its newfound wealth on roads, not schools.

Despite the darker side of the South, there were plenty of joys in Mississippi and at Keesler. New Orleans was a quick drive away, and, while I may have disliked flying into hurricanes, I certainly enjoyed drinking them on Bourbon Street. The Biloxi casinos were a fun place to lose money. It never got too cold on the coast, and let's not forget the nurse trainees.

Then again, I was a very bad gambler, and the two Air Force nurses who moved in next door to me were male—at least they looked male. For those reasons, and because it was hot as hell, I decided to look for a public affairs job someplace a bit more north of the Mason-Dixon line, someplace where gambling was done by Air Force personnel in the air, not in the casino.

First Impressions

Since my departure from Bellingham, Washington, aboard the 408-foot *MV Matanuska*, Alaska had loomed just out of reach for the better part of two days. I saw shoreline mostly, crowded with legions of spruce trees and rock and, through the thick fog it seemed, the glowing eyes of wolves and bear. On the other side of the ship, a woman proclaimed, "Ooh, ooh, ooh!" Everyone recognized that as the universal signal for a humpback whale sighting. The boat listed to the port side as a dozen or so people on board fought for space to watch. There were two whales, one leading, the other following on her wing. They showed above the surface for a while, then disappeared under the ice-black water. With nothing left to take pictures of, the people went back to their seats in the big room with a TV, where *A Walk in the Clouds,* starring Keanu Reeves, was playing for the third time that day.

I found Mike sitting with a group of teenaged girls toward the front of the boat. He was telling his life story to one of the girls, who was pretending that she was old enough to actually get to know the guy. He broke contact with her when I sat down.

"She's like ten," I said.

"Fifteen at least."

Mike was also in the Air Force; he was an aircraft technician who was heading to one of the squadrons at Elmendorf Air Force Base in Anchorage. I met him the day we left port. Although I never got his last name, we became shipboard soulmates.

"Should be getting into town soon," I said.

"Which one?"

"I think it's Wrangell."

"What's the book say?"

I had picked up the *Alaska Almanac.* It said Wrangell was a "major city, population 2,536."

"I guess that's big up here," Mike said.

After a week of traveling from Mississippi, first by car, now by ferry, I could barely wait to touch Alaskan soil. All I had read about the place, all I had heard from people who had been there, and all I knew from watching *Northern Exposure* convinced me that I was heading to someplace more amazing and quirky and dangerous and beautiful than any other in the world. Would I see an Eskimo? Would there be totem poles? Would there be a moose in the street? Worse yet—what about a bear!

John Muir, the famous naturalist and founder of the Sierra Club, described Wrangell in 1879 as "the most inhospitable place" he had ever seen.

> The Wrangell village was a rough place. No mining hamlet in the placer gulches of California, nor any backwoods village I ever saw, approached it in picturesque, devil-may-care abandon. It was a lawless draggle of wooden huts and houses, built in crooked lines, wrangling about the boggy shore of the island for a mile or so in the general form of the letter *S*, without the slightest subordination to the points of the compass or to building laws of any kind.

The weather was not great. A misting rain hung in the air. A two-foot layer of snow was visible on the ground. The man standing at the ramp that led to the dock cautioned Mike and me against slipping. We acknowledged him, then both slipped halfway down the gangway. It was a half-mile walk into the devil-may-care town, and Mike and I headed off for our first taste of Alaska.

Wrangell did not seem to be a "major" anything, and it was far from the lawless morass Muir described. The streets were deserted save for a passing pickup truck without license plates. Fog hung just above the roofs. The houses seemed normal enough. The pizza place we sat in could have been in New York (in looks, not quality). In general, my first stop in Alaska seemed about as unremarkable as a stop in Iowa.

"Hey, the pizza's ready," Mike shouted to me as I gazed disappointedly around the streets.

"How much is it?"

"Thirty bucks."

"No, seriously. How much?"

"It's thirty freakin' bucks, man."

Perhaps Muir was right. Wrangell was a lawless draggle. We dejectedly boarded the ship, hoping that the next town along the way might show us the *real* Alaska, the one I had heard so much about.

The Only Volunteer

A cable-channel documentary provided me with my first up-close look at the Air Force in Alaska. Camera crews captured F-15 fighters as they soared off the runway, silhouetted by impossibly tall mountains. There were features on the military in Alaska and stories about the people, land, and wildlife of the state. I had already started looking for a new assignment when the documentary aired. After I saw the pictures of Alaska on TV, I knew for sure where I wanted to go—Elmendorf Air Force Base.

On the outskirts of Anchorage, Elmendorf, known as Elmo, had every modern convenience and was within easy reach of all that Alaska had to offer. I met several people in Mississippi who had served at Elmo. Each one of them loved it and hoped to get stationed there again. Mike was excited, too. He spent a good deal of time on the ferry looking in real estate magazines for homes in Anchorage. "Man," he said, "I've heard some people go there and never leave."

The problem was that there were no openings at Elmo for a public affairs officer. "Don't worry, lieutenant, there's an opening for an officer at Eielson."

Eielson Air Force Base was the *other* base in Alaska. About four hundred miles north of Anchorage, Eielson was in the forbidding interior. There were no big mountains there, no good fishing, and no good hiking. The nearest city was Fairbanks, an outfitting town for the remote reaches of Alaska. There were only about thirty-five thousand people in Fairbanks—most of them men, or women who looked like men. It was cold there, too cold to go outside, and it was dark most of the year. "You've got to be screwed up in the head to go there," one airman told me. "If you're not . . . you will be when you leave."

Surely it can't be as bad as Mississippi. I applied for the position.

"We've got a good feeling about you. We think you're the right person for the job," Captain Sandy Troeber, the chief of public affairs at Eielson, said to me over the phone. She neglected to mention that I was the only one who volunteered.

Still No Sign of Alaska

Back on the boat, Mike tried to assure me it would be okay. "You will be hating life. Elmo is where it's at." What a pal.

"He's right, you know," said a woman standing nearby. "Fairbanks stinks. Nobody even goes there to visit, let alone live there."

Joe McGinniss described Fairbanks in his 1980 book *Going to Extremes* as a blue-collar town filled with teamsters, drunkards, and pimps. "There were drugs and whores and trailer camps, and disputes among residents were less likely to be settled in small claims court than by small-caliber—or large-caliber—pistol." *Hmmm. My new home.*

Fairbanks was still a long way off as the *Matanuska* pulled up to the dock at Petersburg, the next town on my journey to Alaska. Founded in 1897 by a bunch of Norwegians, Petersburg was a rough fishing town with little to offer for a couple of Air Force guys, but Mike insisted that we stroll into town and see if we could find a local bar. Like any good military man, Mike figured he had a chance to meet the love of his life (and get some action) in the ninety minutes we were docked in the town.

As in Wrangell, there was nothing to see, this time because of the darkness. It was about nine P.M. when we sauntered into a bar that bristled with crab traps and those little striped buoys that New Englanders tie to their mailboxes. It was dark inside, the only light coming from a neon Rainier Beer sign and a plastic lamp hanging over the pool table. There were a few women there, but based on the snarls from the fishermen, they were clearly not available. I ordered two Alaskan Amber beers from the bar, then met Mike over at the pool table. There was already a game racked up on the tabletop. Mike picked up a pool cue.

" 'Ain't your game," one of the fishermen said from the darkness. (This is the scene in the movie when all the locals surround the out-of-towners.)

"Let's go," I whispered.

Mike agreed. We quickly left behind a couple of half-full beers and headed back to the ship just in time for its departure. It seemed we would have to wait for the next village to really see Alaska.

With hundreds of island communities and no roads connecting them, southeastern Alaskans rely heavily on the Alaska Marine Highway System to get around. The ferry runs year-round from Washington State and British Columbia to dozens of towns along the coast. Many travelers use the ferries as an inexpensive alternative to the cruise ships that ply the same waters. It cost more than a thousand dollars to ship me and my car, however, so I was glad the generous taxpayers of America were footing the bill.

We docked at Juneau the next morning. Shoehorned into a strip of land at the base of sheer mountains, Juneau is the sea-and-mountain-locked capital of Alaska. Founded on Joe Juneau's gold mine in 1880, the city became the capital of the territory in 1912. At the time, Juneau was the gateway for the gold fields in the Klondike. Since the rise of Anchorage and Fairbanks in the 1970s, Juneau's significance has dwindled. In 1974, the state voted to move the capital to a central location between Fairbanks and Anchorage. However, the funding was never allotted, and as late as November 2002, voters reaffirmed Juneau's standing as the capital. And a good thing, too. If not for its role in governing, this city of thirty thousand might be little bigger than Wrangell or Petersburg today.

The weather in Juneau was clear, affording me a good view of the mountains that rose steeply from sea level a few hundred yards from the shoreline. There were two of them, Mt. Roberts on the right and Mt. Juneau on the left. A blanket of snow extended from them down to the street level. Mike and I walked from the ferry terminal to the downtown area, which could have been Any City USA if it weren't for the odd totem pole or grizzly bear statue.

Finally, we thought, *the real Alaska. A glacier on the mountain! A totem pole just like in the videos! A grizzly statue! The distinctive Alaskan flag with the Big Dipper! An old gold-mining saloon! A McDonald's! Two of them! And a Burger King and Pizza Hut and Taco Bell and Subway! This is great! We can eat!*

Alaska finally presented us its majestic mountains and native culture and glaciers and everything that makes the place a frontier. Nevertheless, after two days of shipboard food and one pizza of questionable quality from Wrangell, Mike and I headed straight for the Golden Arches and expended what little shore leave we had. Our voyage was almost complete; later that day, we would disembark for the last time in the town of Haines, the armpit where southeast and south-central Alaska meet. After some crisp fries and a Coke, we strolled back to the ferry terminal and left perhaps the most historic and beautiful city in Alaska without writing a lyrical ballad or even taking a picture. In doing so, however, we were no less eloquent than John Muir, who, in his *Travels in Alaska*, wrote that "Juneau, on the mainland opposite the Douglas Island mills, is quite a village, well supplied with stores, churches, etc." Muir stopped in the town, got some travel information from the locals, and went on his way. Had there been a McDonald's when Muir visited, I expect he would have had a bite to eat, too.

The Road Less Traveled

The ferry pulled into Haines around two P.M. on December 3. Two days of hard driving lay ahead. Back in Mississippi I had picked up a Ford Bronco from a very reputable used car dealer named Catfish, a chain smoker with bad teeth, sweaty armpits, and plaid pants.

"This here nineteen-hundred and ninety-one Bronco is about all you need. She's only got but a hunnerd and sixty-five thousand miles on her, she's got four-wheel drive, and I could probably let her go for about ten thousand dollars." Which came to about $175,342 after the trade-in and the interest. It made me sick to pay that much for anything, but the truck looked pretty cool.

I stopped at an auto parts store in Haines to buy a few emergency items for the trip. I had already bought tire chains for the truck, but I wanted to get some more oil, a fan belt, a towrope, a saw, and an air freshener in case I had to eat moose or grizzly or something else that didn't agree with me. The man at the auto parts store asked me where I was headed.

"Eielson," I said.

"I hear they got a cold snap. Your truck winterized?"

Before I left Mississippi, I was given stern warnings from several sources to winterize my truck. Accordingly, I bought several items to heat various parts of the vehicle—a battery blanket, an oil pan heater, a transmission case heater, and an engine block heater. All of these should have been installed before I left, but in my rush to see Alaska, I put it off. After all, I had heard it wasn't that cold yet in Fairbanks. Surely I could have everything installed there.

"You better not turn your truck off at night unless it's real warm."

"Why is that?" I asked.

"You turn it off, your engine block freezes solid. Without that block heater installed, you'll never get it started."

He laughed at me for a little, then recommended I take the truck to a garage as soon as I arrived at Eielson. He also suggested that I place some cardboard in front of my radiator to keep the cold air from blasting it directly. I sheepishly thanked him and considered suggesting that he clean his fingernails and see a dentist.

Haines is the bald eagle capital of the world. About 3,500 of them flock to the town every November to feast upon a group of slow-witted salmon that find their way into the town's streams. There were still several eagles around in early December, and I saw scores of them perched in the trees resting before their next meal. I would have stopped to watch a bit, but Mike and I had joined a convoy that was headed from Haines to the interior.

In just fifty-eight miles, the Haines Highway climbed from sea level to 7,200 feet and crossed into Canada's Yukon Territory. Covered in snow and ice, the road surface was terrible. I switched into four-wheel drive almost immediately. In front of me, Mike's two-wheel-drive economy car fishtailed out of control most of the way.

With the minor exception that I was—for the moment—in

Canada, it was my third day in Alaska, and so far I had seen very little of the Great Land. Now, driving along mountains that seemed on top of the world, I saw even less, my impression of Alaska being shaped by my other senses. With zero visibility at times, I crept forward using the lip on the side of the road as a guide. If I felt my tires fall off on the right, I would adjust, and the same for the left. I was now in the lead, and the others were supposed to follow my taillights closely. Had there been any oncoming traffic, we would have collided. Fortunately for us, only cheechakos drive in that sort of weather. When the snow finally cleared that night, I pulled over and had to wait an hour for the last of our convoy to appear.

We pulled into a motel in the village of Destruction Bay. I parked next to a truck that had passed me rather speedily earlier. It was 20 below zero. Unsure whether my truck could survive at that temperature, I left the engine running. We had all made it to the hotel in one piece and retired to the bar/restaurant for dinner. I wound up playing pool with the guy who owned the speeding truck.

"You guys drive pretty fast on that snow," I said.

"Yeah. You can tell a Yukoner by how fast he drives."

He was not from Destruction Bay but lived and went to school there for the winter. Like many in that part of the Yukon, he said, there was no school near his home, a fact that foreshadowed the remoteness of the far north.

Nobody had ridden off with my truck overnight, so we set out early and made it back to the Alaska border that morning. You didn't need a sign to tell you that you had changed countries. Once we crossed back into Alaska, the road turned into a sea of potholes.

At least that section of the road was paved. There were still some sections of the Alcan that were not. Built in 1942, the Alaska Canada Military Highway stretches 1,422 miles from Dawson

Creek in British Columbia to Delta Junction just east of Fairbanks. The highway was built in just nine months by the U.S. Army. Makes you wonder what the U.S. government is *really* capable of.

Our convoy remained intact until we reached Tok, where the second of Alaska's four major roads led south to Anchorage. Mike and I stopped at a gas station to bid each other farewell. It was a quick good-bye as the −30 temperature drove us back to our cars. While Mike headed for the warmth and excitement of Anchorage, I placed a call to my future boss, Sandy Troeber, to tell her where I was.

"Get a hotel," she said. "It's too cold to drive in here tonight. It's about forty below."

With only two hundred more miles left on my five-thousand-mile journey, it was hard to sit still. "Yes, ma'am. I'll drive a bit and find a place to stay if it gets too cold." In other words, *I'll see you around five.*

A few frigid hours later, the mileage counter indicated that I should be getting close to Eielson. If I was, I couldn't tell. A thick cloud of fog blocked me from seeing more than a few feet in front of me. It was now colder than −40. Several cars appeared mysteriously from a road on my right. Taking a chance, I turned down the road and stopped the Bronco near a barely visible guard shack and visitors center. I stepped out into the fierce cold and headed to the center, where I twisted open the metal doorknob with my bare hand. That was a big mistake. It initially felt like I had grabbed hold of a hot iron. I jerked my hand away, but it was too late. For the rest of the day my hand throbbed in pain from the cold metal. It was December 5 and a balmy 43 degrees below zero. The word "cold" does not describe what that temperature feels like, but the sound of someone screaming in pain might.

January

Authentic Frontier Plumbing

More Oxygen for Me

Forty below zero. Yet the pedestrian I was about to pass on the Richardson Highway was wearing only a T-shirt and jeans. *A cheechako dumber than me?* There wasn't a home, a bar, or any other vehicles around. *What was this guy thinking?* I pulled the Bronco over to give the moron a ride. He opened the door as if he had been expecting me. The strong smell of alcohol followed him into the truck.

"What the hell are you doing? It's forty below. You don't even have a jacket on," I said.

"Nothing."

"You know you could die out there like that."

"Whatever."

He was maybe seventeen or eighteen and too drunk to comprehend what I was talking about.

"Where are you going? I'll drive you there."

"It's up the road a bit."

It was actually about five miles up the highway and down a snow-covered dirt road that led to a couple of small homes. He got out and walked to one of them without thanking me. Had I not picked him up, the combination of alcohol and extreme temperature would have ensured that he never made it to his next six-pack.

If you watch *Friday the 13th* movies, you know not to pick up hitchhikers. In New York, and most everywhere else I had lived, people followed the rule pretty well. With a large population of ex-criminals, rugby players, and other malcontents looking for a new life in Alaska, you would think the hitchhiker rule would apply here in spades, but when it's 40 below, it's not a question. You pick them up and hope they are not carrying a pickaxe. I have even heard that motorists could be found guilty of man-slaughter if they drive past a hitchhiker at those temperatures. The same general rule applies with homes. Cold strangers are completely within their rights to break into a cabin or house, build a fire, and eat what they need to survive, provided they intend to make repairs and restock the pork rinds and beer they consumed should they ever be rescued. Many people with remote cabins even leave chopped wood and supplies of food just in case someone gets lost and needs it, and in most cases they can count on that person cutting more wood and restocking the food down the road. It is the unwritten law of the land. In Alaska, survival against nature is the number-one priority, and anyone who lives there will tell you, what goes around comes around.

Later that winter, I saw a minivan swerve off the road and into a ditch. I pulled up to the accident. The woman behind the wheel stayed in the warmth of her van and gave me a signal that she was okay. From the back of my Bronco, I pulled out the towrope I had purchased in Haines and attached it to the two vehicles. Mean-while, another truck had pulled up, and the driver had attached his rope. We nodded to each other and pulled her out of the ditch together. Once the van was out of the ditch, we unhooked our ropes. The woman gave us a quick wave and drove off. I gave a nod to the man with the other truck, and he drove off. During the entire event, not one word was spoken. We just did what we had to do and went home.

Then it was my turn. Driving in the same area days later, I lost the grip of the road and landed in a ditch as I tried to make a turn. Surveying the scene, I quickly surmised that there was no way I could get out. Within minutes, a man who had been working at a garage nearby saw the accident and drove over in a Bobcat tractor. He asked if I had any rope. I offered my towrope; he said it was too small and left to get a larger one. When he came back, he latched one end to the Bronco and began pulling with the Bobcat. I was out in minutes. Before he left the scene, he gave me the larger rope. He said that mine was too wimpy for Alaska and that he had another anyway. I have used his rope dozens of times since.

Most people who survive in Alaska for any period of time obey these rules of mutual support and common sense. Unfortunately, many people who come to Alaska try to go it alone. Christopher McCandless was one of them. After roaming the country, first by car, then by foot, McCandless found his way to the wilderness around Denali State Park. He didn't have much with him for his journey—and most of his food had been given to him when he hitchhiked to the forest. He survived for a while but ultimately starved to death in the abandoned bus he called home. His story was told in the book *Into the Wild* by Jon Krakauer. It struck many of its readers in the Lower 48 as sad and tragic, but most Alaskans I talked to just thought the guy was an idiot. There are plenty of ways to get killed in Alaska in your own backyard, let alone on a solo trip to the Denali wilderness.

"Serves him right," said Kevin Groff, my buddy from the rugby team, after reading the back cover of Krakauer's book at a store in Fairbanks. "Besides, that leaves more oxygen for me."

Hundreds of cheechakos move to Alaska every year intent on making it. Some are fishermen. Some are waiters. Some are dreamers. No single organization sends more fresh meat to Alaska every year than the U.S. Armed Forces. With several Air Force bases, Army posts, and naval facilities, thousands of cheechakos in uniform proceed into the wild every year. Since much of their work takes place outside, military cheechakos are often more likely to encounter Alaska's dangers head-on.

Viper Envy

Eielson Air Force Base is located twenty-six miles southeast of Fairbanks along the Richardson Highway. Its 63,195 acres are home to the 354th Fighter Wing and its 6,800 airmen and their families. The wing's mission is "to deploy combat-ready forces anytime, anyplace." Its primary combat aircraft include the F-16 Fighting Falcon (Viper) of the 18th Fighter Squadron and the A/OA-10 Thunderbolt II (Warthog) of the 355th Fighter Squadron. The Vipers train to blast other planes out of the sky or to rub buildings off a map, and the Hogs train to fly low and slow to make sure nobody messes with U.S. ground troops. The Alaska Air National Guard also maintains units at Eielson. KC-135 Stratotankers from the 168th Air Refueling Wing serve as flying gas stations, and two HH-60G rescue helicopters from the 210th Rescue Squadron stand by to pick up any unlucky aircrew stranded in the bush or hikers caught in bear traps.

All of the buildings on Eielson, and I mean every single one, are painted tan with brown trim like a chocolate layer cake. The largest of them is a hangar called the Thunderdome. Built to house two B-36 Peacekeeper aircraft (each about the size of forty-two Ford Expeditions), the Thunderdome's arches rise more than 140 feet. Four regulation football fields could fit under the hangar without difficulty.

The headquarters building of the 354th Fighter Wing is adjacent to the Thunderdome. Outside its front doors stand a miniature F-16 and A-10. The A-10, a stubby, slow-flying jet, is considerably bigger than the sleek, modern F-16, but the minia-tures in front of the headquarters make the A-10 look like a little toy compared to the Viper. In the military, size does matter. The off-scale model essentially said that all 355th pilots were chumps. In truth, the A-10 pilots, in their role of close air support for ground troops, often risked more than the F-16 jocks.

To scale or not, the models in front of the headquarters build-ing made it clear that Eielson was above all, a fighter base. That was, however, just its latest incarnation. Eielson traces its roots back to World War II. With much of its land occupied by Nazi Germany, the Soviet Union reached out to its ally the United States for help. One of the answers was the Lend-Lease program, which provided the Russians with American-built aircraft. The Lend-Lease planes originated in Great Falls, Montana, and were hopped from runway to runway until they reached Ladd Field, an Army post in Fairbanks. At Ladd, the aircraft were turned over to Soviet pilots for transport to Russia.

In 1942, the cold winter resulted in heavy ice fog over Fair-banks. Unable to find Ladd Field, many pilots ran out of fuel and crashed. To solve the problem, the Army decided to build an alternate airfield near Fairbanks but far enough away that ice fog would not be a problem. Completed in October 1944, the alter-nate was named "26-Mile Strip" because of its distance from Fair-banks by road. The airfield was a major asset to the ferrying operation, and by 1945 nearly eight thousand Lend-Lease aircraft had been flown through Alaska to our Soviet allies.

Only a year later, the Soviets became our primary adversary. By 1947, the Air Force had become a separate entity from the Army and looked to its two airfields near Fairbanks for a home for its strategic reconnaissance squadrons. Surrounded by rivers, Ladd's runway could not be extended, and the Air Force gave the field back to the Army, who renamed it Fort Wainwright. That left 26-Mile Strip. The runway at 26-Mile was extended from 6,625 feet to 14,507 feet, making it the longest runway in the world. The strip was renamed Eielson Air Force Base after an Alaskan aviation pioneer, and the 97th Bomber Group of the new Strategic Air Command moved in with B-29 bombers. Dozens of flying units and aircraft came and went over the next forty years, each with the mission to defeat the Soviet Union in a first-strike capacity. It was not until the end of the cold war that Eielson's mission changed to its current role. With virtual disregard for Russia, Eielson today emphasizes the forward, or offensive, deployment of fighter jets to hot spots around the world.

According to my new boss at Eielson, me and my kit bag full of public relations stunts (we called them "strategies") were going to help make the Air Force's mission in Alaska possible.

Spin City

Sandy Troeber, a captain with a master's degree in public relations, was the top PR flack at Eielson; her job was to manage the nine-person staff. I met her at the base headquarters when I arrived. Her first order of business was to locate a mechanic who would install my engine block heater. Her second was to introduce me to the intelligentsia of the base, including the tobacco-chewin', squirrel-shootin', rugby-playin' Kevin Groff. Getting me mixed up with a guy like Groff was Troeber's first mistake. Her greatest and ongoing error, however, was her overvaluation of public relations and the importance it had for Eielson's combat mission. A casual observer at the public affairs office might conclude that publishing the base newspaper *was* the mission of Eielson Air Force Base.

Master Sergeant Reggie Dawkins was the senior enlisted member of the office. A former Air Force security policeman, Dawkins transferred to the well-heated office of public affairs to ride out his career. He embodied the wisdom of a grizzled veteran. Anytime Troeber or I came up with a harebrained scheme, we could count on him to give us a reality check. Reggie's greatest strengths were his cool approach and his ability to focus us all on what was really important in Alaska—fishing.

Ken Beyer, the technical sergeant in charge of community relations, had gone native some years before. He had cajoled his way into multiple back-to-back tours at Eielson, a process the military calls "homesteading," and he made no bones about where he wanted to retire. "I'll quit before the Air Force makes me leave Alaska." That would have suited Sandy Troeber just fine. Troeber and Ken agreed on only one thing: enmity for the other.

Staff Sergeant George Hayward and Senior Airman Jenny Hartwig made up the staff for Eielson's newspaper, *The Goldpanner*. Inventive, creative, and highly competent, George ran the paper and was constantly looking for ways to make it better. On the other hand, Jenny Hartwig, the second most junior person in the office, struggled with her role as a military journalist. After George's editorial tirades against her pieces, it was a miracle she ever came back to the office at all.

Staff Sergeant Jackie Boucher, a very pleasant mother of two, sat in the newspaper office playing solitaire most of the day. I still have no idea what her job was, but I'm told she was very good at it.

Keeping us all together were the administrative airman, Senior Airman Carla Pollack, and her daughter, Julie. A single mother, Carla often brought Julie by the office when child care was not available. The Air Force hadn't quite worked out the way Carla wanted, and she looked forward to the day she could return to Texas to be with her mother. In the meantime, she did her job extremely well and smiled more in a day than most people smile in a year. I was first assigned to Carla when I arrived at the office.

It was her job to get me through the maze of official steps required to process into Eielson and Alaska.

The Origin of Moon Boots

Expecting their airmen to show up unprepared, the units at the base made sure their new arrivals were well warned and well equipped to deal with just about anything. "Newcomers orientation" was a day of required briefings for all new airmen at Eielson. Filled with warnings about the weather and the wildlife, the day of lectures could also have been known as "How to Scare the Hell out of the New Guy 101." The class started out with a briefing from instructors from the Arctic Survival School who immediately showed a video of a moose trampling an old man that seemed to be minding his own business. The scene had taken place at the University of Alaska in Anchorage. The moose, like many moose in populated areas of Alaska, had become a regular feature on the campus. She appeared to be friendly and became something of a mascot. Still, with the possible exception of the Crocodile Hunter, no one can read the mind of a wild animal. LESSON ONE: In general, the survival instructors advised that we stay away from animals six times our size. Good tip, but it's not that easy to do. You may try to avoid Bullwinkle, but moose may not try to avoid you. It was not uncommon for me to wake up in the morning and see a moose at my front door. There was little I could do but wait for it to leave.

Alaskans are always getting tangled up with moose, whether they hit one on the highway or cruise into a family along a dogsled trail. The beasts are about as common as rats in a New York subway. According to the Arctic Survival School instructors, though, most moose incidents—like all common accidents in the Great Land—are highly preventable.

Consider the story of the high-heeled female airman from Eielson. Dressed to kill for a night out on the town in Fairbanks, she found herself stranded in a broken-down car on the side of the road about a mile from the Eielson front gate. Although it was 40 below zero, she thought her best bet for survival was to walk back to the front gate of the base and ask for help. The good news is that she made it to the gate. The bad news is that she suffered extreme frostbite and had both her feet amputated. LESSON TWO: Keep the high heels and miniskirts in the trunk. In Alaska, it is better to *feel* good than to *look* good. (Sorry, Fernando.)

Not all cold-weather injuries happen due to the wrong clothing. A sergeant from Fort Greely, about an hour east of Eielson, decided to walk from his post into the nearby town of Delta Junction for some groceries. Again, the temperature was in the negative 40s, but the sergeant, well versed in arctic conditions, dressed for the occasion. Unfortunately, the temperature dropped even more—to about 60 below—so instead of carrying his peanut butter and jelly back to Greely, the street-smart soldier went to the pay phone outside the grocery store to ask a buddy to pick him up. The phone did not feel cold through his gloves, but it left its mark on his unprotected left ear: contact frostbite. LESSON THREE: Insurance does not cover the medical bills if you cut your ear off to send to your girlfriend, but it will pay if you lose your ear due to an "accident."

"Now, airmen," the instructor said, pointing to a couple of teenagers in the front row, "don't dare your buddies to lick the flagpole outside of headquarters. Two soldiers at Fort Wainwright did just that to their pal. Granted the guy was an infantryman— and clearly not as intelligent as you and I—but anyone should know not to lick the damn flagpole. Can anybody guess how they got the kid's tongue unstuck?"

"Hot water?" one of the young airmen replied.

"Well, maybe you aren't much brighter than an infantryman," the instructor said. "Warm water don't do too well when it's forty below! They had to get a dang blowtorch out there to heat up the pole!" LESSON FOUR: Review *A Christmas Story* or *Dumb and Dumber.*

"And you officers," he said, looking at me, "don't you think it's just the airmen who do stupid things like that."

With an accusatory tone, the instructor described an Army officer who forced his driver to go outside and start the truck so the officer could get some junk food in town. When the soldier said the truck wasn't working, the officer told him to go fix it. Not wanting to get in trouble, the young man obliged, but it was so cold, and so difficult to work on an engine in the subzero temperatures, that the soldier had to come back in occasionally to warm his hands. "Stop malingering," the officer said. "Get your ass outside and don't come back until the truck is running." Again, the soldier complied. When he returned, he informed the officer that the truck was now running. Unfortunately, the driver said, he would not be able to drive for him. His hands had frozen solid. When they thawed out, the soldier lost three fingers on one hand and two on the other. The officer was given a reprimand. LESSON FIVE, YOU DAMN OFFICERS: If you forget all other lessons, remember to take care of your men first!

Then there were the bear stories. While practicing his land navigation skills, a lieutenant at Fort Wainwright found he was being stalked by a large grizzly and her two cubs. Remembering that it was smart to play dead, the officer dropped to the ground and lay motionless as the bear lumbered over to him—and then on top of him. The grizzly placed her head right up against the man's face and began licking the salty sweat off him. Eventually, the licking stopped and the bear moved away. Unsure where the bear was, the lieutenant lay still for six hours before taking a look around. When he saw nothing, he sprinted for the nearest road unharmed. It's a great survival story, and when the same thing happened to another soldier the next day, he tried to follow the lieutenant's actions to the letter. Instead of lying motionless for six hours, though, the soldier lifted his head up for a look around after just two. To his horror, the grizzly was sitting thirty meters away from him—and staring right back. Before he could do anything about it, the powerful bear was on the soldier tearing him to shreds. Despite the pain, the soldier again managed to play dead, and the bear ultimately lost interest. The soldier escaped with only three hundred stitches and some pretty vivid nightmares. LESSON SIX: Don't join the Army.

Confronting a black bear requires a different skill, the instructor said. While training in river navigation, a man who failed to heed lesson six told the driver of the boat to pull over to the shore for a bathroom break. The boat pulled over, and the soldier scrambled up the pile of logs that had collected along the side of the Yukon River. "Here, little bear. Here, little bear," he called jokingly to the other side of the woodpile. How could he have known that a black bear was actually there looking for something to do? When the animal popped its head up over the log pile, the man—knowing that playing dead for a black bear is foolhardy—screamed and ran, with urine flying everywhere, for the boat. The bear, no doubt thinking it was a game of fetch, gave chase. The soldier dived into the boat, as the trainer stood on the bow, aiming his shotgun at the bear, but before the trainer could fire, the boat driver slammed the craft into reverse, sending the man with the shotgun overboard into the icy Yukon. By now, the bear had made it into the water and was pursuing the man overboard. Luckily, the guy grabbed the side of the boat as it came back for him and ultimately dragged him to the relative safety of the middle of the river. LESSON SEVEN: If for some reason you find yourself in the Army, be sure to get out as soon as possible.

Pictures of frostbitten feet and ears and noses were followed by pictures of stitched-up heads and legs and arms. Despite the warnings, we all essentially agreed—as had every soldier and airman that ever set foot in Alaska—that mistakes in the arctic were essentially reserved for morons and that none of those things could ever possibly happen to us.

After orientation I headed for the supply warehouse to pick up my winter issue. I wasn't given anything when I was assigned to Keesler. Then again, in Biloxi you didn't face death every time you went outside—unless there was a large hurricane named Camille nearby. The word must have spread that I had arrived in Alaska without a jacket, because they loaded me up with enough arctic gear to walk to the North Pole. For the body: three sets of polypropylene long underwear; a Gore-Tex rain jacket and pants; wool insulators to be worn under the Gore-Tex; insulated "fat boy" pants that looked like something a firefighter would wear; and a thickly insulated parka with a fur-lined hood. For the head: a Gore-Tex ski mask with Velcro straps; a balaclava with a pom-pom on top; and another thickly insulated hat with side flaps that could be worn over the ears or buttoned up to the sides of the hat to make you look like one of the Darryls from *Newhart.* For the hands: one set of Gore-Tex gloves and giant overmittens that, if you stand them on end, look like the hat the pope wears. Finally, for the feet: six pairs of wool socks; a pair of insulated combat boots; a pair of bunny boots—thick-soled rubber boots that could withstand 50-below temperatures; and a pair of the military's version of the Native Alaskan mukluks—lightweight boots that don't keep your feet warm but look and feel pretty cool. You may remember the commercial version of the mukluks, Moon Boots.

It was about 30 below the day I picked up my winter issue, but as I looked outside, I didn't see a soul wearing any of the very warm stuff I had just received. I learned that many of the men at Eielson, like the guys at the ice rugby game, viewed it as unmanly to wear the heavy clothes I had just been issued—unless it was *really, really, really* cold. Thirty below didn't qualify.

Between the rugby game and the arctic clothing issue, I began to get the feeling that there was a simpler explanation for the insane behavior of many of the men I had met in the interior. Basically they're all just afraid of being called a wimp. Any guy can appreciate that. The survival instructors warned us, though, that machismo might be more dangerous on the frontier than the weather.

The Fourth Estate, All Three of Them

Of all the gold discovered in Alaska and the Yukon near the dawn of the twentieth century, only the interior still yields the precious metal en masse. Since resuming operations in 1996, the Fort Knox Gold Mine alone has produced about 350,000 ounces of gold each year from the same hills where the yellow stuff was first discovered by Felix Pedro in 1902. Pedro's discovery and the rush that followed resulted in the city of Fairbanks. Named after Senator Charles Fairbanks of Indiana, the city was founded twelve miles south of Pedro's strike, where ships traveling the Chena River could unload their supplies. Today, the site where the first ship dumped its supplies features the statue *The Unknown First Family*, of an Athabascan Native family and their dog bracing themselves against the savage cold. Surviving several booms and busts, Fairbanks has become the center of the interior.

In any other part of the country, a town the size of Fairbanks would not merit a sizable media community. Then again, there were no other broadcast signals or newspaper delivery vans that could reach Fairbanks easily. More than that, Fairbanks also served as the hub for the entire interior, from miniscule Native villages to isolated oil refineries. To get news in the interior, you had to go to Fairbanks. To meet this need, Fairbanks boasted a daily newspaper, two radio news programs, and three television news stations. Where there is media, there are public relations weenies trying to spin a story to their benefit. The Air Force is no exception.

In an effort to promote Eielson's activities, Troeber made me the head of media relations. While most officers on the base were busy training for potential conflict, my combat mission was to head downtown and pitch stories to the distinguished local press.

My best pitch that winter was about cold-weather survival. Captain Scott O'Grady had been shot down in Bosnia a few years before. Should another pilot be shot down or a soldier be lost in winter conditions, he would need to employ survival techniques to stay alive in the cold. All Department of Defense personnel who are required to attend arctic survival training visit the "Cool School" at Eielson. Of course, the pitch was more lowbrow than all that, and the tie-in to Bosnia was a stretch. I simply planned to tell the media that the instructors teach students how to make fire, show them how to catch wild animals with their bare hands, and may even kill a rabbit for dinner. The coup de grace was the rabbit eyes. "I can't promise you anything," I'd say, "but we might catch the instructors making one of the students suck out the rabbit's eyeballs."

I called the local NBC affiliate and caught their rookie reporter, Curtis Smith, on the line. There was no real news value in the story, but I tried to play off Curtis's sense of adventure. It worked—but mostly because I caught Curtis at the right time. He would have done anything to come up with a story before his news director, Charles Fedullo, a short Italian-American from Philadelphia, leaned against Curtis's desk and asked, "Whatchya got?" in his best gangster impression. Although new to the job, Curtis had decided that he was the best reporter Fairbanks had ever seen (*just ask him*) and could not tolerate Fedullo's probing questions.

"Flynn was pitching an adventure on this day, and I was listening," Curtis later said. "*Cool School*. It had a nice ring, and I was anxious to say those words on television—like I was the first man ever to put them together. Because I had already suffered through a handful of brutally cold winters in Alaska's interior, I was a quick study on what Flynn was selling, a day in the woods with a small group of Air Force pilots. We would be like 'manly men' and learn how to survive in the arctic. All I needed was heavy winter gear— and a five A.M. wake-up call. With my news director stirring and heading in my direction, I told Flynn I was in."

Wow! I couldn't believe I got a bite on my first pitch. I arranged a time to meet Curtis, then proudly strolled into Captain Troeber's office to tell her how great I was (*just ask me*).

"Assist him in getting any of the footage he needs," Troeber said. "Just make sure he doesn't tape the survival instructors committing politically incorrect acts like killing rabbits and sucking out their eyeballs."

I met Curtis Smith at the front gate. He was both the reporter and cameraman for the story. He threw his equipment into the back of my Bronco, and we headed to the survival school headquarters, ironically just across the street from a Burger King. The hall of the Cool School looked a lot like the inside of the bar at Pike's Landing. The mounted animals included grizzly bear, moose, caribou, reindeer, musk ox, wolf, mountain sheep, and salmon. Off the main hallway was a "survival museum" that featured exhibits of common survival gear and techniques. One display showed clothes and boots that had been worn by students who got a little too close to the fire: burnt mittens, burnt boots, burnt socks, burnt hats. The exhibits made it plain to me why it costs the government a couple thousand dollars to buy a hammer.

The school trains about 650 students a year. Many of them are pilots who would be flying in Alaska. Others are Army infantrymen with a very cold assignment at nearby Fort Wainwright. The first half of the class, principles and procedures, takes place in the warmth of the school. The second half, fieldcraft and techniques, subjects the students to the arctic wilderness. By the time Curtis and I arrived at the school, the students were already in the woods practicing their fieldcraft. After a quick interview with the commander of the school, Major David Jones, we immediately headed out to where the action was.

It was warm that day, about 25 below. I was snug in my mukluks and parka. Curtis wore a pair of bunny boots. (Alaskans, not just soldiers and airmen, prized these boots and acquired a pair whenever possible. By the time I left, they had become even more valuable since the manufacturer had ceased making them.) The students wore clothes similar to mine and were hard at work building individual snow shelters, a sort of igloo made by sticks and covered with heaps of snow. The instructors informed us that such a shelter would stay at about 22 degrees above zero inside even if it were as cold as 60 below outside. In some cases the shelter was so good that the body heat from its inhabitant would cause it to melt. Most students spent nights during Cool School in such shelters, but pilots who flew solo in Eielson's F-16s and A-10s were taught another technique. Their survival kit included an inflatable raft with a spray shield that could serve as a cocoon for pilots in all environments. When covered with snow, the raft's cushion of air warmed markedly, keeping the pilot alive, but just barely, according to Lieutenant Colonel Scott Adams, an A-10 pilot and a student at the school the day Curtis and I showed up.

With highs of only −18 forecast during our visit, the pilots who were scheduled to sleep solo were given the opportunity to stay inside a large group snow shelter, but Adams wanted to test the actual gear he would be left to survive with should he have to eject over the interior. "I . . . chose the outside option, and it was a rough night," Adams said. "The breath you exhaled froze against the raft's spray shield so that every time you bumped the raft a shower of frost fell in your face."

But he survived. "The challenge of staying warm and not making a mental mistake that would cause a cold injury was significant, and it was good to see how difficult that would be in an actual ejection situation," Adams said. "I was satisfied with what I learned about myself and gear, and I didn't change the way I dressed, or the gear I took with me on daily flights. While I was chilled sometimes [at the Cool School], I never remember being as cold as I have been in Florida in January."

Adams, who later became Eielson's safety officer, became a disciple of the Cool School and its techniques. "One pilot told me he didn't think there was any way he could survive an ejection and a winter night out in Alaska. I felt that knowing you could survive was so important that I grounded him and sent him home with a book I had about Alaska survival stories. He came back ready to fly and to at least give survival an effort."

Adams did a great job at survival school and learned skills that would help him down the road, but the older lieutenant colonel was a little more straitlaced than the cocksure young pilots who also attended the Cool School. While some aviators like Adams were trying to go by the book, guys like Stoli, the F-16 pilot I met at the ice rugby game, were generating the heat another way. Instead of sleeping in their inflatable survival rafts on the "solo" night, the younger guys dragged the rafts through the woods to Eielson's ski slope, only a few hundred meters away, and spent the night zipping down the hill. This proved good for three reasons: First, walking back up generated body heat. Second, it was fun. Third, there was cellular phone service at the ski area. Within an hour, the pilots were chowing down on stuffed-crust pizzas. So much for rabbit eyeballs.

The only thing Curtis and I saw the students eat was an MRE, which stands for "Meals, Ready to Eat." Served in vacuum-sealed brown packets, the meals are universally disliked. Having gone to survival school myself, though, I can tell you that an MRE beats an eyeball any day. Curtis interviewed the men as they ate around the fire. They laughed and told stories and complained about the food. It seemed a lot like an overnighter in the Catskills. When I jokingly asked where the drinks were, the instructor, always the hard-ass killjoy, noted that a person could die from drinking alcohol in this weather. Instead of freezing, alcohol would drop to the outside temperature of 10, 20, 30, 40 below. If taken at those temperatures, it would freeze the throat instantly and likely cause death.

We spent the day with Adams and the other students. They worked on one task or another and appeared warm the whole time. Curtis, who was born in Alaska, wore less than everyone else but never got cold. I, on the other hand, was freezing and longed for a warm flight into a tropical hurricane. My feet were still frozen and quite numb when we left the survival area. Unfortunately, even though I knew LESSON EIGHT (frozen feet may impair your ability to operate a motor vehicle), a streak of machismo caused me to drive my Bronco beyond my capabilities. The steep hill we drove down came upon a sudden curve, and my numb foot missed the brake. We went off the road and nearly drove over a fifty-foot cliff. Another foot farther, and Curtis's soft feature on survival school would have been the hard headline news story.

Indoor Plumbing and Moose Nuggets

Still freezing, I returned to my room at Eielson in hopes of a life-giving hot shower. Like virtually every hotel in the Lower 48, however, my room on the base had almost no water pressure. In the arctic, a hot shower capable of leaving welts is a necessity. For that reason, and because all of my earthly belongings would be arriving from Mississippi shortly, I set out that weekend to find the ideal Alaska home with a hot tub and a great view of the mountains. I may as well have added palm trees and a golf course to the wish list.

One classified did catch my eye: "Rustic cabin, 12×14, wood stove, secluded, $350/month." What luck! Where better to live in Alaska than a rustic cabin? I could nail snowshoes on the wall, hang caribou antlers over the wood stove, and lay a bearskin rug on the floor. Real Alaskans live in cabins—and I wanted to be a real Alaskan. So I set off to the village of Salcha. Sixteen miles or so southeast of the base on the Richardson Highway, Salcha boasted a year-round population of about 250. It was less a village than coordinates on a map.

The cabin in question was located at mile 43 of the Richardson Highway. Many addresses in Alaska are nothing more than mile markers, which is a lot more accurate than saying, "Turn left after the second stream from the Salcha River, just before you get to the radio tower. If you've made it to the tower, you've gone too far. Turn around and look for an abandoned bulldozer in the woods on the right. It's just a ways up from there, near the stand of birch trees that got blown over last May."

In Alaska, all things are relative. By rustic, what the landlord meant was that the run-down woodshed I kept driving past was actually the "cabin." Just beyond the cabin was a smaller building that turned out to be an outhouse. That would be a problem. The idea of relieving yourself in a shed better suited for West Virginia was bad, but you'd have to be nuts to do it at 40 below. No thanks, I prefer to read the Victoria's Secret catalogue in the warmth of my own home, within earshot of the television if I'm lucky. That's a tall order in Salcha. The Alaska Labor Department estimated in 1999 that 44 percent of residences in Salcha did not have indoor plumbing. That means most people living in the town can't shake hands with at least four of the ten people they know.

Later that year during a trip to Eagle, population 209, when I asked where the bathroom was at the public library, I was told to "head down the hall, take a right, and head out the back door— just past the woodpile." The outhouse was fairly typical by Alaska standards. Made all of wood, it sat on cinder blocks and had a pair of rusty hinges screwed into a three-quarter-inch plywood door with a crescent moon cut out of it. In the winter, the plastic seat was usually hung indoors next to the wood stove for added warmth. A busy outhouse may also have a pole to knock down any frozen waste that has built up to the seat level. I ultimately used scores of outhouses in Alaska and became quite an aficionado, grading various outhouses on their style, uniqueness, and literature selection. Old *Playboys* got a top rating. Antigovernment literature worried me.

I ultimately settled on a two-bedroom apartment in a complex between Eielson and Fairbanks. All of the wonderful images I had of my home in Alaska were now officially dashed. I had dozens of people within spitting distance, the woman next to me blared dance music all day, and I would leave the shower with third-degree burns any time a neighbor flushed a toilet. The worst was my unwanted wake-up call. Since the walls and ceilings were no thicker than saltines, I awoke every morning at 6:15 to the sound of the man upstairs urinating—and believe me, he was always well hydrated.

Cheap housing is a good way to make money, and Alaska was built by people seeking to make a buck. The Russians came for furs. The Americans came for gold. The Texans came for oil. Everyone else would service these people by building cheap housing or by picking up pieces of wood from the forest and selling them as "real Alaskan walking sticks." The next great industry was tourism, and nowhere did Alaskans exploit this better than in my new hometown of North Pole, Alaska. Just off Santa Claus Lane, my new apartment was a short walk to the official Santa Claus House, complete with a reindeer petting zoo and a fifty-foot Santa. Everyone in North Pole got into the act, including the Catholic priest: Saint Nick's Roman Catholic Church was only a block from the Santa Claus House. It was Christmas every day in this made-for-tourism town with a 98.3 percent indoor plumbing rate. Like a perversion of *Miracle on 34th Street*, even the government recognizes North Pole as the official home of Santa. All mail addressed to the fat man at the North Pole is forwarded to the red, green, and white post office in the middle of town, then farmed out from there to scores of organizations, including Eielson Air Force Base, for "authentic" Santa responses.

It was fun to live in North Pole. I was able to mail all my Christmas packages in December with the North Pole postmark. When ordering over the phone, it was after stating my proper address of Santa Claus Lane, North Pole, Alaska, that I was usually hung up on. It was fun, but as I contemplated the reindeer petting zoo and giant candy canes, I realized I would never find the real Alaska at this North Pole. I imagined that it was somewhere farther away, perhaps somewhere a cheechako wouldn't find in a guide book, maybe a place with only a 2 percent indoor plumbing rate.

February

Why There Are No Sheep in Alaska

Where Only Maverick Could Find a Woman

There aren't many fringe benefits afforded a public affairs officer in the Air Force. You don't get to fly jets, which means you
don't get to wear those really cool leather jackets or have cool
nicknames like Maverick or Goose or Ice Man, which ultimately
means you don't get first pick at any available women in uniform.
In most parts of the country, that's not a big problem. Instead of
cruising for chicks on the runway, you can simply cruise down to
the local mall and hang out at the food court. In interior Alaska,
however, the nearest food court is a five-hour flight away in Seattle. That meant the other support officers and I had to compete
with the fighter pilots. If you've seen *Top Gun,* you know that we
were at a major disadvantage. When you consider that there were
only three eligible women on all of Eielson, you know that we
didn't stand a chance.

Let me explain. The military has strict rules about who you
can and who you can't hang out with. It's called "fraternization."
In general, military members of different rank cannot socialize,
let alone date one another. For the lieutenants at Eielson, including the pilots, the policy meant that nearly a thousand otherwise
single women were off limits. Here's how it works. There were
about 6,800 people on Eielson Air Force Base. Of that number,
more than half represented spouses and children. Of the 2,600

people that were in the military, only 500 were officers. (Remember, we couldn't date the enlisted women.) Of that 500, only 60 were female. Of that 60, only 15 were single. Finally, of that 15, only 3 were lieutenants like me. One, two, three.

Fortunately those three women were at the officers' club every Friday night. Unfortunately for desk weenies like me, there was a score of fighter jocks there, too. They stood around the bar in their slick flight suits and leather jackets, tracing flight paths around the girls' heads with their hands. I, on the other hand, sat in the back of the club—without a drink, since I couldn't penetrate the wall of pilots nestled around the bar. At least I wasn't alone. My rugby buddy Groff was also a support officer and, lucky for him, married. He believed that being married in Alaska was great for two reasons: First, he did not have to worry about competing with everyone else for the "two available girls in Fairbanks and the three in Anchorage." Second, he never had to wonder how he would satisfy his manly needs. "I get it whenever *my wife* wants it," Groff said. Instead of tracing flight paths to impress the women, he used his hands to describe how Dale Earnhardt or A. J. Foyt or somebody won the Daytona 500 despite suffering from yellow fever or scurvy or some such disease common in West Virginia.

The female scene at the officers' club was so dismal that many of us were forced to try our luck in downtown Fairbanks, which is like going to a singles bar in Mayberry. Some of the guys chose the Great Escape (a.k.a. the Great Mistake) dance club. Others stuck to the local strip bar, Reflections Lounge. Not being able to dance or afford the strip club, I usually found myself at the Dog Sled Saloon in the Captain Bartlett Inn. A pint of beer was only $2.50, and there were barrels of free peanuts within easy reach of all the tables. Here again, though, the competition was fierce. Fairbanks's semipro hockey team, the Gold Kings, owned one section of the bar. The rugby club owned another corner. A large group of infantrymen from nearby Fort Wainwright occupied by force yet another area. And, of course, there were always some pilots standing around looking down at everyone else.

As if there wasn't enough competition in the bar already, I often went there with Curtis Smith, the journalist I had taken to the Cool School in January. He had a primitive yet effective way to gauge whether he might hook up on a given night, which he called "the bar test." The first thing he looked for after walking into a bar was a woman worth staying for. The second thing he looked for was a man who might beat him to her. If the competition was too tough, he would move on to the next dive. The fact that he had no problem hanging out at the bar with me spoke volumes. If a woman ever made it as far as our table, she immediately fell for the good-looking news anchor. At most, she would ask me for a pen so she could give Curtis her number. I started bringing Groff instead. He would regale me with tales of his 1970 Chevy Nova muscle car, which sat on cinder blocks on his front lawn next to the old washing machine.

Alaska has almost everything a guy could want: fishing, hunting, and hiking; the chance to get rich quick; the chance to prove your manhood on a daily basis. Alaska even has a few of its own breweries. Despite the state's lack of a professional football team, high school sports, college basketball, and semipro baseball and hockey more than satisfy a man's primeval urge to watch real athletes run faster and hit harder than he ever could himself. Yeah, Alaska would be a dream come true for most American men—if it wasn't for one small exception. Women.

There just aren't that many single women in the state. In places like the interior, it's even worse. Shortly after I arrived at Eielson, *Alaska* magazine published an article that said the guy-gal ratio could reach 35-to-1 around military bases. Fairbanks had two of them. Of course, adverse odds have never stopped anyone in Alaska. If life hands you a bucket of moose crap, shine it up, place it on a stick, and sell it to tourists in a package labeled "authentic Alaskan moose nuggets." They are a top seller in most novelty shops.

The Goods Are Odd

When the Russians weren't busy killing off the sea cows and seals and otters, they were busy finding women among the Native Alaskans. When the Americans finally came in large numbers during the gold rush, they found their women the old-fashioned way—in the yellow pages. Miners weren't the only ones getting rich in Alaska in the early 1900s. With a never-ending sea of men flooding the land, any woman of questionable moral character stood to make a fortune. Many of them did.

In 1904, thirty-three saloons were doing steady business along First Street in Fairbanks, according to my pocket guide called *Alaska's History,* by Harry Ritter. If a miner could stumble to Fourth Street, he would find a three-block-long red-light district known simply as "the Row." Comprised largely of one-room huts, the Row was ruled by one Cheechaco Lil, a famous madam who had earned her first fortune in Dawson. Fairbanks would be her crowning achievement.

Today, the flavor of the Row is re-created every summer during Golden Days, a week-long celebration commemorating the founding of Fairbanks. During the week, Miss Ricky, a woman of poor moral standards, assists the "sheriff" with a horse-drawn paddy wagon. Looking sumptuous in her best turn-of-the-century barroom lace, Miss Ricky plies the streets of Fairbanks, Fort Wainwright, and Eielson Air Force Base looking for people not showing the Alaska spirit by wearing a Golden Days pin. (It should be noted, though, that being arrested by the buxom Miss Ricky is not all that terrible.)

Since the gold rush days, prostitution has moved underground, but people are still making a bundle off the lonely men of the frontier. Leading the effort to help the men sitting around the Dog Sled Saloon is *Alaska Men* magazine, a monthly publication that spotlights a hundred eager bachelors from the Great Land for about twenty-five thousand subscribers living all over the world. A featured Alaskan could receive up to five hundred calls; one candidate even received two thousand. The catch: It costs nearly six hundred dollars to get spotlighted. For many Alaskan men, it's money well spent. For many others, it's a waste. For the owner of a chain of not-quite-fast food joints and chicken wing stands in Fairbanks, it was only a small drop in a deepening bucket.

The problem, Jay Ramras told *New York* magazine, was that there weren't enough Jewish women in Alaska. In Fairbanks, the Jewish population reached only about 570, and by the time he was thirty-three years old, Jay said, he had ruled out all the local gals and needed to branch out. Where would an eligible Jewish man go? The Upper West Side of New York, of course. Jay sublet an apartment in the fall of 1997, with the goal of finding a bride by January. After he took his plea to an area synagogue, *New York* picked up his cause and began a weekly column titled "Nice Jewish Boy Seeks Hot-Blooded Jewish Girl for Love in Colder Climes." The women flocked to Jay, and he extended his trip to March. By the time he booked a flight back to Fairbanks, he had been on eighty-seven first dates, spent $16,250 in rent, and been covered by the national media including *Good Morning America,* CNBC, Fox 5 News, *People* magazine, the *New York Times, USA Today,* and countless others. Despite his efforts, he failed to convince anyone to return to the frigid north with him.

How could a man have such bad luck? When *New York* first championed Jay Ramras, it forgot to warn its readers about Alaskan men. It has long been known by women who have looked for love on the Last Frontier that in Alaska "the odds are good, but the goods are odd." Perhaps Jay should have stuck with the girl who proclaimed to him one morning, "It's a great day when you pee and it doesn't sting." Now, that's a woman ready for Alaska.

Sleeping with Seattle

I met my first real live Alaskan woman during my first week in the interior. In fact, she tackled me pretty hard during the ice rugby game. With no regular female rugby teams in town, Elaine was forced to take her aggression out against the men's team. She hit us hard, and despite our gentlemanly upbringing, we had to hit her back hard—or else get hurt. She was tall, extremely tough, hard-drinking, and ruggedly attractive. Ultimately, she became the standard to which I compared all other Alaskan women. They came in different shapes and sizes, but they all seemed to fit the same mold, according to Curtis's mother, Gail Peterson, who grew up in the Native town of Bethel and later Anchorage. When not working as a singer or dancer, she was learning to fly herself around Alaska's vast bush country or was just plain fixing things.

"Alaskan women have a great degree of independence and self-worth," Gail told me one day. "Because if you want something done, you have to do it yourself. There is nobody to call. You have to learn to do it. You don't say no. You just do. It takes a lot of grit and an inner strength."

Huddled in the corner of the Dog Sled Saloon, I scanned each potential prospect, looking for her "inner strength" as she came in through the swinging door. The Alaskans were the ones wearing jeans, boots, and flannel. They drank the cheap pints of beer or shots of whiskey. Then there were the military women. They dressed as if they were going out to someplace nice—a real stretch for this saloon, which boasts the motto "No cover, no dress code, no taste." They all drank light beer in bottles or cheap wine. The tourists were the next big group. They dressed like models for an L. L. Bean catalogue and all drank Alaskan Amber.

These differences in Alaskan women were important to note since they dictated how much of a chance you actually had. The Alaskan women generally avoided the military men, who were often looked on as an occupying force staying just long enough to make some extra money and get a nineteen-year-old pregnant. The women who were in the military often favored other military men because they knew that if they were married, they wouldn't be stuck in Alaska, but again, most of these women preferred fighter pilots, who were given large cash bonuses for the burden of wearing the leather flight jacket. Then came the tourists. In February there weren't that many, but as the weather got nicer they would flock to the state for vacations and summer jobs. These were generally adventurous women and often, if they were inclined to date at all, wanted to go out with a real live Alaskan. Accordingly, the military types didn't stand much of a chance with them, either—except the fighter pilots. They can pretty much score anywhere.

Guys like me were up the creek. We had the bad haircut but no cool leather jacket to make it okay. We lived in Alaska but weren't accepted by the locals or tourists. We were so far away from anywhere that we couldn't drive to some other state on the weekends to visit our college sweethearts. There was only one thing left to do—call Seattle.

Pre–Bill Gates Seattle owes much of its fortune to Alaska. When gold was discovered in the vast empty lands to the north, Seattle businessmen quickly realized they could make a killing. Virtually every gold miner who worked in the Alaskan goldfields was outfitted by Seattle merchants and transported by Seattle steamships. When they returned, they also came through Seattle, often depositing their newfound wealth in the city's banks. As the gold dried up, fisheries became king. Again Seattle businessmen would have their way with Alaska. By the end of World War I, however,

Seattle was beginning to feel the sting of foreign competition. Overland shipping routes through Canada had been established, and foreign-flagged vessels were moving into the Alaskan waters.

To protect their stranglehold on the territory, Seattle businessmen persuaded their senator, Wesley L. Jones, who happened to be head of the Senate Commerce Committee, to lead the passage of the Merchant Marine Act of 1920, a.k.a. the Jones Act. The act authorized foreign shipping competition for all of America's states and territories—except Alaska. Anything heading to or from Alaska had to be carried by an American vessel. As intended, the law created a very profitable shipping monopoly for Seattle businesses. Unfortunately, it came at a high cost to Alaskans.

In his book *The State of Alaska,* former governor and all-around Alaskan hero Ernest Gruening cites the law's effect on a resident of Juneau who had a business foresting Alaskan spruce for airplane manufacturers in the Midwest. Before the Jones Act, the businessman shipped his goods for five dollars per part through Vancouver. After the act, he had to ship them through Seattle at eleven dollars per part. The obscene 100-plus percent increase in shipping put him out of business immediately. In general, Gruening said the act more than tripled shipping costs for any Alaskan freight. The Supreme Court later stated that the Jones Act did discriminate against Alaska. However, the Court also said that Congress had the right to discriminate against a territory, so the act stood, and Seattle held the monopoly over shipping until Alaska became a state in 1959. I'm not sure of the lasting effects, but I would wager that someone in Seattle had a hand in the thirty-dollar pizza I ordered in Wrangell two months earlier.

For me, sitting at the Dog Sled Saloon eating peanuts and listening to Groff spout off *Dukes of Hazzard* trivia, Seattle still had something I wanted. Like Jay Ramras, I had to look for love outside Alaska. Fortunately, I had already done my field research and found a woman who was at least willing to visit while I was serving in the far north. My girlfriend, Lori Ann, had moved to Seattle several months before. It wasn't Alaska, but it was a hell of a lot closer than New York. The flight to Fairbanks from Seattle cost around four hundred dollars at the time. Although I had no money, I put down my credit card immediately in hopes I could keep the long-distance romance alive.

Military men are notorious for the long-distance relationship. At least half of all military members have someone waiting for them under an apple tree in the greater Niagara Falls region. It's a direct result of the relative youth of the military forces and the constant travel required of them. After all, it's pretty hard to sneak a nineteen-year-old former prom queen onto a six-month-long submarine tour, but it's also pretty hard to keep the love flowing from four thousand miles away. Between all your "good buddies" checking in on your loved one back at Salina County Community College and the suspicions created by missed phone calls and answering machines, it's a wonder any of the thousand-mile relationships work at all.

Dear John,

Hope you are doing well. Things here are okay! Matt came by last week. He's really nice!! He asked about you and when you were coming home. I really like him best of all your friends!!! He asked me to ask you if he should check in every now and then. I told him that you would think that was a great idea!!!! How's everything at Ranger School? Geometry is such a pain in the ass!!!!! I knew I should have paid attention in math class. Called you a few times last week. I guess you were out or something. Tell those Ranger guys to let you call me!!!!!! Anyway . . . I have to run. Matt says hi.

    XOXOXOX

Love,

Mary

P.S. What do you think about seeing other people?

My best bet would have been to ask Lori to move to Alaska with me, but I had asked her to come live in Mississippi and was shot down miserably. *What are you, nuts? You'd have to drug me, tie me up, and lock me in a suitcase. Then you might as well kill me when we get there. It would beat having to look for something to do. Why don't you just give me a lobotomy now!*

At least Mississippi was warm. "Oh, no," Lori said after running back inside Fairbanks International Airport in February. "I can't go back out there! I can't even breathe. It's too cold. It's too dark. It's like the moon! I can't even see out there. Oh my God . . . if my father ever knew it was like this up here, he never would have let me come. I can't go back out there! I won't go. Does your truck even work when it's this cold?"

"It's fine," I said. "I left it running. It should be nice and warm in there."

"Nope, I'm not walking out there. I can't breathe. You'll have to pull it around."

Lori arrived for her first visit to Fairbanks in the middle of a cold snap. Expecting her to be underdressed, I brought my military issue cold-weather parka for her to wear, but it seemed like nothing short of a quick flight to Hawaii would help. Lori stepped from the airport as I pulled up to the curb. Before I could tell her not to, she grabbed the metal door handle with her bare hand—resulting in an immediate case of contact frostbite that was still hurting when she got back to Seattle the next week.

Dear Sean,

Had a nice trip. It was nice to see where you live. Kind of dark though. And definitely too cold. Disappointed that I saw no moose. My hand still hurts. Thinking about letting a friend of mine take a look at it. You'd really like him. He's a doctor here. I met him the other day at massage therapy school. And you'll never guess what he did before he became a doctor! He was an F-14 pilot in the Navy!! You guys have so much in common!!!

The Meek Shall Inherit the Earth

In most parts of the United States, deals are made on the golf course. There are two courses in Fairbanks, the North Star Golf Club and the Fairbanks Golf and Country Club. Unfortunately, they are only open in the summer, both days of it. Therefore, many deals are made over the card table. Unbeknownst to me, two Fairbanksans were about to deal me a royal flush. The first was the wing commander of Eielson Air Force Base. The second was Billy Bob Allen, a former mayor of the Fairbanks North Star Borough and a successful real estate developer. Both happened to be Texans.

Billy Bob had a problem out on Harding Lake. The lake, which lay almost an hour outside Fairbanks and twenty-five minutes past Eielson in Salcha, was the summer weekend retreat for Fairbanks's elite. Since it was largely abandoned in the winter, and since the closest police department was at least thirty minutes away, thieves and vandals found the elaborate cabins adorning the lake easy targets. For the second time that winter, they had hit Billy Bob's cabin, so he asked the commander for a hand. Maybe the general knew a nice, responsible officer with no pets who would be willing to live out at the cabin for free. When summer came, the officer could stay at the cabin during the week and live in Billy Bob's house in Fairbanks on the weekend—only a ten-minute drive to the Dog Sled Saloon!

Somehow my name came up, and I was invited to have a look at the place. The fact that it was in Salcha made me a bit nervous—I had become pretty attached to indoor plumbing and wasn't ready to give it up—but one look at this cabin made my mind up for me. It was a two-story cedar home sitting right on the lake. It had a satellite dish, a wood-burning stove with a picture window, a couple of snowmachines to use in the winter, and a boat and Jet Ski to abuse—I mean *use*—in the summer. Would I be interested? Are you kidding? Does moose crap look like peanut M&M's?

Sometimes the stars shine in your favor. They certainly did for me that month. I was far from the ice fog of Fairbanks, the gaudy commercialism of North Pole, and the thundering roar of Eielson. I had simultaneously cut my rent payment to nothing and moved closer to the real Alaska I had dreamed about when I first learned of the assignment. The first night I stayed at the lake, I saw the northern lights again. This time, instead of freezing my tail off outside, I gazed at the heavens through large picture windows that framed the lake, its surrounding hills, and the brilliant night sky. It was perfect. More important, if things ever fell through with Lori Ann, the cabin was a babe trap beyond compare. The pilots may have had the slick jackets and cool nicknames, but none of them had a remote cabin with a Jacuzzi. My stock was up.

Alaska the Muse

Despite the woman-catching potential of my new cabin, the reality out at Harding Lake that winter was a solitary one. With nothing but empty weekend homes for neighbors, the only contact I had with other human beings was through my satellite dish. Even so, unless I *accidentally* found adult programming on one of my four HBO channels, I often just turned the television off.

I didn't need TV that winter, anyway. The aurora borealis was "out" almost every night, and even with dozens of hours of gazing, it was something I could never quite get enough of. The large picture window in the living room gave me a spectacular view of the lights and their slow dance of blue-green streaks arcing across the sky—first in one direction, then smoothly back in the other. On more than one night, the sky was so brilliant, I was literally forced outside to take it all in. With my extreme-cold-weather parka and bunny boots, I was able to shuffle out to the middle of the lake, where I could view the sky from every angle as if I were floating around with the lights, the moon, and the stars myself. A moment of Nirvana here on earth. From one horizon to the other, the night sky was a miracle of lights that could humble even a fighter pilot (although I doubt he would ever admit it).

Alaska was simply another world. I couldn't send enough letters to family and friends to describe the bizarre planet I had landed on. I spent hours on the phone trying to describe everything I had seen: a moose casually walking through a parking lot; a drunk wearing only a T-shirt stumbling down the street at 40 below; the miraculous appearance of the northern lights. It was so different from anything my family in New York had ever known. In fact, it was the exact opposite. New York was one of the original thirteen states; Alaska was second to last. New York has 11 million people; Alaska has about 600,000. New York has the Yankees and the NFL; Alaska has dog mushers and outhouse racing. New York has the Beastie Boys at Madison Square Garden; all Alaska has is a crusty old guy I saw picking a guitar at the Crazy Loon Saloon.

I had done some writing for the weekly newspaper at Keesler Air Force Base, but Alaska had inspired me to write even more. The result was a proposal for a weekly newspaper column for *The Goldpanner* based on my experiences as a newcomer in Alaska. I called it "Cheechako."

The audience for the column would be the men, women, and families of Eielson. Many of them hated their assignment. Many more loved it. Either way, most knew little about Alaska. My goal was to intertwine humorous stories about daily life in the state with some Alaskan history. If I were lucky, I could entertain my readers and perhaps teach them a little about the state. If I were really lucky, I wouldn't get in trouble for writing it.

I spent several days preparing the proposal and some sample columns. To say the writing was not standard fare for a military-sponsored newspaper would be an understatement. In one sample column I equated all Alaskans to the Unabomber. Even so, Captain Troeber reluctantly approved the idea, and we took it down the hall to our boss, General Richard E. "Tex" Brown III, the commander of Eielson and the guy who recommended me for the cabin-sitting gig at Harding Lake.

With the discovery of oil in Alaska in the late 1960s, many Texans like the general began to look at Alaska like a little brother—even though the Great Land was more than 2.2 times the size of the Lone Star State. While Alaska had land, it had no oil expertise. That all came from Texas, and the cowboys who came north to get the oil out of the ground let everyone know where it was that they were from. Pick any summer lake community in Alaska today, and you're likely to find as many Texas flags flying outside the cabins as Alaska flags. Tex Brown was no different. If anything, Alaska made him more eager to show his colors. Shortly after arriving, he began signing his name over an outline of his home state. Alaska may be bigger and produce more oil than Texas, but trying to convince a Texan fighter-pilot general of this was next to impossible.

The atmosphere in General Brown's office was tense. The two fighter squadron commanders and the operations officer had just concluded a meeting with Tex about the fighter wing's preparedness to deploy jets to potential war zones in the Pacific in less than twenty-four hours. In other words, they were talking about some pretty serious stuff.

"Okay. So what's this urgent meeting with the public affairs staff all about?" Tex said, hands on his hips, general's stars gleaming on his shoulders. "What's going on? Are we the target of a *60 Minutes* investigation or what?"

"Well, not exactly."

Tex could be a very approachable man. He was often eager to meet new people and talk about the good ol' days in Texas. Then again, you could also catch Tex, a former A-1 Skyraider pilot with

140 combat missions from Vietnam under his belt, standing at his full six feet, six inches and very busy being a fighter wing general. At those times, unless you had a flight suit on, you better have something really, really good to say.

Instead I handed him my sample columns. "Sir, the men and women of Eielson will really like this kind of thing. It will help their morale and get them to read all the other important stuff in the paper. In short, General Brown, adding this column to your paper is really important to the success of your mission." *You know—to deploy fighter jets to war zones, meet new and interesting people, and kill them.*

"Is that so," he remarked.

"Yes, sir," I said confidently.

Deep down inside, all Air Force personnel know that the most important jobs at a fighter unit are flying and fixing aircraft. Everything else is pretty much secondary. But the military simply doesn't work without its support infrastructure. Driving trucks, cleaning teeth, cooking chow, and managing the payroll become as important as flying jets in the long run. One could even make the argument that the mission of the public affairs people rates as high. As Tom Wolfe's would-be astronauts proclaimed in *The Right Stuff*—no bucks, no Buck Rogers. By promoting Air Force programs, public affairs geeks were going a long way to secure the sexy jets flown in Alaska.

Twisting that reality a bit, I reasoned that a humor column was also key to mission success. If the articles entertained airmen, morale would be higher, and we'd win wars quicker. Americans would celebrate in Times Square, and gas prices would drop back to one dollar a gallon.

Am I full of shit or what? Tex thought so. He quoted my material as he read the sample columns.

New York City has culture . . . but all Alaska has is a crusty old guy pickin' a guitar at the Crazy Loon Saloon.

The person approaching me was actually a big, bearded, meat-and-potato-eatin', dog-mushin', Carhartt- and bunny-boot-wearin', tobacco-chewin', moose- and grizzly-shootin', ice-fishin', four-wheeler- and pickup-drivin', beer-drinkin' Alaskan named Fred, the toughest woman I had ever seen . . .

I want to watch the WWF from my toilet if possible . . .

Aren't the female characters in Disney cartoons hot . . .

By the way, the Dallas Cowboys suck!

"You must be kidding me. My mission is to deploy combat forces anytime, anyplace—and I will be able to do that better now that I know where you like to go to the bathroom?" Tex asked. "What about this one? This will go over really well at the chamber of commerce next week. *If you have seen a picture of the Unabomber, you have seen an Alaskan.* How can we possibly publish this in *my* newspaper?"

"Well, sir . . ."

"Well, at least you try to compliment Alaskans here . . . *Most fellas have great fashion sense—flannel shirts, a four-wheel drive, and a drill press.*"

Captain Troeber chimed in to help out. "Why don't we give it a try, sir? If it doesn't go over well, we'll stop doing it," she said.

Tex flipped the pages from one column to the next. *Things to Do with an Ice Auger. You Really Can Drool on Someone You Don't Know. Heather Locklear and Cappuccino—The Fall of the Rough Alaskan Image.*

"I don't know," he said. "I just don't want to offend anyone."

Long pause.

"Okay . . . just take out the bit about the Dallas Cowboys. That there is America's team."

The first column ran that week.

THE DRILL PRESS EXTRAVAGANZA

Between the gold mines and the oil wells and the canneries and the military bases, Alaska can be downright Spartan. This austere environment has led to the creation of a mythic figure that is revered by men and desired by women outside the state. The figure is the Alaskan man. According to the myth, the Alaskan man is big. He is tough. He can do just about anything that needs doing.

And, the myth follows, the Alaskan man is lonely. The myth, which men say was created by women, assumes that the starkness and the alleged loneliness are bad things. Publicly, Alaskan men say otherwise.

They say Alaska is one of the few places in the United States where a man can be a man. He can spend all his money on a pickup truck with a lift kit. He can stay out all night drinking beer. He can burp and belch and curse and throw peanut shells on the floor. He can wear really ugly out-of-fashion clothes—and nobody will think any less of him. For the Alaskan man has nobody to answer to. He has no one to impress.

This freedom—this extravaganza of manliness and machismo and drill presses—is due, many Alaskan men would say, to the lack of women in the state. Without women to judge them, the men are left free to be the rugged individuals they grew up reading about and watching in the movies. The Daniel Boone of Bethel. The James Dean of Delta.

But that is where the *real* myth of the Alaskan man comes in. It does not take long for any male just arriving in country to see that rugged individualism is the exception among men in the state, not the rule.

For men, one commandment supersedes all others: *Thou shalt not covet thy neighbor's goods. Thou shalt get thy own and outdo thy neighbor.*

From the gold rush to the oil boom, men have historically come to Alaska to get rich and outdo their friends. The evidence is still readily seen in Alaska today. To rank among other Alaskans, a man needs to have a snowmachine, a boat, and a monster truck, and those machines need to be bigger and stronger and faster than his neighbors'. A man must hunt and fish and hike, and the moose he shoots must be older, the fish larger, and the hike longer than his neighbors'.

A cheechako usually has none of those machines. A cheechako may not even own a gun, let alone know that you don't catch fish with a rifle. Unless he acquires those tools and learns to use them, he will forever remain an outsider, unable to outdo his neighbor, unable to wear the mythic label of "Alaskan man."

So what? What's the big benefit of being an Alaskan man? Who wants to be a big, tough guy who spends all his money and time acquiring big, tough machines? Doesn't it get boring? What's the point?

The point, of course, is to impress all those Alaskan women the men claim are not around. Some are, though—and even more can be flown in.

The truth is that the myth of the Alaskan man was created by none other than Alaskan men so that women around the world will find them more desirable. The big machines, high-powered rifles, and worn-out clothes just keep the myth alive—a myth that is much bigger, stronger, and more impressive than any myths from Texas or California.

It doesn't take long for a cheechako to see that he better start toeing the company line. After all, why would any woman want to go to Alaska to date a New Yorker?

All in the Family

I was not the first in my family to work on a military newspaper in Alaska. Realizing that he and the one-legged guy two houses down were the only young men left on the block, my grandfather Eugene Phelan left his comfortable job at the *Daily News* to enlist in World War II. Already thirty-six years old, Gene was not selected for the infantry. Rather, the Army—in a move rarely seen since—assigned my grandfather to a job he already had the skill for. As an Army journalist, Private Phelan—call sign "Grandpa"—was attached to an engineer battalion headed to the Pacific theater. Where better to be a soldier-journalist in 1943? While the infantrymen slugged it out on Corregidor and Guadalcanal, he would be able to write about the fight from a warm Australian or Polynesian beach with a fruit drink in hand. After leaving San Francisco, however, the ship turned north. Days later the sun disappeared behind a curtain of clouds, reappearing for only minutes over the next two years. By the time land came into sight, the cold had arrived with a wet, windy sting he had never felt on the banks of the Hudson River.

"Where the hell are we?" he asked his partner Charlie Laloma, a Hopi Indian from Oklahoma.

"Alaska."

"Alaska! Jesus, Mary, and Joseph, what the heck are we doing here? There's no Japs here."

Not anymore.

The Thousand-Mile War

> At 2000 we assembled in front of headquarters. The last assault is to be carried out. All patients in the hospital are to commit suicide . . . Gave 400 shots of morphine to the severely wounded, and killed them . . . Finished all the patients with grenades . . . Only 33 years of living and I am to die here. I have no regrets. Banzai to the emperor . . . Goodbye Tasuko, my beloved wife.
> —LT. NEBU TATSUGUCHI, MAY 28, 1943*

The 800 men slipped quietly from their posts. They were all that remained of 2,300 who had captured the island of Attu the previous summer. Now, in a last-ditch effort to hold the barren

---

*This quote and many of the facts regarding the Japanese occupation of the Aleutian Islands come from Brian Garfield's incredible book *The Thousand-Mile War: World War II in Alaska and the Aleutians*. It was the first book I read in Alaska and should be required reading for all military personnel assigned to the Great Land.

rock, the survivors slipped through enemy lines and prepared to charge the hill that held the American artillery. If they could capture the hill, Colonel Yasuyo Yamasaki would turn the guns against the 15,000 Americans who had landed on the island two weeks before. With only bayonets and rifle butts, the charge was a gamble, but if they surprised the Americans, it just might work.

The hill was lightly defended, and the GIs who were there, combat engineers mostly, shivered in their foxholes. More than 1,100 of their fellow soldiers, outfitted in uniforms better suited for North Africa, had already suffered severe cold injuries in the wet and freezing weather. At least they were alive. More than 500 of their buddies were not, buried under the permafrost or lying out of reach on the tundra-covered slopes with only a shroud made of fog.

It was a strange place to fight over: the last island in the Aleutian chain, closer to Russia than to the North American continent. Almost the only people who ever lived there were Native Aleuts who had adapted to the wicked weather over thousands of years. Even they were accustomed to strife. Russian fur traders had come nearly two hundred years before and killed dozens of defenseless natives—an act immortalized by the aptly named Massacre Bay.

The Japanese didn't have big plans for Attu and the Aleutians. The main reason they invaded the island chain was to divert American forces away from a larger operation they planned in the North Pacific. Expecting the Americans to split their naval forces to defend Alaska, Japan was planning to ambush the main American fleet near Midway Island. With the U.S. fleet destroyed, Japan's hegemony over the Pacific would be uncontested. Fortunately for the Yankee navy, somebody cracked the Japanese encryption code. Instead of a major victory at Midway, Japan lost several ships and 3,000 men in a battle that has been called the turning point of the war in the Pacific.

To ease the blow of Midway, Japan committed all it had to the Alaskan campaign. Starting with an unsuccessful air attack on Dutch Harbor, the Japanese set out to control the thousand-mile-long Aleutian chain. With no ground forces, the Alaskan Command relied heavily on its planes. The 11th Air Force, which still commands Alaskan skies today, launched 297 missions against the Japanese. Despite flying an out-of-date fleet built around B-18s, B-36s, and PBY float planes, the 11th only lost thirty-five planes to enemy contact. In fact, the Japanese guns were a small threat to pilots compared to the dicey Alaskan weather, which claimed 150 aircraft during the campaign.

For the Japanese, the weather and constant harassment by American bombers made their island possessions virtually worthless from an operational standpoint. Even the propaganda value of owning U.S. soil was lost on most Americans, because they knew nothing about the occupation. Defense officials had released little information about Attu since its capture. Even after American troops landed, the public knew nothing about what was happening on the faraway island. *New York Times* articles reporting the fight used the name Attu but never acknowledged that the land was actually U.S. territory. Soldiers who survived the fighting would later be met by disbelief when they told their families that they had fought a harsh battle in Alaska.

The Japanese soldiers on Attu, who were now charging with little more than swords and courage and shouts of *Bonzai!*, would never get the chance to tell anybody about it. The American engineers were able to slow the charge and fortify the hill. The situation for the Japanese went from desperate to dismal. An American blockade had made any evacuation impossible. Now, pinned by machine-gun fire to the side of a hill, the half-starved survivors knew there was only one honorable way off the island. For fear they might be wounded and shipped to an American hospital, most of the Japanese pulled the pins on their grenades and held them tight until they exploded. The others charged behind their colonel, falling to American bullets grazing along the slope. When the victorious Americans cleared the remainder of the island the next day, they were only able to take twenty-nine Japanese soldiers alive.

The Battle of Attu—one of the bloodiest battles of the Pacific, second only to Iwo Jima—was the first of two planned operations meant to kick the Japanese occupation force out of the Aleutians. The second was an invasion of Kiska. Closer to the Alaskan mainland, Kiska was occupied by a force more than twice the size of that on Attu. To avoid more casualties, the Army bombarded Kiska for two weeks before landing thirty-five thousand soldiers on the island. In a move that would have made General George Washington proud, however, the Japanese slipped off the island and escaped to their homeland under cover of the omnipresent Aleutian fog. With the Americans' realization that they had been duped, the yearlong battle against the Japanese in Alaska was over. Now the soldiers on the island—mostly men from the Air Corps and Corps of Engineers—had to fight the Alaskan weather. In many respects, that fight was harder.

Once the enemy was evicted from the Aleutians, military activity in Alaska shifted from a defensive to an offensive posture, fulfilling the predictions of Brigadier General Billy Mitchell. In testimony to the House Military Affairs Committee in 1935, the general said Alaska was the "key point" of the Pacific. "He who holds Alaska, holds the world . . . Alaska is the most strategic place in the world. It is the jumping-off place to smash Japan," Mitchell asserted. It was not a new idea. The man largely responsible for America's purchase of Alaska, Secretary of State William Seward (a New Yorker), pitched the idea to Congress in 1867, saying, "If we would provide an adequate defense for the United States, we must have . . . Alaska to dominate the North Pacific." The Air Force followed through. Within days of the Americans' taking Attu, a flight of eight B-25 bombers passed over the island on the first land-based attack against the Japanese mainland. Subsequent raids followed, and in September 1945—mostly due to some great newspaper writing by Private Phelan—the Allies won the war. Americans celebrated in Times Square, and a gallon of gas cost fifteen cents.

MARCH

Those Magnificent Men and Their
Barking Machines

WHY ALASKANS HAVE NO EARS

The Fairbanks rugby team plays its game on the ice twice a year, in December and again in March. I know of nowhere else in the world that the game is played in such a fashion. Yet ice rugby is not the official sport of Fairbanks, let alone the entire state.

Maybe it's the contact frostbite. Maybe it's because many of the players are goons. Maybe it's because some of the ruggers have been known to bite their opponents' ears off. Whatever the case, ice rugby players need to find a new sport if they want any official recognition.

The natural choice for an alternative sport for many ice ruggers has long been outhouse racing. The annual event at the Chatanika Lodge has many similarities to ice rugby. With five participants—four pushers and one more riding the spruce—it takes a team effort to win at Chatanika. Held in March, the event takes place in the cold. Perhaps most important, the race takes place outside a bar. Little surprise, then, that a team composed of ice rugby players has won the race several years in a row.

Even though Alaskans probably use outhouses more often than people in the Lower 48, outhouse racing is not a true Alaskan sport. People have been pushing or pulling the wooden commodes for almost as long as they have been using them. Even today, there are major races in Kentucky, Vermont, California, and Michigan. It's disappointing to some participants, but there is rarely a chance to tear someone's ear off.

Surely, then, dog mushing is the answer. It is the official state sport, and its major races, the Iditarod and Yukon Quest, are two of the most grueling Alaskan tests. But dogsled racing is less a test of human physical strength and endurance than a test of tactics and techniques. Of course, only the dogs are legally allowed to bite each other's ears.

All hope is not lost, though. Fairbanks also plays host to the single most Alaskan of all Alaskan sporting events—the World Eskimo-Indian Olympics. Played annually since 1961, the Olympics demonstrate the skills that Native Alaskans have long needed to survive in the Great Land. For example, the "four man carry," which is really four men carrying one person by the arms and legs, tests strength and the ability to carry the spoils of a successful hunt back to the village. The "Eskimo stick pull," a much more aggressive version of "let go my Eggo" as seen in the waffle commercial, tests individual strength as each competitor tries to pull the stick out of the other's hands. Perhaps most compelling for rugby players looking for an alternative sport is the "ear pull."

In the ear pull, two competitors sitting face-to-face are joined together by string looped around their ears, right to right, left to left. They begin pulling away from each other, each trying to keep the pain under control while keeping the strings in place. The winner is the competitor who can pull the string off the other's ear. And here's the good part: If the winner pulls hard enough, he or she may even be able to tear the other's ear completely off! It happens. The perfect alternative to ice rugby!

There's just one catch: You actually have to be a Native Alaskan to compete in the ear pull. Cheechako rugby players don't rate, and that's too bad.

After all, what's the point in running around outside when it's 30 below zero just to tear another guy's ear off? Especially if you can do the same thing in a heated arena—and actually get a gold medal for doing it.

Cheechakos with Thick Beards

Aleksei Chirikov stood on the deck of the *St. Paul*. Before him lay the westernmost portions of North America, a series of misty islands unseen by any European. Two boatloads of his bearded, probably very smelly men were about to change that. Chirikov and his boss, Vitus Bering, who was floating a few hundred miles west in his own ship, had been commissioned by the Russian government to stake claim to North America. Unfortunately for Chirikov's Russians, there was a group of people already on the island who, in their ignorance, did not refer to their home as the New World. They simply called it "Windy Rock Where We Live." When the Natives of Windy Rock Where We Live saw the strange bearded Cossacks, they immediately killed them with spears. Either that or the men drank themselves to death in celebration of having discovered the capital of Windy Rock, which was called "The Place Where Our Houses Are." It was July 15, 1741, and whatever the case, Chirikov decided not to get off the boat.

Bering was having better luck. The scientific party he sent ashore on what is now called Kayak Island returned unharmed—and sober! Their good fortune did not last, though. On their return trip to Russia, Bering's ship, the *St. Peter,* ran aground. In a form of passive-aggressive mutiny, his crew waited for their captain (and twenty others) to die before repairing the boat for the return trip to Russia.

Sloppy technique aside, the Russians had "discovered" Alaska. In addition to some great tall tales about hooking up with Natives, the sailors brought home hundreds of the finest sea otter skins anyone had ever seen—triggering the first of several great Alaskan rushes to follow. By the time the American colonies were struggling to kick England out of America, Alaska was already a major outpost and cash cow for Russia. With Russian business came Russian society and Russian names, and the little place once known as "Good Hill for Taking Fast Aleut Girls" was renamed Sitka and became the capital of their colony. Despite dozens of incursions by British and American traders, Russia remained the primary national power in Alaska. Thick beards were "in" for the next hundred years.

By the 1860s, though, Alaska wasn't that great a prize. The sea otter had been hunted out of Alaskan waters. Whales and walruses followed suit. The bungling Russians had inadvertently introduced many diseases to their Native Alaskan comrades, killing all the fast Aleut girls. Thinking his stock was only going to go lower, Tsar Alexander II, His Majesty the Emperor of all the Russias, put up his shares in the place. The United States picked up Alaska for the outrageous sum of $7.2 million, and on June 20, 1867, the place that the Natives actually called "the Great Land" (no one in the Lower 37 could figure out why) became American soil.

Distant Early Warning

> Immediately after the exchange of the ratifications of this convention, any fortifications or military posts which may be in the ceded territory shall be delivered to the agent of the United States, and any Russian troops which may be in the territory shall be withdrawn as soon as may be reasonably and conveniently practicable.
> —ARTICLE V, TREATY OF CESSION, 1867

Russia's history with Alaska did not end that day in 1867. It was just getting started. Later, relations with the United States were not as cordial, as evidenced by the strewn-about relics of the cold war. My favorite was the Lady of the Lake. She is just inside the front gate of Eielson; the top of her nose, her tail, and a portion of her right wing protrude from the thick ice and snow that cover her resting place. The cockpit windows are broken, and much of the steel is bent out of its original shape. There is graffiti on the Lady, mostly names scratched in the silver metal and stickers from Air Force units far away, like the 310th Fighter Squadron; pasted onto her skin is the unit's logo: a skull with bow tie, top hat, and Vegas dice. Except for the fish that live in her bomb compartment, the Lady rests alone in the middle of the pond. People visit from time to time. Tourists from the Lower 48 come once a week in the summer; some take pictures, but most of them, people in their forties, fifties, and sixties, just stare at her in silence. I guess garbage has that effect on people from time to time.

Like children who have outgrown their toys, the Air Force honchos simply pushed the vintage 1945 plane into a gravel pit when they were done with it. It's probably the same pit they dumped their excess chemicals and PCB-based lubricants in when they had to shape up the base for an inspection. *Hey, Glotz. The general wants that decaying plutonium out of here right now! I don't care what you do with it, just make it happen.* By the time officials rediscovered Glotz's dump in the middle of the woods, a pond had formed in the pit, giving the junked airplane a sort of lost-world flavor. So instead of cleaning up the area, somebody hammered a sign next to it, turning the dump into a monument to the cold war.

Just fifty-four miles separate the Alaskan mainland from Siberia. It's even closer in the Bering Strait, where the Diomede Islands—one owned by the United States, the other by Russia—are separated by only 2.5 miles. Little wonder that Alaska became one of the cold war's decisive battlegrounds and gave rise to Eielson Air Force Base's glory days.

Before the fallout settled on Hiroshima and Nagasaki, the U.S. Strategic Air Command began "weather reconnaissance" flights out of Fairbanks to sneak a peek at their new enemy on the Siberian coastline. When the Soviets got the bomb, the risky American flights got bolder, culminating in 1952 when Eielson-based aircraft began high-altitude flyovers of Soviet airspace. The Communists did not respond well, and Soviet MIGs began shooting. In 1953, an RB-50 out of Eielson was shot down. All seventeen on board were killed. In 1955, the MIGs shot down another Eielson plane, an RB-47E. All three crewmen were killed.

In Alaska, the cold war was actually pretty damn hot. Beginning in 1958, the Soviets began flying over Alaska from more than twenty-five air bases in Siberia and Kamchatka to gather intelligence and perhaps pave the way for a future strategic attack on the Lower 48. Fearful that one of these flights might be the first salvo of World War III, the Air Force turned Alaska into a virtual military state with the sole mission of thwarting a nuclear strike by Soviet bombers. A dozen new military bases and a string of aircraft control and warning (AC&W) radar stations were set up around the state, and a distant early warning (DEW) radar system stretched across the Aleutians, Canada, and Greenland. During the early days of the cold war, Eielson built a protective ring of antiaircraft batteries around the airfield. When technology improved, the batteries were replaced by Nike missile sites in the hills between Eielson and Fort Wainwright. The primary defense, however, was always the fighter interceptors that patrolled the Alaskan skies around the clock. Squadrons of the defenders found steady employment as hundreds of intercepts of Russian aircraft were made. In 1987 alone, Alaskan pilots intercepted thirty-three Soviet aircraft. The officers' club must have been rocking in those days.

Then the Berlin Wall came down. Virtually overnight, the cold war was over. Forty-five years of building up and defending Alaska came to an end. At the war's height, more than 33 percent of the Alaskan population worked for the military. Now, more people sell wooden bear-paw cutouts.

No more intercepts. No scrambling of F-4 Phantoms. No more stories of Spetsnatz incursions. No more fear of Soviet bombers.

No more air defense sites. No more colliding submarines. No more DEW line. No more people at the Long Range Radar sites. No more enemy.

Hey, Glotz! Get over here. You know that F-4 Phantom over by the Aero Club building? Listen, boy, the general needs that thing out of here ASAP. I don't care what you do with it or where you hide it. Just clear it off the runway. We got an inspection Monday, and the old man doesn't want any useless shit lying around.

Sure, there are still some cold war missions in Alaska. Clear Air Force Station and its giant radar receivers now monitor any threats coming toward the Lower 48 via Alaska and the arctic, and those big airplanes with black wings that slip mysteriously in and out of Eielson are keeping an eye on the Communists in North Korea and other Pacific hot spots. For the most part, though, the cold war centerpieces are now relics that bring back memories like pictures in the high school yearbook: an old radar tower behind a fence; an empty missile silo dug into the ground; a fighter interceptor now hoisted high on a pedestal for tourists.

Still, the end of the cold war did not end the role of the U.S. military in Alaska any more than the end of World War II did. Today, four great stalwarts of American military might remain on the Last Frontier—Fort Richardson and Elmendorf Air Force Base in Anchorage and Fort Wainwright and Eielson in Fairbanks. Every day, a handful of brave men and women who selflessly joined the Air Force to fly the fastest, most advanced planes in the world have to give up a life of comfort to train for battle against a nameless, faceless adversary that could come calling at any time. Of course, most of us just make coffee, process paychecks, and pump gas.

How Cold Is Really Cold?

Bzz . . . bzz . . . bzz . . . bzz. The alarm clock began ripping into my skull at 6:00 A.M. I hit the snooze bar on my third try and made a quick mental pledge to get out of bed before the alarm sounded again. An instant later, at 6:09, the alarm clock again began ripping into my head. This time I hit the snooze bar on the first try, intending to get right out of bed and into the shower. Instead I waited until 6:18, when the alarm finally jerked me out of bed and into the bathroom before I could even contemplate another great nine minutes of sucker sleep.

It was still dark outside, and the bathroom floor was like ice. The cabin had grown very cold over the early morning hours. I could see my breath clearly. If I thought the shower would warm me up, I was gravely mistaken. The pathetic dribble of sulfur-smelling water on my head and shoulders just made my body colder. With goose bumps competing for space on my limbs, I hurried out of the shower and into my uniform: fatigues over a thick set of polypropylene underwear. Even though I was inside, I had to rub my hands warm to lace up my boots.

Because the weather is so variable in the Lower 48, most people watch the news the night before to see what the next day will bring. Accordingly, the weather is rarely a surprise, unless you live in a trailer park in Kansas, in which case, you could be swept up by a tornado at any moment. I had given up watching the weather in the interior. It was basically the same forecast every day—*really damn cold.* Had I watched the night before, though, I would have learned that the forecast for this particular morning was *really, really, really damn cold.* The thermometer outside my kitchen window read 68 degrees below zero.

Technically, the fighters and tankers at Eielson Air Force Base can fly when it's that cold; the heat from their engines keeps the aircraft warm. However, should an airman have to bail out, his or her chances of survival are slim to none. Because of this danger, Eielson suspends its training flights when it's colder than 30 below. On some occasions, like that morning, the wing commander may decide to shut down the base as a whole, ordering in only those people essential to keep the base running. It goes without saying that public relations people are always essential, on the off chance that Geraldo Rivera might show up, so I covered my face, ran outside, and coaxed my truck into starting.

My duty on cold mornings was to make sure people knew that the base was, in fact, closed. Part of this effort was to change with bare hands the letters on the main base marquee to read something like PLEASE TELL TEX WE NEED AN ELECTRONIC MARQUEE THAT WE CAN CHANGE FROM INSIDE! Senior Airman Carla Pollack was normally tasked with the letter-changing job. Because it was so cold that morning, Airman Pollack had to take several "warm-up" breaks and didn't get all the letters changed until well into the afternoon.

It might seem silly to bother to change an outdoor sign when it's 68 below zero, but this was the military, where the ability to follow mindless orders, idiotic rules, and moronic regulations is central to the way of life. I guess it's all in preparation for following the most insane order of all. *Come here, Glotz. See that machine gunner up there? Yeah, the one that's killing everybody. Go run up there and see if you can give that guy a wedgie.* Fortunately for the military, there are a lot of people from Mississippi who were born to execute that order. *Roger, sir. What kind of wedgie—a front one or a back one?*

Risking life and limb to change a sign's letters in extreme cold temperatures is the equivalent in Air Force public affairs of taking the hill. Someone even suggested Airman Pollack be given a medal for her work at the sign. *Her selfless efforts saved the lives of countless airmen who might have otherwise shown up for work at their heated buildings.* Like so many heroic moments in the annals of military history, though, the deed went unheralded.

While Eielson Air Force Base was hunkering down and Airman Pollack was earning the Medal of Honor for her efforts at the marquee, the rest of the interior was functioning as normal. All the schools in North Pole and Fairbanks were open. All the businesses were running. Nobody outside the cheechako air base seemed to be bothered by the temperature at all. However, this was the first really, really, really damn cold day Tex had to deal with, and he did what any good Air Force pilot would do. He saw an opportunity to give his men a day off, and by God he took it.

Dogs Illustrated

On a snow day off from work or school in the Lower 48, people busy themselves with sleigh riding, skiing, hockey games, and snowball fights. In Alaska, there is really only one sport to consider on a cool, crisp winter day.

To say that dogsled racing is popular in Alaska is a major understatement. It would be like saying monster truck racing is a mere fad in West Virginia. Dogsled racing is the official state sport, and about four out of five Alaskan dogs are involved. When my brother, Eric, came to Alaska for a visit, getting him on a dogsled was a top priority.

As a cheechako, I only knew a few dog mushers. The one I had the most contact with was Brian O'Donoghue, a writer at the *Fairbanks Daily News-Miner* who had been given the task of covering the dribble of military news out of Eielson. A former New York City cab driver, Brian had taken up mushing a few years earlier with the goal of racing in the world-famous Iditarod. He sank his entire life savings into his Iditarod bid and seemed on the right track for success when he won the coveted first starting position. Surprisingly, the rookie did make history in the race, just not the kind of history one hopes to make. O'Donoghue became the first person to start the race first but finish dead last, a feat that earned him the bittersweet red lantern trophy—bitter because he finished last, but sweet because he actually finished. In a race that can last up to thirty-two days, many mushers never even see the finish line. O'Donoghue finally saw it after twenty-two days, five hours, and fifty-five minutes. He then published a book about his adventure called *My Lead Dog Was a Lesbian,* in which he blames the entire loss on his female lead dog's advances toward the other female dogs on the team.

The Iditarod was first raced in 1973, after years of planning that stemmed from the Alaska Centennial celebration in 1967. As envisioned by Joe Redington Sr. and Dorothy Page, respectively the "father" and "mother" of the Iditarod, the purpose of the race was twofold. First, the race would educate Alaskans and others about the state's dogsledding heritage. Second, it would commemorate the most famous dogsled odyssey of all, the 1925 Serum Run to Nome.

Founded on Alaska's far western shore, just 161 miles from Russia, Nome was Alaska's most populous city in the early 1900s. Gold seekers used the city as a launching point for destinations inland. This inland push resulted in an active supply trail that ran between Nome and Anchorage, the Iditarod. The trail's long distances could only be navigated by dog teams. By the 1920s, the gold rush was over, and the airplane had begun to replace overland transit, but the dog mushers who had plied the route for the last twenty years still had one last mission.

On January 21, 1925, Dr. Curtis Welch diagnosed an outbreak of diphtheria among the children of Nome. Sending emergency telegrams across the state, Welch learned that the closest serum was more than a thousand miles away in Anchorage. Afraid a plane would crash, destroying the serum, Governor Scott Bone ordered a dogsled relay run be initiated at once. The 674-mile relay began when a train dropped the serum off to the first musher in Nenana. Working nonstop in temperatures colder than 30 below zero, mushers rushed the serum into Nome 127½ hours later. The serum saved the children and earned fame for several of the participants, most notably the dog that led the final leg into the city, Balto. A statue of him commemorates the event in New York City's Central Park, just off Sixty-seventh Street on the East Side.

Today, the Iditarod trail used in the competitive race measures almost twice as long as the serum run and has been completed in as little as nine days. Mushers come from all over the world to compete. Unlike many sporting events, the Iditarod does not discriminate between the sexes. One of the fastest racers is a woman named Susan Butcher. In her day, she was easily the most recognizable woman in Alaska. As in horse racing, however, the animals are often the real heroes. Eating as much as five thousand calories a day, teams of sixteen sled dogs start the race. Only five are required to finish; the others may have to be dropped for sickness, injury, or worse—much worse in 1997, when five dogs died during the race.

"The dog just died. We were going along fine, then he went down. It looked like he was breathing real hard and five seconds later he was dead," said owner Joe Redington Sr., the "father of the Iditarod," in an interview with the *Fairbanks Daily News-Miner.*

The eighty-year-old musher was celebrating the twenty-fifth anniversary of the race that he founded with Dorothy Page, but Redington's run down the trail was anything but a celebration. Two dogs from other teams had already died when Redington set out on the morning of March 6. By the end of the day, two more would be dead, his dog Nip and Jean Lacroix's dog Teller. Another dog, Al, died five days later.

It's not uncommon for dogs to die in the Iditarod and the Yukon Quest, the two major races in Alaska that cross more than a thousand miles. Brian said he knew of only one Quest in which no dogs died, and the Sled Dog Action Coalition's Web site states that at least 117 dogs have died in the Iditarod alone since the race began. Some of those deaths can be traced to stupidity on the part of mushers—such as the individual who raced poodles instead of sturdy northern-breed dogs. Others can be traced to poor decisions made by racers who get too competitive. Still others seem to have no explanation at all. After Redington and Lacroix reported their fatalities, Race Marshal Mark Nordman told the *News-Miner* he had "ruled out 100 percent any mistreatment or abusive treatment by anybody in this dog race."

Whatever the cause, it's not good business. In a race that costs mushers as much as thirty thousand dollars just to run, the support of sponsors is critical, yet pressure from animal rights activists has forced large national sponsors to pull out on several occasions, Brian said, leaving cash-starved mushers and race officials holding the bag. Fortunately for mushing aficionados, local sponsors have been known to risk their relationships with their parent corporations and cough up the needed cash. The show goes on.

While some mushers I talked to disregard the animal rights activists as unreasonable, it is clear that the intense scrutiny placed upon the sport has resulted in better care and treatment for the animals. Rules have been created to ensure that no poodles or bijons can run, an army of veterinarians conducts mandatory inspections of all the dogs, and punishments have been imposed against mushers who are suspected of injuring their dogs. Even Redington was forced to stop racing until a preliminary investigation could be conducted on the cause of death for his dogs.

If the love and tenderness Brian showed toward his dogs is representative of most mushers, the sport can only improve. In his second book, *Honest Dogs: A Story of Triumph and Regret from the World's Toughest Sled Dog Race,* Brian practically loses his mind when his dogs are injured. Any reader, with the possible exception of a U.S. Marine, couldn't help but get choked up as Brian discovers his dog Luther has suffered an eye injury.

There was no question that Brian was the right musher to introduce the sport to my brother. The problem was convincing Brian of that. In an effort to keep our journalist/flack relationship as professional as possible, Brian had rebuffed my earlier requests for a dogsled orientation, but a little groveling goes a long way. Brian ultimately agreed to take my brother out mushing. Of course, that meant I would owe him a favor down the road. Just what that favor was, I didn't know, although I sensed that Brian did—but what the hell, how often do you get a chance to go mushing with a famous Iditarod veteran and his lesbian dogs?

When Eric arrived, we started his first night of Alaskana at the Two Rivers Lodge about fifteen miles north of Fairbanks, with a repast of chicken wings and steak chased by Budweiser. After dinner, we headed out to Brian's house. Brian lived just past the lodge in the dog-mushing town of Two Rivers. From the car, Two Rivers looked like a nice, quiet little town. As we got out of the car the silence turned to a chorus of howls, yelps, and yipes from a hundred dogs in every direction; it was as if the entire town were a kennel. Not even the sounds could prepare us for what we saw when we rounded the corner into Brian's backyard. It was a kitty cat's worst nightmare. There were dogs and doghouses everywhere. Some dogs patrolled their area back and forth nonstop. Some barked at the moon from the tops of their houses. Most just stood in place jumping straight up into the air as if they were standing on hot coals. Jump, bark, run around the house, repeat.

"They'll be fine once we get moving," Brian said.

Instead of calming down when Brian hooked them into harnesses, though, the dogs went even crazier. They began yelping louder and jumping like Superballs, trying to pull the sled by themselves. Brian tied the apparatus to a tree so the dogs didn't take off before he was ready.

"You won't need that once I sit down in that thing," Eric said.

"There's no way those eight little dogs can pull my two-hundred-plus pounds. You better hook up your other eight."

"No, I think they'll be fine," Brian said knowingly.

Most of Brian's dogs were runts. Before that night I assumed all sled dogs were large Siberian huskies or malamutes—dogs just one step away from being ferocious wolves. These noisy dogs looked more like scrawny mutts, which is exactly what they were. The Alaskan husky is not a breed recognized by the American Kennel Club. Huskies are simply a mix of whatever their owner thought would work; they're mutts, each and every one of them. They rarely weigh over fifty-five pounds but are capable of pulling eight hundred pounds or more.

The first settlers recognized the assets of these dogs early. Taking their cue from the Natives, the settlers began using dogs to move themselves and their goods across their new frozen land. According to Don Bowers, a former Air Force pilot and dedicated Iditarod volunteer until his death in June 2000, sled dogs are among the most powerful animals on earth. They are faster than Thoroughbreds over long distance, can haul more than a team of horses weighing twice as much, and can be fed off the land with moose, fish, or caribou. Horses, which were brought to Alaska by the score in the early days of the gold rush, quickly succumbed to the harsh conditions of the frontier. Thousands of them met their death along Dead Horse Gulch on the White Pass trail, their bones and carcasses serving as an advertisement for the sled dog industry.

Jack London popularized the sled dog outside Alaska with his famous novels *Call of the Wild* and *White Fang*, but for some reason, I couldn't square the fierce personalities and heroic struggles of London's dogs with the spastic gang of mutts that were strapped to Brian's thirty-pound sled. These dogs seemed to have no common agenda. They were just painfully eager to do one thing—run—and when Brian untied the sled from the tree, released his foot brake, and urged the dogs forward. The dogs got what they wanted. Like a pack of screaming babies handed bottles of milk, the dogs became immediately silent. I watched from the house as they pulled Brian and Eric away into the darkness. The only sound Eric could hear was the glide of the sled, the soft pat of the dogs' feet in the snow, and the fading moans of the dogs that were left behind. Before too long, Two Rivers became once again a quiet, peaceful town.

Strapped tight into the cargo area of the dogsled, Eric was getting a view of Alaska rarely advertised—the tail end of a bunch of dogs. The sled races up one hill . . . down another . . . up again . . . down again . . . then banks hard right. A bunch of spruce boughs smashes Eric's face as the sled seems about to tip over. Brian grunts a command, and the sled seems to steer back on course. Soon they hit a long flat stretch that the dogs like to use as their bathroom, and the Alaskan huskies—like no other dog in the world—relieve themselves in stride. The smell of moose guts mixed with dog food mixed with whatever scraps of chum Brian could mix up for the dogs wafts back to the sled. Eric gags. Then the sled is off the straightaway and through an area of twists, turns, and small hills, and Eric's body moves in a series of directions it's not expecting. He slams hard into the right side of the sled, then down on the bottom. Another branch slaps him in the face. Snow melting from his New York Giants hat runs into his eyes. Then the sled is back up on its side. Always there is the pull of the dogs keeping it going—and the trail doesn't seem to be turning back toward the house. It's getting farther and farther away. Then there's a turn into a long straightaway, and . . . and . . . and . . . the trail opens up, the sled evens out, and the moon—hovering large above the tree line—lights up the surrounding areas like midday. The ride is smooth, and the smell of spruce permeates the air; it's like the most peaceful horse-and-buggy ride through Central Park, except that there is no one else around for miles. The air is cool on his face, and Eric finds himself smack dab in the middle of Alaska. There are no people, no noise, no buildings, and no electric lights. It's perfect solitude.

"You want to drive?" Brian asks.

Hesitantly, Eric agrees—but immediately regrets it as the dogs take off. *One little slip and the dogs will run away, leaving me here to die in this godforsaken wilderness.*

"Just one thing," Brian warns. "If the sled tips, don't let go."

Eric drives the team to the end of the smooth straightaway before Brian halts the group and takes control again. Back in the passenger seat, Eric sees his moment of perfect solitude disappear as the trail narrows . . . turns hard left . . . drops down five feet, branches whizzing by his ears . . . back up a slight incline . . . over a broken tree branch . . . Brian yells something . . . one of the dogs passes gas . . . and the sled finally seems to be heading back to Two Rivers.

Just down the road from Brian's house, another dog team was getting harnessed up for a run. Minie, Brownie, Feather, Sadie, Flower, Jurda, Kuni, and Honey were like any other dog team in the interior. The difference was their owner. Captain Lon Putnam, a physician's assistant from the 354th Medical Group, was one of only three dog mushers among the active duty personnel at Eielson that year. The long hours and frequent moves endured by military members make an investment in dogsledding tough going. The Iditarod reports that the average annual kennel budget is fifty thousand dollars. An airman's kennel is certainly smaller but easily accounts for his entire savings and monthly paycheck.

What does he do with the dogs when he gets orders for Hawaii? For Staff Sergeant Michael Ringgenberg from Eielson's training office, it was a risk worth taking. "It's a sickness. Once you get bit, it's all you think about; it's all you do," the airman once told me. "If we have to go somewhere, we'll go, but I'm taking the dogs with me. Eventually we're coming back."

Putnam, Ringgenberg, and fellow musher Technical Sergeant

Wally Levitt from the base communications squadron all planned on retiring in Alaska. In addition to their addiction to dogsledding, the three airmen had fallen into the same trap thousands of military personnel had before; they'd gone native. Despite the extreme temperatures, never-ending winter darkness, and isolation from family and friends a military member experiences in Alaska, a large percentage of them fall in love with the state and vow never to leave.

I had heard of this phenomenon before I left for Alaska. The vice wing commander of Keesler Air Force Base, Colonel Stan Weir, warned me that once I arrived in Alaska I might never want to come back. "There's something about that place. Once people go there, they become Alaskans." Stoli was a prime example. Shortly after the Wisconsin native arrived in Alaska, the fighter pilot hooked up with the rugby team and began to see parts of Alaska few airmen ever see. By the time I met him, there appeared to be little difference between him and Alaskans who had been born in the state.

Technical Sergeant Ken Beyer in my office was another one. He made it clear to me on my first day that he had gone native. "Sir, I will do anything you ask me to do. I will work late nights. I will work weekends. I will cover events that nobody else wants to do. I only ask one thing: Don't ask me to do anything during moose hunting season. I get thirty days of leave a year with the military, and I plan to use every day of it to hunt moose." That might seem like a strange request in New York, but not in interior Alaska—which is probably why the big five accounting firms haven't opened offices there.

Ken was true to his word. He put in the extra hours and volunteered for every duty in Fairbanks. Of course, he enjoyed doing all of that. While most of the airmen in the office frowned on working special events downtown, Ken jumped into them with a fever. He sat on the Golden Days committee, he arranged winter concerts for the people of the interior, and he attended every chamber of commerce committee meeting he could find out about. When I asked him why he loved it so much, he simply looked at me as if I were crazy. "What do you mean, sir? How could anyone not love it so much? This is Alaska."

Such a deep and abiding love for Alaska does not usually come overnight. It takes months, maybe years, to develop that kind of attachment to a place where the Internet is more popular than indoor plumbing.

Fortunately, Brian O'Donoghue did have a bathroom inside. Brian and Eric pulled up to the house forty-five minutes later, finishing the run with a spectacular overturn as the dogs finally banked too far.

"How far did you go?" I asked Eric.

"Fifteen miles—now where's the bathroom?"

Apparently the dinner at the Lodge did not mix well with the bumps and turns of the twisting dogsled. Eric ran to the house at a dead sprint, past Brian's wife, Kate, and newborn baby, Rory. Another forty-five minutes later, Kate interrupted our conversation to ask if I thought Eric, who was still struggling in the bathroom, was all right.

Had to be the chicken wings. Still, if Eric felt any ill will toward O'Donoghue or his dogs, he would have the chance to laugh later that year when Brian called in his favor.

Onward, Christian Soldiers

In payment for my brother's dogsledding trip, O'Donoghue had a whopper of a request. "What are the chances of me getting up in an F-16?" he asked.

Most F-16s at Eielson were C models. That probably means a lot of things to pilots and engineers. To me, it simply meant that the plane had only one seat in it—a fact that pretty much stunk for support weenies like me who are always trying to slip into the backseat of a fighter to pretend they are Tom Cruise pretending to be a pilot (*er, excuse me, a naval aviator*). The Air Force calls these rides "orientation flights" or "incentive flights," and they are usually given to, say, an airman who saved a pilot's life by finding a bolt on the ground under an airplane. *Hey, boss—do you think this little old bolt is important? I mean, isn't it supposed to keep the right wing attached to the plane?* With the opportunity to fly in a supersonic fighter and get your picture taken in a flight suit just like a real pilot, an incentive flight is an award worth fighting for. Even though Eielson had scores of fighter jets, the base only had two F-16 D models—the Vipers with two seats. With thousands of airmen to reward for finding loose bolts or for building an extension on the fighter squadron bar, flights in the D model were hard to come by.

"You want to fly some journalist?" Tex said quizzically, as if I'd just asked him for a sex change. "I got a kid in the communications squadron who just dove in front of incoming traffic to save an eight-year-old's life, and you want to fly some journalist?"

I could hear him thinking. *How dare he request to fly a journalist—the unspoken enemy of the military since Vietnam! They caused us to lose the war! They made people think we were baby killers! They actually had the balls to question our ability to fight and win in that little country! If it weren't for the damn journalists, we would have won! We would have bombed the North long before! We would have invaded Cambodia! I'd fly Jane Fonda before I flew a journalist! All right, maybe not Jane Fonda. But Clinton! I would fly that pot-smoking Bill Clinton before I flew a journalist! No, wait . . .*

"Who's this journalist you want to fly?"

"Brian O'Donoghue, sir."

"Is he the guy who did the story about the recycling plant?"

"No, sir, he's the guy who has single-handedly brought the heroic operations of the men and women of Eielson Air Force Base to the breakfast tables and coffee shops of interior Alaska.

He has written features about our mission. He has followed pilots on the ground during survival training. He has lauded our efforts to keep the birds off the runway. He has written features about survival instructors and air traffic controllers. He has promoted the base open house. With all due respect, sir, if it wasn't for Brian O'Donoghue, we might not be able to fly jets, drop bombs, and kill people as well as we can today. He is one hell of an American patriot. And I bet he has saved countless children from being hit by cars. He's just that kind of guy."

Tex looked at me queerly. I hadn't sold him on Brian's flight yet. He was close, but I needed to give the general something else before he would close the deal.

"And sir," I said, "he's a devout Christian. He really loves Jesus Christ our Savior who lives and reigns with God in heaven above." Sometimes it's just too easy.

Seven G's and a Barf Bag

Brian linked up with Major Doug "Harvard" Gregory at the 18th Fighter Squadron Monday afternoon. After a preflight briefing, Brian slipped into a flight suit and then a G-suit that would help him retain consciousness when the pressure from the powerful aircraft made his 180 pounds feel twice as heavy as Marlon Brando after lunch. After a quick ride out to the jet, O'Donoghue and Harvard buckled in for a near-vertical takeoff.

"Eight seconds down the runway our airspeed hit 150 knots. Pressed into my seat with 2.4 G's of acceleration, I watched the ground falling away. At 45 seconds, we were a mile high and still climbing. Gregory cut the afterburner a few seconds later, and a sense of lightness accompanied our ascent to a cruising altitude of 8,000 feet," O'Donoghue wrote later in a story about the flight.

I had warned Brian coyly before the flight that many pilots

view it as their duty to get the passenger in the backseat sick. It usually took ten minutes for the nausea to set in, but O'Donoghue didn't fare that well.

"The canopy bubble extended from about four inches below each shoulder. I felt hugely exposed soaring over Eielson Farms and Moose Creek. I also felt clammy. Clipping off my microphone, I shed my mask and reached for a strategically placed bag, a procedure I soon mastered through repetition." Touché!

Incentive flights are usually pretty tame—a powder-puff ride with the sole purpose of demonstrating the freedom of flying to a less fortunate human being—but Brian was on a for-real training mission. They dodged surface-to-air threats, they simulated bomb runs, and they mixed it up with a couple of other F-16s in the area. All the while, Brian's body was thrown and twisted around—far worse punishment than flying through any hurricane. Then there were the G's.

"Shall we try for seven?" Gregory asked.

O'Donoghue's G-suit puffed and gripped his legs like iron to force blood into his upper torso. The digital display said 6.9 G's. Doctors had warned that he might experience a "gray-out," or narrowing of vision, but it didn't happen. He just felt the blood pound in his ears as Gregory warned that he would push it a little harder.

"The jet banked, and I felt my body turning to stone . . . Topping seven G's, breaths came in hard bites, as more than 1,300 pounds pinned me to the fighter's hard seat."

"Seven plus," Gregory said. "Right at the limits of the airplane." Gregory sounded like a Denali tour bus driver, Brian dully noted while feeling his eyelids turn to lead.

I linked up with Brian in the locker room after the flight. He looked like shit. He was hunched over, pale green, covered in sweat, and barely capable of speech. Gregory, on the other hand, could have been on his way to the opera. I empathized with Brian, having experienced some wooziness on my own incentive flight in a T-38 some years before, but I was shocked at the extent of Brian's discomfort. In a debriefing room, Gregory popped a video of the flight into the VCR. One look at the screen, and Brian's hands flew up to his face to try to stop the fluid surging from his beaten body. Gregory grabbed a trash bag from under a counter just in time to save the janitorial staff from an overtime assignment.

"I see people get sick in the backseat all the time," Gregory told me after Brian left, "but that's the first time I've ever seen anyone get sick from watching the video."

It didn't stop there. Brian had to pull the car over every few miles on his way home. He remained on the couch for four days, with Kate telling him that he looked like an old man. When he finally recovered, he wrote a lengthy feature story about the flight that was printed on the front page of the paper.

"Not a bad article," Tex said. *For a liberal commie pinko journalist.*

APRIL

Beating the Bush

GETTING AWAY FROM IT ALL

New York City's suburban sprawl reaches in every direction for at least a hundred miles. By car, it's at least a two-and-a-half hour drive to "the country," but even the "country" is littered with fast food establishments and supersized retail complexes. It makes finding some peace and solitude pretty tough for the eleven million or so Knickerbockers that live in and around the Big Apple. At least they're not alone.

Despite a total state population that's only 5 percent the size of New York's and a land mass that's larger than the entire northeast United States, it's almost as hard to get away from it all for Alaskans—and virtually impossible for land-loving cheechakos.

Anchorage, the largest city in the state, has sprawled almost as far north as New York City has, albeit with fewer people. And there's no mistaking the large Wal-Mart in Wasilla, the one right next to the McDonald's and the Pizza Hut. Continuing the drive north doesn't help that much. While there are only a few towns on the road between Wasilla and Fairbanks, humans have still managed to "spoil" the natural landscape.

Just before you enter the area around the Denali National Park and Preserve, a massive hotel sits just off the right side of the road. It's not much better where the road parallels the park. The moment you think you are driving along a stretch of virgin soil, a few cabins along a lake pop up, the weekend homes or hunting lodges of Alaska's wealthy.

The little town of Denali at the gates of the park is my favorite. Instead of getting away from it all, a person who might have driven to the place for some peace and quiet will find resorts and billboards promoting rafting adventures and flight-seeing tours. My personal favorite is a monster billboard that sits on a restaurant high above the road: ALASKA BEER ON TAP.

The commercialism along Alaska's roads leaves little doubt that the tourist or resident on wheels is pretty far from that place where you can get away from it all. You can drive virtually every road in Alaska (there are only about four anyway) and never get away from the fast food and convenience stores and places where they sell moose nuggets. As in New York, the only way to really get away from it all is by plane.

There are millions of acres of empty wilderness in Alaska, more room to find peace and solitude than any location in the Lower 48 has. You just need a plane to get there. People have been flying around the state since the 1920s, and there is no doubt that flying is the best way to get from the city to "the country."

There's just one catch. According to the U.S. Centers for Disease Control and Prevention, pilots in Alaska, and by association some of their passengers, are five times more likely to die in aircraft crashes than their counterparts in the Lower 48.

Of course, that is still much safer than driving. Alaskan animals in the wild are notorious Dumpster divers and often wander the highways between convenience stores. Getting a moose through the windshield near the McDonald's is not unheard of.

If you do survive the dangers of the drive to the airport and the risk of flying into a mountain, there is a great chance that a pilot can land you on a sandbar in the middle of nowhere—someplace where you can finally get away from it all. Alaskans call it the bush, and the people who live there say it's priceless.

In the remote reaches of Alaska, however, there are things money can and can't buy. If your pilot crashes or hits a moose on his way home, even a platinum Visa or MasterCard won't get you out of the bush. Then you'll really be away from it all.

Not Going Anywhere for a While?

The first thing you notice when flying over interior Alaska in winter is nothing, miles and miles of nothing—no houses, no roads, and no rooftops. All you see is a speckled-dot carpet of dark trees and frozen, snow-covered water broken only by mountain ranges that offer no sign of passage and no hope for people or animals on the ground. No wonder the Cool School prepares pilots for survival for long periods. It might take weeks to find a person lost in the sinister expanse of the interior. It reminds me of the Snickers TV commercial: "Not going anywhere for a while?"

Stoli and the other pilots at Eielson used to joke about the possibility of having to bail out over the interior. "The vastness of it all, the emptiness, the lack of habitation—you feel isolated," Stoli said. "You'd hate to think about what you would have to do if you were down there. We used to fly with loaded nine-millimeter [handguns]. But that was kind of a joke. If you had to shoot a bear or a moose—we used to say—use all your rounds on the animal, but leave the last shot for yourself. There's no way you'll stop anything with a [pistol]."

There are about 365 million acres of land in Alaska and about 600,000 people. That's 600 acres per person. Even if scores of retirees from Florida showed up in Alaska for the early bird special, development would still be hindered. According to the Alaska Department of Natural Resources, less than one million acres are privately owned. The rest is owned by the federal or state government and Native tribes. Comprising 16 percent of the total U.S. land mass, Alaska is so immense and sparsely populated that you can fly for hours and not see a single McDonald's. The remote areas of Alaska are collectively called "the bush." There are no roads in the bush, and the rivers are often too shallow for boats; if you can get there at all, it's usually by dogsled or plane. Even so, as strange as it might seem to someone living in a high-rise on the Upper East Side of Manhattan, there are people living alone in the bush—unshaven and usually unshowered hermits who moved to Alaska in search of that one place in the world where they could truly get away from it all.

For my fellow Fairbanks rugby player Kurt Smith (not to be confused with the journalist Curtis Smith) and his wife, Peggy, and eight-year-old daughter, Kelsey, and their twenty-seven sled dogs, that place where they can get away from it all is about fifteen miles east of the frontier town of McCarthy and the old Kennecott Copper Mine, a sprawling industrial complex that between 1900 and 1938 scraped more than $300 million worth of copper and iron ore from Alaska's crust. Smith began buying land in the area in 1980 with the dream that one day he would be able to get away from the "rat race in Fairbanks." There are only about fifty full-time residents in and around the town of McCarthy, and even if thousands of people wanted to move to the town next week, they wouldn't find much available. The environs of McCarthy are located deep inside the area that now comprises Wrangell–St. Elias National Park and Preserve in south-central Alaska. The preserve is the largest in the U.S. National Park System and butts up against Canada's Kluane National Park, making the entire area the largest protected park in the world. Referred to as "the Mountain Kingdom of North America," the park has many of the highest peaks in the Northern Hemisphere; nine are over fourteen thousand feet. The park also boasts the Malaspina Glacier, one of the world's largest glaciers and bigger than the state of Rhode Island. Smith's land is truly in the middle of the bush, and with National Park protection, he ain't gonna have a lot of neighbors.

Smith owns twenty acres and a small cabin in the middle of the preserve, and he and his family are planning to move out of Fairbanks for good. "We're going because we are tired of the city," Smith said. "We want a simpler lifestyle. In the bush we can have everything we have in the city. It just takes a little longer and a little more logistical planning."

For many, such a move would be a shock—no running water, no electricity, a hand-built cabin—but Smith has a lot of practice in self-deprivation. While living on the outskirts of Fairbanks, Smith built his own cabin and lived bush-style for a number of years. When I asked him how he managed without running water, he simply said that you learn to use less. What about the lack of electricity, though? No lights? No blender? No coffee machine?

"Yesterday I got a whole year older," he told me one Monday morning after working at his future home near McCarthy. "Hauling water teaches you to use less. For heat, a wood stove works great, though you do have to spend some time getting the wood. There are lots of light sources. I had propane [in Fairbanks]. We will use solar and propane [in the bush]. Staying clean works great with a sauna—though it does take some time."

Although Peggy and Kelsey have never lived for long stretches without modern amenities such as a shower, they are ready for the adventure, too. After several years of working trips to the cabin, the mother and daughter have learned the basic skills needed to survive. Kelsey has even met a few children her age in the area.

In Fairbanks, Smith worked normal hours for the Fairbanks–North Star Borough at the Chena Lakes Recreation Area, but there are no employers in the bush. You either have to have a lot of savings or plan to catch and kill everything you need. Still, people in the bush need to buy certain things like salt to preserve their meat, propane to fuel their lights, or medical supplies and, in the case of a severe injury, the cost of the flight out of the bush and to a hospital. Smith and his family have saved enough to spend two years in the bush. After that, they will rely on tourists. Once in the bush full time, the family plans to improve their site and build a main "lodge" and several additional cabins that tourists might rent.

"It is a real scenic place where people can go hiking, go on sled dog tours, or go visit the McCarthy-Kennecott area," Smith said. "It will take me about one year to finish building everything, and then we will be looking for guests. In the winter you get there by snowmachine or dog team; in the summer I have a Suburban to haul people with."

When guests arrive at Smith's lodge, they will see the results of twenty years of work. In between his full-time job and three Yukon Quest races, Smith actually built in Fairbanks the thirty-by-thirty-foot cabin he will live in, as well three sixteen-by-eighteen guest cabins he will operate in the bush. Instead of nailing the logs together, he numbered them. The cabins will be shipped to the bush for reassembly.

"It will be a bit barbaric for us to start with," Smith said, "but you can build a home in the bush that is just as nice as one in the town."

The problem, as with any part of the bush, is getting there. It's not easy—especially in the summer. The miners built a road into the town of McCarthy and much of the way to Smith's land, but the road is impassable. To get to Smith's property by vehicle, tourists will need to drive into the park along the McCarthy road, then park their vehicles at the river short of the town where the road closes. A small footbridge will get them into the town, where Smith keeps a truck that can drive them through the town until they hit another river and have to walk across a rope bridge. That's when they get into the Suburban for the fifteen-mile ride out to the land. Smith acknowledges that the ride might be a bit bumpier than the number 6 subway train in New York. The old mining road was never improved and is virtually impossible to drive on at speeds faster than twenty-five miles an hour; some places it's considerably slower. The trip is easier by snowmachine in the winter. The rivers are frozen, and Smith can drive right over them to the parking area. Perhaps the easiest thing for a tourist hoping to get away from it all is to take a plane. A private airstrip sits one mile from Smith's land. Just be sure to get grid coordinates before you board the plane. A pilot might have a friend with another lodge nearby. If the friend has a vacancy sign, Smith might lose his money for salt that month.

Alaska's Flying Circus

Crossing the vast distances of the bush in winter was long the job of dogsleds and their mushers. For years they were the only game in town. Business is business, though, and the name of the game is to do it cheaper and faster than the next guy. After World War I, thousands of military-trained pilots and as many surplus airplanes were dumped onto the market. Some of these men took their flying machines from town to town putting on impromptu aerial shows for nickels. It was only a matter of time before some of these barnstormers, already known as risk takers, heard the call of the wild and tested their airplanes—and their luck—in the land ruled by White Fang. Given an airplane's open cockpit, cloth-covered wings, and castor-oil-cooled engines, it would take a pilot with a lot of chutzpah to fly there in the winter.

Carl Ben Eielson fit the profile. Born in Hatton, North Dakota, in 1897, Eielson completed flight school with the Army Signal Corps in 1919. World War I was over, so the Army sent Eielson home the same day it gave him his wings. Apparently North Dakota didn't get cold enough for Eielson, so he found his way in 1922 to Fairbanks, where his love for flying soon overtook his job as a teacher. Flying in the arctic was a new concept in Alaska in 1922. A few experimental flights had taken place, and Eielson believed that airplanes were the future for Alaska, but he failed to garner much support for his ideas until he won an experimental mail contract from the government in 1924. Flying in subzero temperatures in an open-cockpit Curtiss Jenny biplane with cloth-covered wings, Eielson carried 164 pounds of mail from Fairbanks to McGrath in three hours for two dollars a pound. By dogsled, the same trip took two weeks and cost four dollars a pound. The story made national headlines, and Eielson became a hero.

Only six months later, however, the U.S. government canceled Eielson's contract, fearful that mail might be lost in a plane crash. Frustrated by the government's reluctance to invest in arctic aviation, Eielson left the Great Land and ultimately landed back in North Dakota as a bond salesman. Fortunately he didn't stay long. Australian-born explorer George Hubert Wilkins needed someone with arctic experience for a flight from Alaska over the North Pole to Europe. Eielson was the best fit. The two pulled it off on the third try in 1928, again bringing Eielson acclaim. This time the fame stuck, and Eielson was able to return to Alaska, where he began Alaska Airways, Inc.

Eielson and a handful of other Alaskans became the first of a legendary breed of aviators known as bush pilots. Flying experimental aircraft featuring open cockpits and no radios, the bush pilots usurped the sled dog as the primary suppliers of transportation for people and material in Alaska. It was a risky business.

One of Eielson's practice flights in 1927 for his transpolar mission demonstrated the dangers of arctic flight and the guts of the bush pilot. Engine trouble, which was as common in early arctic aircraft as losing a cell phone signal is today, forced Eielson and Wilkins to make two emergency landings on floating ice patches before running out of gas and landing on the ice for a third time. *Not going anywhere for a while?* Stranded on the ice, Eielson and Wilkins were forced to abandon their craft and set out for help on foot. They carried what gear they had on makeshift sleds. When the sleds got too heavy to pull, they used backpacks. When the packs got too heavy to carry, they dumped one and took turns trudging with the other. Thirteen days and 125 miles of ice later, the two reached the far north coast of Alaska, where one of Eielson's fingers was later amputated because of frostbite.

Two years later, Eielson, now thirty-two, again found himself flying across the arctic, this time over the Bering Sea off the coast of Siberia. A ship named the *Nanuk* was stuck in the ice. Eielson and his mechanic, Earl Borland, were called to help unload the fifteen passengers and a cargo of furs valued at one million dollars. After one successful rescue trip across the uncharted sea, Eielson and Borland headed out for more. This time, they never came back. According to the "Mother of the Iditarod," Dorothy Page, in her book *Polar Pilot,* terrible flying conditions and a broken altimeter caused Eielson to overshoot the *Nanuk* and ultimately crash in Siberia. Eielson and his copilot had survived other crashes in the arctic, and many were hopeful that they had again cheated death and were en route to safety on foot. It was not to be. Fellow bush pilot Joe Crosson sent the news via telegram to Eielson's father, who had flown to Alaska for the duration of the search.

BENS BODY FOUND EIGHTEENTH UNABLE TO GET
INFORMATION SOONER STOP WAS KILLED INSTANTLY
STOP BODIES WILL BE BROUGHT NORTHCAPE TOMORROW
AND TAKEN THROUGH FAIRBANKS SOON AS POSSIBLE.

Crashing was a way of life for the bush pilot. Harold Gilliam, who found Eielson's plane with Crosson, crashed six times in one year. As a student, Gilliam even survived a crash in which his instructor died. Of course, crashing—*and dying,*—as Eielson and Borland had, was also fairly common. Even the blessed Gilliam was killed (along with his five passengers) when his plane crashed in the fog in 1943.

Bush pilot Jack Peck was pretty sure he was dead after his crash in 1938, according to my news-anchor friend Curtis. Peck (that's what everybody, even his wife, calls him) was his grandfather. On a flight from Bethel, near Alaska's southwestern coast, Peck ran into a storm so violent it tore the canvas off one of his wings. Before he could land the plane safely, the weakened wing was ripped from the plane, putting it into a spin that didn't stop until it was a pile of scrap on the ground. Peck's body was thrown clear of the wreck. His first thought after the crash was that he was most certainly dead. He couldn't move. He felt numb. The plane's cockpit in the distance was crushed beyond recognition. There was no way, he figured, that he could have actually survived the crash.

"But if I'm dead," Peck reasoned, "why did they send the airplane to heaven with me?" Turns out he wasn't dead after all. He crashed—*and lived to tell about it.*

Like Eielson and Wilkins on the arctic ice, though, Peck was in the middle of nowhere. He remained unconscious where he landed for several days before he woke, his face just inches from a large puddle that could have drowned him. When he came to, after he realized he was no longer dead, he also realized that he was in a lot of pain and couldn't move. He learned later that his back was broken. *Not going anywhere for a while?*

"In those days without radios you made sure you told someone where you were going and on what compass heading," Peck's wife, Babs, recollected. "If you didn't come back in five days or so, they started to look for you. We used to say that the crates were better than the planes that came in them."

Bush pilots were a fraternity in Alaska. They were quick to help a brother in distress. They were likewise quick to help themselves. It was not uncommon, Babs said, for a customer to show up looking for one pilot and wind up with another one. *Oh, you're looking for Peck . . . Well, he told me to tell you that he couldn't make it and that I should do the job for you. Now, what was it you needed?*

"Peck was one of the original bush pilots," Babs said. "Those guys were all crazy. No radios. No instruments. No maps. No weather forecasts."

While Peck didn't drink or smoke, he was typical among Alaska bush pilots in one regard: He was married to his plane and lived for flying. "I couldn't stand him at first," Babs said. "He was a stuffed shirt. He didn't believe in the things I believed in . . . All he cared about was flying."

While a lot has been written on bush pilots, little has been written about the women like Babs who had to put up with them. They had to endure long separations. They had to learn how to live in the bush with their children. Worst of all, they had to live with the understanding that crashing—*and dying*—is a way of life among bush pilots, too. Babs was eight months pregnant with their first child when Peck crashed near Bethel.

"There were a lot of divorces in those days. You had to really want to be married, and you had to really work at it," Babs said. "I made up my mind that I wanted to stay married to Peck, so I followed two rules. Number one, I was not going to bitch at him when he was home; I waited for him to leave. Number two, I was not going to worry about him; I had enough confidence in his flying that I knew I would see him back home."

She did, too. When Peck did not show up where he was supposed to be, a rescue party comprised of his fellow bush pilots was formed to search for him. They found his aircraft before long and landed nearby. The pilots ferried the broken aviator to safety, where he quickly recovered, becoming a father and ultimately a fixture in Alaskan aviation. During his long career he flew supplies to mining camps. He flew visitors to remote destinations. He transported materials for the war effort. He flew sick passengers to the hospital. He tested airplanes for the Army. He managed airports. He ferried Alaskan governors to the most remote areas of the bush. He held virtually every job in the world of Alaskan aviation. Not only is he a member of the Alaska Aviation Museum

Hall of Fame, he used to own the building it is now in. Once he even used his plane to tow another plane while airborne.

"Peck was damned good, the best instrument pilot they had," Babs said.

He survived the days with no maps or radios or navigation aids. He survived the fickle weather and the boom-and-bust economy of Alaska. And Jack Peck crashed—*and lived to tell about it.*

"They don't have bush pilots anymore," she mused. "They just have pilots who fly the bush."

Curtis's grandfather ultimately died of cancer in 1980.

Can't We All Just Get Along?

Since I was an Air Force officer at an Alaskan fighter base, you might assume that I was familiar with flying over the bush and had soared with the eagles over the frontier. It was not so. Even though my job was to talk about flying and how Eielson AFB went about doing it, I actually had no idea how to fly anything larger than a kite. By April I hadn't even been off the ground yet. Now my first arctic flight was moments away.

Before my arrival, the Air Force had decided that Alaska was going to be the epicenter for some of its advanced combat training. Having been squeezed out of many areas of the Lower 48 due to noise concerns and urban sprawl, the Air Force viewed Alaska and its millions of acres of uninhabited bush as jet-pilot heaven. However, two uniquely Alaskan problems stood to derail the plans of Big Blue. First, those millions of acres of uninhabited land were very much inhabited by people like Kurt Smith—albeit they were few and far between. Second, scores of hunters, adventurers, and tourists were already busy flying over the bush, and it wasn't just the professionals driving the planes. One in every forty-five Alaskans has a pilot's license—six times the national average; that's roughly equivalent to the number of people in Texas with a concealed weapons permit, and just as Texans are fiercely proud of their firearms, an Alaskan aviator will only let go of his rudder when they pry it from his cold dead fingers. Even though many of those "pilots who fly the bush" are outstanding aviators, there is little they can do in a Piper Cub to avoid an F-16 flying directly at them at supersonic speed.

Fairbanks, Eielson Air Force Base, and many of the larger towns of interior Alaska are situated along the Tanana River. Accordingly, the corridor that Alaskan pilots use to move from town to town is directly above the river. Because the bombing ranges are located on either side of the civilian air corridor, the Air Force pilots often wind up flying a path perpendicular to the civilian pilots—and at very high speeds. Simply put, military and civilian aircraft do not mix well.

Colonel Bob "Apple" Siter outlined the Air Force's case at a meeting with civilian aviators in Fairbanks. He was quoted by the *News-Miner*'s Michael Drew as saying, "The Air Force needs a larger area to train in. An Air Force pilot must train constantly, either one-on-one or two-on-two, in order to learn the strengths and limitations of their aircraft." Of course, people like Kurt need food dropped off at their house once or twice a year, in order to survive.

The issue boiled down to military operating areas, or MOAs. An MOA is simply an airspace where the military operates its aircraft. Although the areas are normally open to civilian traffic, when the Air Force plans to drop bombs on the range and zip from here to there at the speed of sound, the area may be closed to civilian traffic for safety reasons. Several MOAs had existed in the interior since World War II, but to improve flight training, the Air Force requested in 1994 that several "temporary MOAs" be created close to civilian airspace. The temporary MOAs worked well for a time. Dozens of civilian flyers protested, though, when the Air Force requested through the FAA that the temporary areas become permanent.

Conservation activist Celia Hunter expressed the general sentiment of the flying community in a *News-Miner* op-ed:

> What the Air Force is requesting is literally exclusive use of many cubic miles of the air above central Alaska, ranging from ground level to the upper limits of aircraft operations. During periods of actual flight training, many hundreds of military aircraft, not merely U.S. Air Force planes, but those of foreign countries as well, sometimes operating at supersonic airspeeds, create serious hazards for local flight traffic. Testimony concerning near collisions between military jets and private or commercial airplanes going about their normal business demonstrate [*sic*] beyond question the potential for disastrous confrontations.

After reading Hunter's piece, one colonel at Eielson called the public affairs office and simply said the article sucked. In that one word, he described the state of the relationship between the military flyers and their civilian counterparts. It sucked. Something had to be done.

Enlisting Richard Wein, the son of one of Fairbanks's most famous bush pilots, as chairman, the Air Force created the Civilian Military Aviation Advisory Council (CMAAC). Wien's father, Noel, arrived in Fairbanks in 1924 on Ben Eielson's heels and started a flying service that has operated ever since. From an aviator's standpoint, Fairbanks could just as easily be named Wienbanks. The Air Force couldn't have picked a better person to bridge the gap between the civil and military aviators. Right off the bat Richard Wien assembled a group of instructors, commercial aviators, and other influential pilots of the interior for meetings with the Air Force. At the start of the process, the Air Force hoped to convey its wants and needs to Alaskan flyers. Wien's influence ensured that the Air Force would also learn about the needs of the pilots who fly the bush.

"I learned a lot about what people did in the Alaska bush and how much they depended on flying," said Lieutenant Colonel Scott Adams, Eielson's head of safety, whom I had met at the Cool School. "There were miners who used aircraft to get to the digs; wildlife biologists who tracked wolves, caribou, or bears wherever and whenever they needed; vacationers; mailmen; medevacs; and, of course, fisherman and hunters."

The learning went both ways. Adams also had to push his message of safety. Based on comments after the first meeting, his message got through. "It's obvious they don't want to hit us any more than we want to hit them," one member of CMAAC told the *News-Miner.*

Still, it wasn't enough to *want* a safe airspace. The civil aviators made it clear to the Air Force that the only way it would get its permanent MOAs was if the boys in blue came up with a reliable and simple system that would tell pilots who fly the bush when and where the Air Force was flying. Moreover, in case a civilian pilot accidentally wandered into active military airspace, there needed to be a system that would prevent the wrong-way pilot from being ingested into the engine of an A-10.

The Special Use Airspace Information Service (SUAIS) and Eielson Range Control did both things. SUAIS is a twenty-four-hour service that assists civilian pilots in planning flights through or around MOAs. The military normally schedules the airspace for a block of time but only utilizes it for a portion of that period. If pilots trying to get to Fairbanks in a hurry don't want to fly around the MOA, they can call SUAIS on the radio or by phone to find out exactly when the MOA will be active. In many cases, the civilian aviators will be able to fly through the MOA, confident they will not get caught in a mock dogfight. If a wrong-way pilot did fly into the MOA when it was active, airspace managers at Eielson Range Control would see the plane on their radar. In that instance, all military traffic would be placed in a holding pattern until the civil aviator cleared the operating area—even though it could result in the cancellation of several exercises involving more than eighty aircraft.

The Air Force's safety measures convinced the members of CMAAC that the military and Alaskan aviators could work together, but SUAIS would only work if all the pilots who flew the bush knew about it. To promote the service, General Tex Brown dispatched three of his staff to all the major civilian airfields between Eielson and Canada. Reacting to criticism that the Air Force spokesman at the first meeting in Fairbanks was "belligerent," Tex recruited the good-humored and down-home-talking commander of Eielson's combat training squadron, Colonel Chuck Brammeier, an F-16 jock; Brammeier's job was to be the pilot's pilot. The safety-minded Scott Adams was also sent, to dispel any fears about the possibility of midair collisions with civilian aircraft. I rounded out the trio to ensure nobody was "belligerent."

Jackbooted Thugs

I had been in a Cessna once before. A pilot friend of mine in Mississippi, call sign "Spot," took me up for a night flight. It was a beautiful flight over the neon-splashed Gulf Coast of Biloxi until we came in too steep for a maneuver called a "touch-and-go," which a pilot uses to practice landings without actually landing. Having flown during several home-computer simulations, I felt that we were a bit too steep, but I didn't worry about it until I heard Spot gasp a simple "uh-oh" over the headset. *What do you mean, uh-oh? That can't be good.* Hammering on the gas, Spot was able to pull the plane into the right attitude the moment before we slapped hard on the runway. We bounced off at an odd angle before pitching down onto the runway again with a second hard bounce. Spot righted the airplane before it smacked down a third time. With a big silly grin that meant *I do this sort of thing all the time,* the aviator looked over at me and said, "Wow, I hope that doesn't happen on the next four tries." *Yes, ladies and gentlemen, these are the people who are protecting our country.*

Spot was a lieutenant and couldn't have been much older than twenty-three when he forced the first gray hair onto my head. Surely, I figured, the older Colonel Brammeier would have slightly better control of the orange-and-white Cessna 172 Skylane that we were planning to fly over the bush. Brammeier and Adams walked around the plane checking things that, I imagine, were very important. They both wore slick flight suits that indicated to any casual observer that these men were pilots and clearly superior to the guy with the pencil in his pocket who watched nervously from a distance. I was wearing a standard camouflage battle dress uniform, the ubiquitous BDU that soldiers, Marines, and nerdy Air Force public affairs officers wear when they are trying to kill the bad guys—spin them to death, in my case.

The Cessna was actually an appropriate vehicle for my introduction to Alaskan airspace. As common in Alaskan skies as MOOSE CROSSING signs are on the roads, the Cessna was built to last in tough conditions. The planes were built so well, the company actually bankrupted itself. Since an old Cessna was just as good as a new one, nobody bothered to spend the big bucks on the new birds.

Still, I found myself slightly uncomfortable for my first flight over Alaska. Planes are always crashing in the bush, even planes flown by Air Force generals. Anything could happen in the Alaskan skies: bad weather, heavy ice, or a loose bolt on the wing. The good news was that two highly trained and experienced fighter pilots were in front at the plane's controls. If either of them had to do anything heroic, I would be able to write all about it. The bad news was that there was nothing I could do if they both had heart attacks at the same time. Well, that's not totally true. I could probably vomit on them.

After kicking the tires and looking under the hood, we loaded the plane, and Brammeier taxied us to the end of the giant runway for takeoff. Nonetheless, it seemed like we only used about ten feet to get in the air. A bump here, a dip there, and we were up high over the interior in no time. Signs of human life disappeared in less than ten seconds. After quick visits to the highway towns of Northway and Delta Junction, we turned north for the Yukon River town of Eagle and its 150 residents.

I had read a lot about the bush and the small villages of the interior prior to the trip, but I had not yet left the confines of the Alcan or the Richardson Highway. Thousands of travelers drove to Fairbanks or North Pole or Eielson or Tok every year. Just eight miles from Canada, Eagle was a little harder to get to. A highway stretched to the town in the summer months, but it was a rare destination for most. If someone went to Eagle, it was usually for good reason.

"I needed some books and some sugar," said Ray (no last name offered). We met Ray at the Eagle public library in the center of the village. His long beard, dirty clothes, and musky odor left no doubt he had come from somewhere in the bush. He had driven his dog team into Eagle that morning. "Damn ice on the Yukon is starting to melt already," Ray said. "I needed to get here and back before the whole thing melts. I went in twice as it was."

Ray spoke as if he had just spent an afternoon at a coffee shop. He smiled like a child at Disney World. His eyes were opened wide and seemed to emit a strange northern light. He gestured wildly with his hands and jumped from topic to topic as he described his trip into the town and his need for back newspapers and his concern about the snow melting before he could get back. "I better get going," he said several times in our conversation.

"Hey, what are you guys doing here anyway?" Ray asked after looking over our uniforms.

"We're here to talk with local pilots and others who want to know when and where we are flying this summer," I said.

"Really? Wow! Hey, do you guys control the jets, then?"

"Sure, to some extent anyway," I said.

"Man, I wish you could tell those guys to fly over a little more often."

"What do you mean—over your house?"

"Yeah. I love when they fly over. The lower the better. I always try to get outside to wave at them. Sometimes they wave back."

Colonel Brammeier, who had been talking with the librarian, came over and joined the conversation. "You really want planes to fly over more often?" he asked.

"You bet! I love you guys. Sometimes you're the only company I get out there."

"Well," Colonel Brammeier looked at me, "I don't suppose there's any problem with that. Do you?"

"No," I said. "At least, I don't think so. You're the pilot."

Brammeier opened an aerial map of Alaska and spread it out on the table for Ray. The bush resident pointed out the location of his cabin in the middle of a military operating area. Brammeier circled the area on the map with a pencil.

"We'll see what we can do," the colonel said with a smile. "Do you want a sonic boom, too?"

"You can do that? Oh, man, that's great, man. Really great, man," Ray said—then snapped to attention. "I mean, thank you, sir. Thank you very much." The raggedy man of the bush snapped a rusty salute. "I'll be waving."

It was a pleasure to meet Ray, but he was the exception in Eagle. It seemed that doors were slamming and blinds drawn as Brammeier, Adams, and I walked down the dirt street of the village. Our uniforms identified us with the U.S. government, and if you wanted to have any credibility in Eagle, the government was the last thing you wanted to represent. Eagle is surrounded on two sides by the Yukon–Charley Rivers National Preserve. For years the people of the village had hunted and trapped in the preserve, but the government, in all its wisdom, was now cracking down on the locals, and they didn't like it one bit. The people of Eagle weren't closing their doors and drawing their blinds because of our uniforms. They were turning their backs on the park ranger who showed us through the town.

"He wasn't particularly liked in town as a government official," Adams recalled. Quite an understatement. The town residents had left garbage on the steps of his government house, let the air out of the tires of his government car, and cut a series of wires in his government airplane.

"They don't like oversight," the park ranger noted.

Alaskans are well known for their strident opposition to big government. They don't want anyone in Washington telling them where they can and cannot drill, clear forests, or catch fish. They certainly don't want a liberal park ranger issuing fines for taking a moose from their backyard. An estimated twenty thousand Alaskans are members of an organization that one day hopes to vote for independence from the United States. More relevant to the people of Eagle, the Alaskan Independence Party (AIP) calls for repatriation of all federal lands (70 percent of the state) to Alaska. It is a major platform item, and it wouldn't surprise me if someone told me 146 of Eagle's 147 residents voted with the AIP. The park ranger, if he was inclined to vote, would probably have "fallen" or suffered some other sort of "accident" on his way to the polls.

Eagle was unlike any town I had ever seen. Its reactionary residents crossed all economic lines. In a village that consists of two streets, the difference in income was blatantly apparent. A brand-new house that would look big in a New York City suburb sat across the street from a plywood-walled, tarp-covered shack that was home to twelve. Internet sites about Eagle describe the town's various amenities, including a K-12 school, bed-and-breakfasts, a cafe in the summer, phones and fax hookups, and a campground. What the Web sites don't say is that those places are surrounded by shacks in various states of disrepair that are littered with car frames, rusted appliances, and all the other wastes of modern life. Despite its often ramshackle appearance, the town of Eagle sat in one of the most beautiful locations I had seen in Alaska. The Yukon River's various arms converged into a wide river at Eagle that turned at a right angle against a giant bluff that seemed to stand guard over the main village. A blanket of green spruces pushes against the place. I guess if you have to live in a plywood-and-tarp-covered shack, it might as well be in a place that beautiful.

If you are a government employee, however, be sure to keep that to yourself. Who knows, even though the AIP rarely gets more than 5 percent of the vote, your days might be numbered.

We departed Eagle after taking extra time for a thorough preflight inspection of our government airplane. We had dropped off maps and pamphlets and pleaded our case with anyone who would listen. It was our last town visit that day, but not the last in, what turned out to be, a successful campaign. After more than a hundred meetings around the state, comments from more than a thousand Alaskans, and more than thirty changes to the original plan, the FAA approved the Air Force's request for permanent MOAs. Today there are sixty-six thousand square miles of military operating areas in Alaska. Still, even with all that space to zoom around in, many Alaska-based fighter pilots manage to find their way from the Yukon River down to a small stream valley where a man who looks like Santa Claus and drives a sled always runs out to greet them with a big smile, glowing eyes, and wild waves of the arm.

"Just stay away from Eagle," a commander might warn. "The

Alaskan Independence Party also believes strongly in the right of the individual to keep and bear arms."

The Last Garden

There is one primary difference between flying over Alaska and flying over most of the Lower 48: no farms. Farms of all shapes and sizes cover the landscape of the Lower 48. There are big square fields in Ohio and round irrigated fields in the dry states. Where farms have gone away, massive red or white barns still dot the subdivided landscape. Alaska, however, didn't seem to have anything approaching *American Gothic*.

Alaskans don't live on moose alone, though. Vegetables and meats of all kinds still crowd supermarket isles. Before our flight to Eagle, I assumed all these products, which cost much more than they did in the Lower 48, were shipped north by sea or highway, but on our return flight, Brammeier took Adams and me over a town called Delta Junction and what looked an awful lot like farmers' fields spreading across the valley.

Despite subzero temperatures, permafrost, and thin soil, the interior supports a handful of farms—although just barely. In 1978, the state began the Delta Agricultural Project, creating a total of thirty-seven farms averaging more than two thousand acres each. Crops in Delta Junction include barley, oats, potatoes, and peas. Much of the harvest goes to feed Delta's dairy and beef cattle. The rest is sold around Alaska and outside the state. The potato crop alone is worth about $2.5 million annually.

Despite some success, the Delta Agricultural Project lives in the shadow of a government-sponsored agricultural failure. In 1934, the government relocated two hundred families to Alaska's Matanuska Valley between the Chugach and Talkeetna mountains. The transplants found it difficult to scratch a living from the soil, and most returned to the Lower 48 by the end of World War II. However, although the Matanuska farm project was a failure for large-scale agriculture, it was a shocking success for the *Guinness Book of World Records*. The region, with its twenty-two hours of summer daylight, is now known for its giant vegetables that include six-foot-wide cauliflower, eighteen-pound carrots, fifty-pound celery, and the granddaddy of all giant vegetables, the Alaskan cabbage that can weigh more than a hundred pounds per head. Visitors to Alaska can view most of these jolly green giants every summer just north of Anchorage at the Alaska State Fair, but they won't enjoy all of the Matanuska's bounty there—unless, of course, they are willing to spend anywhere from ninety days to five years at the Alaska State Penitentiary.

The valley of the giant cabbage is also home to the legendary hemp product called "Alaskan Thunderf——k" by people in the Lower 48 and properly called "Matanuska Thunderf——k," or simply "MTF," by locals. (At least, that's what I heard. As a member of the military, I certainly wouldn't have known anything about such a potent plant firsthand.) According to Scot Dunnachie, the chairman of the lobbying group Free Hemp in Alaska, "MTF" describes an Alaskan strain of marijuana that is "good to sight, smell, taste, and effect." Outsiders have raved about all its characteristics for years and search out the stuff. Unlike the Yugo-like cabbages and baseball-bat-like carrots, Dunnachie says, MTF has nothing to do with the long summer days. "The reason behind it being so good is due to the lack of sunlight in Alaska. Less sunlight means more time in the greenhouse," he said. More time in the greenhouse equates to extraspecial attention and care from its growers, and if anyone should know how to grow marijuana well, it's Alaskans. They've had a lot of practice. In 1975, the State Supreme Court ruled that an Alaskan's right to privacy included the right to use marijuana at home. With the official green light to grow the herb, many Alaskans became marijuana aficionados and talk about it today with a candor not found among the general public in any other state of the union.

"Because Alaskans were so used to growing and smoking their own pot, it's safe to say we think very little of taking a puff today," one of my friends (I'll call him Bill) told me. "I know I don't think much of it, and it's safe to say the majority of the population treats it with a very cavalier attitude."

However, while the feds encouraged farming in the Matanuska Valley in the 1930s, growing ganja was not what they had in mind. Embarrassed by the Uncle John's Band of yahoos on the frontier, the government in 1991 threatened to take away the state's highway funds unless it changed its mind about what people could or couldn't grow and smoke in their own homes. In a land with few passable byways, the threat was taken to heart, and the population voted 54 percent to 46 percent to pave over their gardens—but not all did. Many simply took them underground and perfected their strains of MTF using growing lights and secret greenhouses, and it wasn't just in the Matanuska. Some Alaskans believe that MTF didn't come from its namesake valley at all. Some say MTF was started in Fairbanks but named "Matanuska" just to throw off authorities.

"At least, that's what I heard," Bill said. "As a law-abiding Fairbanksan, I certainly wouldn't know anything about growing such a potent plant firsthand."

Unless marijuana use is made legal again (a bill doing just that lost by only ten thousand votes in 2002) visitors to Fairbanks will be hard pressed to find any MTF or giant cabbage or any other farms in the interior. About the closest they will get is the state-run Creamer's Field Migratory Waterfowl Refuge, a working dairy until 1966. Tourists are not the only people you will see at Creamer's Field, though. In April, Fairbanks residents will begin visiting Creamer's, sometimes spending hours staring at the snow-covered fields in hopes that they will see some of the *other* Alaskan aviators. Man is not the only creature that flies the bush. Birds of all shapes and sizes compete with F-16s and Cessnas for airspace. None is more important to Fairbanks in April than Canada geese. When the first Canada geese land at Creamer's Field, usually around the first or second week of the month, the winter-weary residents of the interior know that spring is finally on the way. In a couple of weeks, they can take their MTF out of their basements and transplant it into their gardens. (At least, that's what I heard.)

MAY

Breaking Up Is Good to Do

WINTER COVER-UP

There is something under the snow in Alaska, but it's hard to make out what it is until the blanket starts to melt. As the white stuff goes, it is easier to identify its characteristics. It's bulky. It's rectangular. It seems to be hollow. The paint on it is white. It has a little rust. Wait . . . it's coming into view . . . yes, just as I suspected . . . it's a refrigerator!

I used to think that littering your property with spent appliances and cars on cinder blocks was a form of art restricted to the Deep South. I couldn't have been more wrong. Heaping waste onto the front lawn or into the woods off the road is almost an epidemic in Alaska. People routinely throw their empty soda bottles and fast food wrappers out the windows of their cars, and many of the yards and vacant lots around Fairbanks are piled deep with junk of all sorts from busted snowmachines and retired Chevys to baby strollers and in some cases even piles of household garbage.

It is as if the environmental consciousness that has taken hold in much of the Lower 48 has yet to be introduced in Alaska. I can sort of rationalize the economic reason why a bankrupt gold mining outfit might abandon its equipment somewhere in the bush, but I cannot come up with any good reason why someone might throw an empty beer can out the window.

Who is there to blame for such poor waste disposal techniques? Can it be the state? Some areas of state-owned land are riddled with the hulks of rusted mining equipment and industrial relics that seem to have died in place. Should it be the federal government? In 1989, researchers identified sixty-six sites contaminated by oil and lubricants and you name it on Eielson Air Force Base alone.

The government and its military should provide an example of how to act toward the environment. In the case of Eielson, they have. Most of the sixty-six sites have been completely cleaned up or are under some form of active remediation. That's just a fraction of the trouble, though.

Environmentalists can still describe areas of Alaska where the government is providing a poor example for its constituents. Radiation from the nuclear weapons it tested in the Aleutians is leaking, fallout is still contaminating the wildlife of the state, and there are many abandoned military facilities that may or may not be environmentally sound. So perhaps the government is guilty of all the littering after all.

Then again, the United States is a government *of* the people. The miscreants who spilled oil or dumped PCBs into a stream or hired the cheapest bidder for the radiation containment area are just regular old citizens. So perhaps it's the other way around. Perhaps the reason the government has made a mess is that the people it has to choose from show no regard for the environment.

So pizza boxes and coffee cups continue to fly out the car windows, and jet fuel and lubricants continue to drip out of the engines, and the great paradise of Alaska becomes more of a great paradox. But only for a few weeks.

Summer is short. When it starts to snow again, even a cheechako can see that the problem will disappear overnight.

Betting on Spring

With the exception of the Happy Meal boxes, beer bottles, and bags of household garbage that often line the sides of roads in the interior, there are essentially three colors that make up the winter vista: white, black, and gray. Snow, ice, and the ubiquitous birch trees are white. Dirty snow, the road surface, and the supposedly ever*green* spruce trees are black. The faces on the people are all gray. These are the gray faces that wait . . . and watch . . . and wait a little more . . . and then finally place odds and two-dollar bets on when Hell will thaw out or—as it is called in Alaska—break up.

The action is at a little town once known as "A Good Place to Camp Between Two Rivers." Now it goes by the name "Nenana," which roughly translates into "A Good Place for Tourists to Stop and Use the Bathroom Between Fairbanks and Anchorage." The name of the game in Nenana is roulette, and Mother Nature spins the wheel . . . April 27 . . . April 30 . . . May 4 . . . 9:00 A.M. . . . 10:00 A.M. . . . 7:00 P.M. The winner is the person who guesses closest to the exact date and time when the ice on the Nenana River breaks up and starts to flow. In 1917, the first year the Nenana Ice Classic was played, the river flowed out at 11:30 A.M. on April 30 for a prize of eight hundred dollars.

The betting begins when a group of very gray, very cold, very depressed residents venture out onto the frozen ice the last weekend of February and erect a large tripod of logs painted black and white. As the ice begins to melt, a wire is attached from the top of the tripod to a watchtower on the shore. The wire is rigged to a clock that will stop the exact moment the tripod moves a hundred feet on the shifting ice. From the first perceptible movement of the tripod, attention from every miserable gambling Alaskan turns to the town, but most just want to know when they can crawl out from under their blankets, put the cap back on top of the whiskey flask, and shave off their Cossack beards.

The tripod has moved out as early as April 20 but usually doesn't break until April 30, the most common day for the start of breakup. My first year we had to wait a little longer. Finally, on

May 5 at 12:32 P.M., the black-and-white tripod moved beyond a hundred feet. At that exact moment, the sun came out. It warmed twenty degrees. The snow melted. The spruce trees became green. The birch trees produced buds. And the gray people rejoiced as life finally returned to the interior.

We Don't Need No Stinking Matches

With the melting of the snow and the budding of the trees and the smiling of the people, I figured—I *knew*—that I had survived my first winter and passed the critical stage in the metamorphosis from cheechako to Alaskan. Nothing could stop me: not 40 below, not ice rugby, not perpetual darkness, and certainly not a little bit of snow at the beginning of the hiking trail to Granite Tors.

Sixty miles north of town, Granite Tors is one of the most popular weekend destinations near Fairbanks. During rugby practice the week before, Groff suggested to me and another rugby player, Mark Bevilacqua, that we give the fourteen-mile loop a try. The payoff for the hike is about halfway through the loop when you come upon a large monolithic formation, the Tor, that goes a hundred feet straight up. A camping area rests at the base of the Tor, where we planned to spend the night and return in the morning.

"You think there's any snow up there?" Mark asked.

"I don't know. Maybe a little. Groff said there would be a light dusting."

"Good. I forgot my hiking boots," Mark said. "All I have are sneakers."

"What the hell, how bad can it be."

The trail follows the Chena River through the lowlands before turning up the mountain. As we headed out, ice still lined the side of the river, but the only snow we could see lay in the shady spots under the spruce trees. It looked to us like smooth sailing.

We posed for "hero" pictures along the stream. What brave, stupid cheechakos we were.

As soon as we began the slightest rise in altitude, the snow spread from under the trees to across the trail. In less than twenty minutes of hiking, we were already walking in a foot of snow. Mark's sneakers began to take on water.

"It's no big deal. As long as we keep moving, my feet will stay warm," Mark said. So we pushed on.

Despite a high level of traffic, Granite Tors can be a dangerous hike. In August 2000, two hikers set out for a one-day stroll around the loop and wound up lost for days. Unlike Mark and me, those guys were experienced hikers. One of the men had completed the Appalachian Trail and hiked from Mexico to Canada along the Sierra Nevada Mountains. The weather in Alaska can fool the best of them, though, even in the springtime. On the Tors trail, the two men encountered wind, snow, and swollen creeks, ultimately wandering off course for three days.

"As I see it . . . we thought we were on the trail and got discombobulated," hiker Greg Selid told the *Fairbanks Daily News-Miner.* Protected only by tree branches and garbage bags, the men began to shiver uncontrollably and had to huddle with their dogs to stay warm. Fortunately, the third day brought sunshine, and their signal fire was answered by an Alaska State Troopers helicopter that had been searching for them.

A year earlier, in May 1999, a woman and her dog lost their way on the trail and survived for three days on mosquitoes, cranberries, and an old stash of Army rations she discovered in a shelter. She lost her dog along the way but ultimately hiked back to the Chena River, where she was rescued by a search boat.

Mark and I soon had the Tor in site, but the snow continued to deepen with every step. First a few inches, then a few feet, and finally Mark, a network administrator who stood at least five feet tall, was up to his waist in snow. The trail had somehow vanished in the deep snow, and the waning sun seemed to be telling us that

Mother Nature was going to punish us for our cavalier attitude toward her daughter Alaska.

But I can see the rocks! I know we can make it. We're men. Alaskan men!

"I don't think we can make it," Mark said. "I can't feel my feet."

"But we just—I can see the Tor."

"Can't feel my legs, either. I need to get warm quick."

Don't worry . . . keep going . . . you can get to the shelter . . . it's not that cold yet . . . his feet are fine . . . it's not like he's gonna lose a toe or a foot or a leg . . . what are the chances?

Mark began to shiver uncontrollably. I probably wasn't that far behind, so I said to myself, *Self, we need to stop here and get a fire going and get warm.*

What a couple of wimps you guys are, said Self back to me.

"Do you have any matches?" I asked.

"Matches? No. Don't you have a lighter?"

"Why would I have a lighter? Are you sure you don't have matches?"

A couple of morons, too, Self added.

Somehow, despite a fleeting notion to double-check our gear, we forgot matches or a lighter or a blowtorch—forcing me to create fire with flint and steel.

"You must be joking," Mark said.

"Seriously, man. We can do it."

Think, damn it. What did they tell you at survival school? How the heck do you light a sopping-wet log with sparks?

Fortunately for scores of gigantic idiots like us, a well-oiled and well-practiced rescue team was sitting around back in their hangar at Eielson. Although their primary mission is to rescue downed airmen from Eielson, a detachment of the Alaska Air National Guard's 210th Rescue Squadron regularly launches its two HH-60 rescue helicopters for civilian rescue missions. At the heart of each rescue are the Air Force's elite PJs, cousins to the Navy SEALs and the Army's Green Berets and Rangers—which is to say, the exact opposite of an Air Force public affairs geek. Public affairs specialists get their training through a military journalism school with no real physical requirements except the ability to sharpen a pencil. Pararescue specialists, on the other hand, spend twelve weeks running, swimming, holding their breath, and pushing the ground at an indoctrination course that is designed to weed out any potential public affairs specialists and earn the graduates the right for more physical abuse at Army Airborne School, Combat Diver School, Freefall Parachutists School, and Air Force Survival School. If they make it through all that, and only a small percentage do, they finally enter the twenty-week long Pararescue School. Upon graduation, the PJs' next reward is deployment to a real unit, where they will accept very little pay in exchange for a good chance of being killed by bad guys or bad weather. It is a job that you might only do once—sometimes just to save a cheechako who thought he was an Alaskan. Since the 210th was formed in Anchorage in 1990, the squadron's PJs and pilots have launched more than five hundred missions, saving the lives of more than four hundred people.

In most cases the people they saved had more experience in the outdoors than Mark and I had, but Mother Nature must have taken her Prozac that weekend. Remembering the little steps needed to pull the job off, we were able to start the fire using the flint and steel. We toasted our cold feet by the flames for a few hours, then slipped into the sleeping bags for a chilly night in a waist-deep "dusting" of snow.

Our foolhardy hike to the Tors was rife with cheechako assumptions. We assumed that there was no snow. We assumed we were dressed properly. We assumed we knew enough about Alaska to venture into the wilderness with nothing more than the average hiker might take to Central Park in New York. We were completely wrong and could have died from our stupidity. However, we learned our lesson. Never again would we approach Alaska so casually. While the hiking trip demonstrated to me that

I was not yet an Alaskan, it also added to my understanding of the power of the Great Land. For the moment, I was content surviving the drive to work.

Voyeuristic F-16 Pilots

The eruption of Mt. Pinatubo in the Philippines began at 1:42 P.M., June 15, 1991. At ten times the size of the eruption of Mt. St. Helens, the Pinatubo disaster was by some reckonings the second largest volcanic eruption of the century. (Alaska's Mt. Katmai eruption in 1912 was the largest.) The eruption blew away one cubic mile of the mountaintop. Nearly 1,000 feet of a 5,725-foot peak vanished into an ash cloud that rose twenty-two miles into the atmosphere. Even though more than fifty-eight thousand people were evacuated by the time the eruption began, eight hundred were ultimately killed, and 70,257 homes were damaged or destroyed, as a tropical storm combined with thirteen inches of ash from the eruption to form rivers of mud that ravaged the countryside. The eruption lasted only nine hours; however, its impact was felt around the world for more than two years. Temperatures on the surface of the planet noticeably cooled, floods and droughts increased around the world, the ozone hole over Antarctica expanded exponentially, and the peace-and-quiet-loving people of interior Alaska got the shaft.

The shadow of Mt. Pinatubo was home to Clark Air Base and its eighteen thousand American military personnel. Virtually all of them were evacuated beginning June 10. None of them ever returned. Few Alaskans knew then that the closure of an air base half a world away would ultimately shatter the solitude and silence they had always enjoyed in the interior. Every year, America's allies in the Pacific Rim brought their fighter jets to Clark Air Base for a small air combat exercise. When Pinatubo closed down the base, the Air Force chose Eielson and Alaska's sixty-six thousand square miles of military operating areas as the new home for Cope Thunder—and thunder it does.

Today more than 2,800 people and up to 240 aircraft deploy to Eielson for one of four very noisy exercises held over the spring and summer. For the air forces that participate, it is one of the best training exercises available. Statistics show that most combat losses occur during an aircrew's first eight to ten missions. Therefore, the goal of Cope Thunder is to provide a vital, gut-check combat simulation without the negative side effect of being blown out of the sky by a surface-to-air missile. Many Air Force, Navy, and Marine Corps veterans of Operation Desert Storm had participated in one or more Cope Thunder exercises in the Philippines and attributed their effectiveness over Iraqi territory to lessons learned in these exercises.

Typical Cope Thunder missions launch at about ten A.M. and again about two P.M. Landings are normally about one and a half hours after takeoff. Before and after, the crews spend hours and hours engaged in threat-and-target study and in mission briefings and debriefings, to maximize the learning from the scant ten or twenty minutes they are actually engaged with other planes in the air or targets on the ground. "I can tell you that when a pilot flies one of these missions, it's as close to real as can be experienced without actually going to war," Tex once said.

If you are a regular old Alaskan minding your own business at your homestead somewhere in the bush, you may conclude that the United States has in fact gone to war over your living room. Not only are there four times as many airplanes as usual flying one hundred feet over your house, there are dozens of unfamiliar markings on the wings. In addition to U.S. planes, aircraft from Canada, England, Australia, the Philippines, New Zealand, Thailand, the Republic of Singapore, and even the Japanese Air Self-Defense Force roar over the interior in a virtual nonstop combat operation that lasts all summer. All that adds up to noise. Lots of it.

"Many Alaskans have laboriously built wilderness cabins as a way of getting close to nature, but their hopes of being able to enjoy the silence and the natural sounds of birds are wiped out by screaming jet engines and the cacophony of sonic booms," wrote Fairbanks environmental activist Celia Hunter in an opinion in the *News-Miner*. "As one witness at a recent meeting angrily declared, 'I have more peace and quiet in the middle of Fairbanks than I do at my getaway cabin up the Salcha [River]!'"

The poor pig farmer who bought a house near Eieslon's flight path in the middle of winter learns in May that the house was so cheap because the only way the previous residents could escape from the noise of the jets was to move to Bora Bora. *That's okay,* he says to himself. *I support the military. It's only a little—okay, a lot of noise.* The farmer thinks he can cope with it, until a few days go by. Then he calls me up in the public affairs office to complain rather vehemently about "that unmentionable plane that's so loud it caused my pig to eat its young!"

That was really what he said! And he wasn't alone:

TOP TEN, NO-KIDDING, EIELSON NOISE COMPLAINTS
10. My car ran into a ditch because of the noise!
 9. Aircraft were flying all around my house, then the jets came to both my windows and looked in!
 8. The boom was so bad, it scared my dog under the cabin!
 7. The jets are circling my house just waiting for me to come outside. Then they dive-bomb me and my car. My car won't start because of them!
 6. My chickens won't lay their eggs for a week after a sonic boom!
 5. The jets came in low to attack, and I hit my head when I went under the cabin, and I need to know who I can sue!

4. The jets rattled my cattle so bad, they trampled almost three acres of oats!

3. The sonic booms caused us to drop a satellite dish we were installing on our roof!

2. I talked to the eagles, and they were upset!

And the number one no-kidding noise complaint at Eielson Air Force Base:

1. MY CAT FELL OVER!

Because I was the primary liaison between the community and the Air Force, the noise complaint issue fell squarely in my lap. Any given day of Cope Thunder flying could result in as many as twenty noise complaints from all over Alaska. Some people called because the noise was so loud they thought an aircraft crashed. They called because the jet noise woke up the baby. They called because the noise caused their bull to jump the fence into the cow pen, which resulted in pregnant cows that gave birth in the middle of winter when it was 40 below. *And if you haven't helped a cow give birth at 40 below, you should come out here sometime and see how the hell you like it, jackass!*

Noise was only one inconvenience. Many callers wanted to know where they could file claims against the government for the damage created by the noise. One who wanted to take more drastic action asked, "Who do I shoot for breaking all the windows in my house?"

Threatening to shoot an aircraft out of the sky was a common reaction. If the caller actually said that to me over the phone, I was required by policy to notify the Air Force Office of Special Investigations. Even though we suspected most people were full of hot air, you never knew for sure which people meant it. Brian O'Donoghue, the *News-Miner* journalist turned dog musher, once received a call from military agents who were investigating a threat against aircraft. The person who made the threat was one of O'Donoghue's neighbors, and the military was calling everyone around to see if the threat was real.

"There were some low helicopter flights over the area for two or three nights in a row," said O'Donoghue as he related the story to me. "Apparently [my neighbor] called and made a threat, something like 'The old boys will be waiting and the sparks will fly.' "

No aircraft were shot at, O'Donoghue said, but the late-night flights over the neighborhood stopped right away. (While it might appear that the caller got what he wanted, I should caution anyone contemplating a similar act. The threat they called O'Donoghue about was before September 11, 2001. I suspect that the military would not be as cooperative and courteous now.)

Other callers actually claimed to have shot at us. One Vietnam veteran who moved to Alaska to get away from it all lived south of Delta Junction in the bush near the Trans-Alaska Pipeline at the foot of the Alaska Range. He swore several times that he shot at our F-16s with shotguns. The first time he called, we took his claim very seriously. Then he swore just as vehemently that the jets would hover over his yard and look at him through his outhouse window.

Threats of shooting at low-flying aircraft actually sparked an idea among the planners at Eielson. In an effort to ensure pilots stayed within their approved lanes, the Air Force placed threat emitters around areas that had been designated as "noise sensitive." If a pilot flew too close to the noise-sensitive area, a warning would sound in his aircraft. To the pilot, it would look and sound the same as if the aircraft had been detected by enemy radar.

That might work for the pilots who were visiting Eielson, but the regulars knew the deal. All over their flight planning charts were little red circles that warned of noise-sensitive areas. They planned their missions around them, but they all knew the little red circles were put on the map because someone was pissed off at the Air Force. Stoli and the other pilots said that sometimes the circles were justified, other times not.

There was a "big red circle" over the village of Circle Hot Springs. As the story went, a pilot earned his call sign of "Boomer" when he did an unauthorized "simulated attack" on the area. Coming in at a steep angle and very high speed, the pilot caused a sonic boom so severe that it smashed several windows and almost killed the local handyman, who was knocked off a ladder. In that case, the noise-sensitive area was probably a good thing—certainly for the handyman, if no one else. The noise-sensitive area around the peregrine falcon nesting area may not have been justified, however. The environmentalists insisted that the area be kept quiet so the falcons could breed. To determine whether the F-16 was a danger to the birds, the Bureau of Land Management (BLM) enlisted an Eielson pilot for a trip to the nesting area to take noise readings. The pilot on the ground coordinated with an F-16 to come in low through the valley so that the BLM worker and the Air Force representative would see how damaging the sound was. When the fighter came roaring through at high speed, the conservationist "freaked out" and ran away screaming to look for cover. The peregrine falcon didn't flinch. Even so, the conservationists won out, and the noise restriction remained.

From the Air Force side of things, many of the calls seemed funny. The idea that noise could knock a cabin off its foundation or cause pigs to eat their young seemed completely fanciful. Despite the seeming hilarity of the thing, however, the noise issue was serious business for many Alaskan residents, and it and the attitude of the Air Force were soon the topics in the court of public opinion.

Celia Hunter wrote in the *News-Miner:* "The widespread public reaction to the excessive noise pollution of present-day fighter aircraft, to the cascading thunder of sonic booms breaking windows and startling everyone within range into convulsive reactions, and the threats to wildlife and birdlife within or adjacent to intensive training operations has caused curtailment of such training in the Lower 48. Alaska, with its abundance of open terrain, is tempting both politicians and military planners to move all such operations northward."

"Northward" was a bit too far north for one resident. "I'm madder than hell, and I'm sad," said Jack McCombs in a meeting of concerned citizens reported by the *News-Miner*'s Kelly Bostian. "The Air Force was an institution I respected and considered a good neighbor, but it has become greedy, and in that sense it has become the enemy."

"McCombs said expanded Air Force activity has in effect robbed him of his retirement home on the Salcha River," Bostian wrote. "He said sonic booms that break cabin windows and globes on propane lights and jet engine noise that makes conversation impossible have changed the character of the place he chose as his retirement home."

Despite numerous calls, McCombs said, the Air Force was not listening. "I feel impotent in dealing with a shifty Air Force bureaucracy and dealing with [public relations] goons with their laser pointers," McCombs said. "It's like David and Goliath and, let me tell you, Goliath is winning." *Those damn public relations goons!*

Every single noise complaint or low-flying-aircraft complaint that came into the public affairs office had to be logged and researched. There were so many complaints during the summer exercises that Cope Thunder appointed one of their own to track down the complaints full time. Captain Doug Kelsch, a KC-135 pilot by training, was my point of contact over at Cope T. The moment I got off the phone with a low-flying complainer, I faxed him the record of our call. He then took the complaint, which included the time, location, and description of the aircraft, into the operations room, where the real-time location and altitude of every aircraft was displayed on overhead screens. Since these displays were recorded for pilot debriefings, Kelsch was able to check the computers to see if an aircraft was where the complaint came from. In most cases, there was an aircraft in the vicinity. More often than not, these aircraft were just above their minimum flight restrictions. The problem was that in many areas that restriction was only one hundred feet. A jet cruising overhead at that level could cause a pig to kill its young, then fry up the bacon in a skillet inside the cabin with the man hiding underneath. So I would call back the complainer and essentially say, "Too bad, so sad."

It doesn't take many conversations with irate Alaskans to feel their pain. I soon got to know many of the callers well. Some were my neighbors at Harding Lake. I truly wanted to help them, but I also realized that the Air Force had a mission. It was a tough position to be in. I had little credibility in the minds of the public because I kept telling them that the jets were in the right place and doing everything properly. I also lost credibility in the minds of the aviators. Every time they flew a mission, it seemed there was a message from me waiting for them that questioned how and where they were flying. Lieutenant Colonel Adams told me later that he thought Eielson's public affairs goons had essentially gone native.

During my first year, Eielson received and processed eighty-one noise complaint calls. More than three-fourths of them (sixty-three) occurred in May, June, or July, during Cope Thunder rotations.

"Only eighty-one?" some of the pilots joked. "There would be a hell of a lot more if the people in the bush actually had phones."

The multitude of calls and, more important, the major negative press spurred us to come up with a plan. We created a program based on the old Vietnam "hearts and minds" concept. Our goal was to spin some sort of message to win the community's understanding and support for why they heard the jets.

WE SAID: *For your safety . . . We are considerate of noise . . . We have concern for the environment . . . We are following flight rules . . . This is critical military training . . . But most important . . . We really care!*

WE MEANT: *Cope Thunder is approaching! So buy a pair of extralarge ear plugs!! Stop bothering us, you royal pain in the ass, or we will fly over your house on purpose!!! Thank you for calling!!!!*

Some eventually got the message. Sadly, they accepted the aircraft and resumed their lives. *Oh, well, Goliath won the battle. Now I need to go hunting so I can eat this winter.*

There were some, though, who would never quite get the message regardless of what we told them or did for them. Most notable in this category was Jeannie Rinear. Middle-aged, with a pleasant smile and streaks of silver in her hair, Jeannie lived with her husband at 21 Mile Chena Hot Springs Road in the Pleasant Valley subdivision north of Fairbanks. They had lived there in peace and quiet since long before Eielson had any loud aircraft. Then the A-10s came in 1988. Despite the fact that the A-10 is a quiet plane as far as jets go, Rinear began a string of complaints that grew exponentially when Cope Thunder came to town. In an effort to defuse the complaints, Eielson commanders called her, visited her house, took noise readings, and, in 1994, placed a 3,500-foot noise-sensitive restriction over her subdivision. The restriction was followed but proved not to be enough for Rinear. She did not want an altitude restriction; she wanted the Air Force to create a no-fly zone over her house.

Acting on advice from the Eielson public affairs office— advice nobody ever thought she would follow—Rinear organized the people in the Pleasant Valley subdivision into a committee, the Chena Noise Abatement Committee. As head of this committee, Rinear circulated a petition requesting Eielson change its flight levels. When the petition and its 135 signatures arrived on his desk, Tex raised the local Pleasant Valley restriction to 5,000 feet. But this was still not enough. She wanted a no-fly zone. She outlined the problem in a letter to the commander of all Air Forces in Alaska: "The jets last year that flew over this area in the north-to-south attitude made tomatoes fall off vines in a commercial enterprise. Who buys bruised or spoiled tomatoes?"

"You're not doing what we want!" she said to me during a call. "This community will declare war—and I'm not kidding!" She revealed her plan when I visited her house that summer. Their goal was to release their cattle on the runway at Eielson during the base's next air show.

"What else can we do that we haven't done already?" Tex asked during a meeting about noise complaints. Colonel Mike Warden, the operations group commander, had the solution. Give Rinear one of the highly valued incentive rides. Fly her over her house and show her why we flew the way we flew. Knowing Rinear better then the rest, I recommended against the idea. In my opinion, Rinear would only be satisfied if Eielson Air Force Base was moved to Florida. Even then she might call. Warden pushed ahead with the flight. It turns out he had a simple plan.

Warden dispatched an officer from the bioenvironmental office at Eielson to take readings of the noise at Rinear's house as Warden and Rinear flew overhead. That had been done before, but this time, Warden told the environmental officer to take readings of other pieces of equipment from around the Rinear house as well. With permission from Mr. Rinear, he took readings of a chain saw, a radial table saw, a cement mixer, a television, a microwave, and a refrigerator. As Warden had expected, the noise around the house rated louder than the noise of the jet overhead.

"Much of the equipment Mr. Rinear comes in contact with around his home produces hazardous noise levels," wrote the bioenvironmental officer, Captain John Bell. "I showed [Mr. Rinear] that much of the equipment produces higher noise levels than the aircraft flying overhead. Additionally, during the course of this survey, a civilian mail plane flew down the Chena Hot Springs Road heading south. Mr. Rinear stated that the aircraft flies that pattern every day. The maximum noise measurement recorded was between 110–120 [decibels]. This measurement was louder than any military aircraft measured during these surveys."

Bell also noted in his report that Mr. Rinear was "fed up with the Air Force and that they were ready to take the Air Force to court." Mr. Rinear didn't call a lawyer that day, but he did make one call. When Warden flew over in the F-16D with Jeannie Rinear on board, her husband went inside to call me in the public affairs office to complain about the noise.

JUNE

Land of the Radioactive
Midnight Sun

THE SAME . . . BUT DIFFERENT

There's an old adage in the media business: It's not news when a dog bites a man; it's news when a man bites a dog. It should be no surprise, then, that what little Alaskan "news" makes it outside Alaska is dramatic. Even a ten-car pile-up that caused the death of a dozen people in Anchorage might not make the news in the Lower 48—unless, of course, the accident was caused by dancing grizzly bears.

No wonder everyone on the outside thinks Alaska is such a bizarre place. When friends learn that you are moving north, they want to share their intimate knowledge of the Great Land.

Wow, I can't believe you're moving to Alaska, man. That's crazy. I heard this story the other day about a guy who was attacked by three grizzly bears right in the middle of his living room. The guy was just watching TV! I didn't even know they had TVs in Alaska. Anyway, the guy lost both his arms and both legs, but they said he's going back to work as a lumberjack any day.

In reality, one of the first things a cheechako learns is that places in Alaska are pretty much the same as places in the Lower 48—and not all that exciting. Local newspapers are filled with reports about politics, business, crime, and sports just like they are in any town in the continental United States. The only difference is content. The political story is about drilling for oil. The business featured is a salmon cannery. The crime report lists a stolen moose rack. The sports page leads with outhouse racing. Alaska is the same—just a little different.

As in New York City, there are places a newcomer should not go in Alaska, but instead of the Brooklyn waterfront, cheechakos need to avoid the Kenai River when grizzly bears are feeding on the running salmon. Like residents of New Orleans, Alaskans are known for their great food, but instead of eating Emeril's creations in the French Quarter, Alaskans eat the moose they shot in the White Mountains. Trying to find an apartment on the Last Frontier is as difficult as it is in San Francisco, but the challenge is not to get a view of the bay; the challenge is to get indoor plumbing.

It's the same—just a little different.

A man from Delta Junction was once quoted in the local Fairbanks newspaper as saying that "people come to Alaska with more dreams than common sense." The dreamers don't know that they need to plug their car in when it's not running, and they don't know that you should play dead if you get attacked by a brown bear but fight for your life if you get attacked by a black bear. That's no different than a man from Iowa moving to New York City. The Iowan doesn't know how to move about the city in a subway, and he doesn't know that he should accept the approaches of an attractive woman in the East Village but seriously consider running from the deep-voiced woman with an Adam's apple in the West Village. The man from Iowa came to New York with more dreams than street smarts.

It's the same—just a little different.

Alaskans are not above taking advantage of their small differences. Both residents and journalists know that the people in the Lower 48 love stories about moose attacks and the heroic actions of bear hunters, and they will use them shamelessly. To look tough, residents will tell harrowing survival tales to cheechakos and outsiders, and to get their "news" stories run around the world, the journalists will follow that other old media adage: If it bleeds, it leads.

Blood, Sweat, and Beers

Summer finally came to the interior in late June, with clear skies and temperatures reaching the high 80s. I was finally seeing the Alaska the tourism companies extol: a lush, green landscape cut by ribbons of clear, fast-moving water that flowed from hills and mountains in every direction.

Too bad I hardly had time to see any of it. Unlike in the rest of the Lower 48, summertime is the busiest time of year in Alaska, from both a working and a playing standpoint. Nobody took time off in the summer. If anything, the amount of work tripled—even in the Air Force. All the major training exercises and community-related events take place in the short warm-weather window. About the only airmen who could get a break in the summer were the instructors from the Cool School. With so much to see and do, it wasn't long before I adopted the Alaskan approach to the season: Work hard, play harder, sleep never. A rugby match, played in much more favorable conditions than in December, was a good start.

I draped my right arm across Kevin Groff's back and grabbed a handful of his rugby jersey as we slammed into the forwards of the opposing scrum. The musty smell of unwashed, mud-soaked uniforms permeated the air. Sweat dripped into my eyes, distorting my view of Mark Bevilacqua. The computer geek I almost died with on Granite Tors was playing scrum-half, the quarterback of rugby. Mark shouted something through his mouthpiece, and I squinted through the sweat so I could see the ball as he rolled it underneath the scrum toward our side. Grunts and pants arose from the mass of men as Kevin and the rest of the beefy Sundawg forwards extended their legs to push the front-row players, the props and hooker, in order to drive the scrum forward. I watched the ball from the left flank as the forwards channeled it on the ground through their legs until it rested underneath the bearded and ever-menacing J. D., the first Sundawg I'd met in December.

My girlfriend, Lori Ann, watched the action from the sideline. Tired of the long-distance-relationship telephone tag, she was visiting from Seattle with her sister Nicole. The two girls watched the scrum from the sideline with my news-anchor buddy Curtis Smith, who discovered that day that rugby, especially as played in Alaska, was an unusual game.

"The first thing I noticed was the ragtag nature of the teams," he said. "Not just the unmatching uniforms—many had the same shirts, but shorts and socks were left to personal taste—but the makeup of the men. Fat, short, bald, and wiry, it was hard to tell this group from Middle America—not what I expected from a game that didn't include time-outs and made heroes out of the bloody. Still, it didn't take long for me to appreciate the numb, bone-against-bone sound that meant the ball was in play. It was the same sound a boy learns when his angry punch lands against his brother or schoolmate. It was a rite of passage of sorts, and because I had two brothers, I knew it hurt."

What to Curtis, Lori, and Nicole looked to be little more than a pile-on was actually a well-practiced maneuver in the art of rugby—and extremely hard to do for many of the players, who were very hung over. With heads pounding, muscles aching, and purple flashes clouding their vision, if they stood up from the scrum too fast, they might just pass out.

Mark moved from the side of the scrum to the back to pick up the ball from the ground under J. D., whose job was to keep possession until the scrum-half arrived to pick it up. The opposing scrum-half from the Anchorage-based Barbarians was right on Mark's heels. As soon as Mark tried to pick up the ball, the Barbarian was going to hit him with all he had. Normally the backup scrum-half, Mark was filling in for the bush-bound Kurt Smith, who sat on the sideline drinking a beer. When the team showed up for the game that morning, coach Jim Whitaker, also a Fairbanks city councilman, made the controversial call to start Mark over the eighty-proof veteran. Kurt wasn't happy about it, but he knew he had lost a little speed in his eighteen years of playing rugby. Besides, there was a fresh keg of Fairbanks-brewed Raven's Ridge ale on the sideline; being benched was not so bad.

Mark quickly grabbed the rugby ball and, diving to avoid the tackle, tossed the ball back to Ray Ray, a lanky and spastic Fairbanks native who began every game by throwing up in the end zone. Already under pressure from the defenders, Ray Ray feinted left and came running back toward the scrum, where he was hit and held up by a defender. I broke off the scrum and ran to Ray Ray to help save the ball for the Sundawgs. As I stripped the ball from Ray Ray, Kevin knocked down the approaching defenders. Back in control, I handed the ball to the other flanker, a muscle-bound advertisement for Gold's Gym named Mace McFarland. Mace ran over four defenders before spinning the ball out to Stoli, who called himself "the best rugby player in Alaska." Like a sleek Viper slicing past a squadron of plodding A-10 Warthogs, Stoli jived, spun, refused to pass, and finally ran the ball into the end zone to give us the go-ahead score in a game that most American-born spectators will never figure out.

Lori Ann, Nicole, and Curtis sat on the sideline with Mace's wife, Kristen, who had set up a beach umbrella, a folding table, and lawn chairs. Kristen had single-handedly turned the Fairbanks rugby pitch into a Miami polo ground. Wearing a large white hat and a sundress, she held a chilled chardonnay in one hand and a cracker in the other. Lori and Nicole wore shorts and sleeveless shirts. Curtis, making sure he could be easily identified by any young women at the game, wore a shirt with the NBC logo.

It was 75 degrees. The sky was a flawless blue. The Alaska Range rose clear and majestic in the distance. The spruce trees emitted their marketable fragrance. The grass was a deep shade of green. A rugby player from the Barbarians who had scored for the first time stripped and celebrated underneath the goal posts naked. It was summertime Fairbanks style.

For Lori, who had only seen Alaska in the dead of winter, the change was unbelievable. With nearly twenty-four hours of continuous sun and temperatures reaching into the 90s, Fairbanks in the summer is the closest thing America has to an Eden, if you forget Hawaii, and the tourists flock north by plane, train, and Winnebago in search of paradise, gaudy Alaskan T-shirts, and souvenir moose nuggets. They come by the thousands to mine for gold, to eat salmon, to hike the hills, to ride the Alaska Rail Road, to snap pictures of moose, and to walk along the Trans-Alaska Pipeline. They check into the fancy hotels on the outside of town and eat at the restaurants with the early bird specials. Then they head to the local theme parks at Alaskaland or to the Ester Gold Camp for a night of poetry reading and singing from the long-ago days when Fairbanks was a new city. Their RVs crowd the streets, and their stomachs crowd the restaurants, but most important, their wallets help out the locals.

I joined the after-match party on the sideline. Curtis, having learned the Alaskan technique for passing the bottle, hurled a cheap can of cold beer at my head. I took a couple of sips, placed my arm around Lori, and soaked in the scene.

Mace wrapped a bandana around his head and sat shirtless drinking a beer next to Kristen. Kurt Smith downed his beer before taking to the field for the second rugby game. Ray Ray pulled a bottle of vodka out of his rugby bag. Stoli worked a group of young girls in Daisy Duke shorts on the sideline. Everyone else told stories and compared scars.

"Now *this*," I said with a big smile, "this is Alaska."

Curtis, who had grown up in and lived in several different parts of the state, looked at me like I was crazy. "Actually, Lori," he interjected, "this is not Alaska, and please don't ever think this is. This is like the WWF, but not as good."

Curtis was a bit of a snob when it came to sports. In general he approved of only three summertime Alaskan sports: fishing, golf, and baseball. On that day, June 21, he approved of only one: baseball. "So if you don't mind, I will leave you bunch of knuckleheads and link up with you later at the *real* game. Then, Miss Lori and Miss Nicole, you will see the *real* Alaska."

A Hard Day's Day

June 21, the summer solstice, is the longest day of the year. In most parts of the country it's no big deal, but in Fairbanks, the solstice means more than nineteen hours of sunlight and a back-to-back dusk and dawn that keeps the interior bathed in light for twenty-four hours. It's not the eighty-four days of continuous sun that the residents of the farthest northern reaches of Alaska get, but it is still cause for a major celebration, the Midnight Sun Festival. Stores and restaurants stay open late, and dozens of booths open in the center of Fairbanks's Golden Heart Plaza, where thousands of Alaskans and tourists mingle to the sounds of local bands. After washing off the blood and grass stains from the rugby game, I took Lori and Nicole straight there for a carnival-style dinner of fried dough and hot dogs. We gorged ourselves, strolled through the gift shops around the plaza, and danced (as only a beat-up rugby player can) to the music. The party in the plaza was just the beginning, though.

The real highlight of the night was the Midnight Sun baseball game at Growden Memorial Park. First played in 1906, the Midnight Sun game brings together amateur baseball teams for what may be the most unusual game of their career. None of the game is, or ever has been, played under electric lights—just the ever-glowing summer night sky.

Growden Memorial is an old-fashioned ballpark with no bad seats and ticket takers and vendors that remember your name. About 4,500 people joined us for the game that night, but it felt like I knew every one of them. There were airmen I knew from Eielson, friends from the rugby team (many not yet showered), and, of course, the local media community. Because it was such a big event, Curtis Smith had an assistant working the camera at the game. They both bumped their way over to our seats, where Curtis began taping an impromptu interview with Lori and Nicole, "two visitors to Fairbanks." Halfway through the interview, the hometown hosts of the game, the Alaska Goldpanners, took to the field amidst great applause. Their red hats bore the number 49, representing Alaska's induction into the United States as the forty-ninth state. Their jerseys simply said ALASKA. Having watched the team take to the field, Curtis turned to us with a big smile.

"Now *that*," Curtis said, "that is Alaska."

The first pitch was thrown at 10:30 P.M. to a batter from the Kelowna Grizzlies, a Canadian team based in British Colombia. The sun had already slipped below the horizon, but its glow still lit the sky as the Goldpanners began a dominating night against the Grizzlies. At midnight, as if to remind everyone that this was no ordinary baseball game, the umpires halted the game for an Alaskan version of the seventh inning stretch. A woman took to the loudspeakers and began to sing the "Alaska Flag Song." "Eight stars of gold on a field of blue . . ." (I'd cite the rest, but it costs $200 for permission to use.)

The game ended around 1:30 A.M. As usual, the Goldpanners won, 8–2. Almost 180 former Alaska Goldpanners have gone on to play in the big leagues, including Tom Seaver, Dave Winfield, and Barry Bonds. More recently, Yankees players Jason Giambi and Christian Parker trace their roots to the Midnight Sun game.

Even though it was late, the three of us were just getting

started. From Growden Park we drove outside the Fairbanks limits to watch the sun rise from the highest point near Fairbanks, Murphy Dome. We were not alone. Dozens of Midnight Sun revelers had also climbed the steep hill. Despite the festive atmosphere down in Fairbanks, those who sat on top of the dome were quiet. It was a moment of spiritual reflection as we watched something one could never see from inside the steel canyons of New York City—a sunrise—and only a couple of hours after the longest day of the year ended, the second longest day of the year began.

Despite an extremely cold winter, the daily sunlight had been increasing by about seven minutes a day since December, but Lori and Nicole had no time to adjust to the longer days of sun and play. Tired and wanting to sleep, we returned to the cabin at Harding Lake around 3:30 A.M. after watching the sun rise. Unfortunately, Harding Lake was the worst place in the interior to try to get some sleep. It seemed the Midnight Sun party had spread to the lake, where dozens of boats, water-skiers, and Jet Skis still zoomed around as if it were the middle of the day. We failed miserably in our attempts to sleep. If it wasn't the Jet Skis, it was the sunlight shining through the window. If it wasn't the sunlight, it was the rogue mosquitoes that buzzed relentlessly around your ear. There was just no rest for the weary.

I finally gave up trying to sleep around 6:00 A.M. I grabbed a bar of soap, some shampoo, and a towel and headed down to the lake for a bath. Jumping in was something of a gut check. The cold water, still barely above freezing, gripped and squeezed and bit at every part of my body as I washed. Still, the fresh air and the clean lake water beat the sulfur smell and low pressure of my shower. The water at the end of the dock rose to my chest, and the dock served as a perfect ledge to hold my supplies. Lori and Nicole came outside shortly after with sunglasses, towels, suntan lotion, and paperback books. One hundred and fifty miles from the Arctic Circle, the two girls lay down to get a tan at 6:30 in the morning. I would have liked to join them, but it was Monday, and I had to go to work back at Eielson.

Alaska in the summer really is the paradise you have heard of and more, but for those who live there, it's also the most demanding time of year. The majority of all work in Alaska is done during the summer. Instead of an eight-hour day, workers can expect a fourteen-hour day, and instead of relaxing after work, people have more to do at home: boating, barbecuing, fishing, jogging, hiking, and so on. It's nearly impossible to get to bed before 3:00 A.M. or get up after 6:00 A.M. in the summer. After two months at that rate, some Alaskans begin to fantasize about winter. (Well—not really.)

Lori and Nicole were finding out why firsthand. Despite their amazing lack of rest, both women found that the sun's rays provided as much energy as a full night's sleep. Having lived in cloudy Seattle for the last year, neither of them was about to pass up any of it. They sunbathed in the morning, water-skied in the afternoon, arranged dinners on the deck in the evening, and then went water-skiing again at night. About the only thing that could slow them down was the unpredictable summer thunderstorms that seemed to appear out of nowhere and ravage Harding Lake. One storm caught them in the middle of the lake. The winds were so furious that the water turned into a wave pool that made it nearly impossible to dock the boat back in the lift. By the time the boat was docked, the sun came back out, and the two fell back into their routine: sunning, boating, grilling, more boating, and, in rare instances, sleeping.

"Now *that*," Lori said, "that is Alaska."

Alaska is a lot of things to a lot of different people. Before June, however, I was really only familiar with what Alaska meant to people who traced their roots to the Lower 48. I hadn't a clue about what Alaska meant to her aboriginal residents. A fire out in the bush and its ensuing political scrum were about to change all that.

The Caribou of the People

Ask any caribou in northern Alaska and they'll tell you: Next to the grizzlies and wolves that try to eat you when you're just a calf, the worst part about summer is the mosquitoes. They're merciless. They swarm around your backside. They fly up your nose, in your ears, and through your teeth, and there are always a couple of the bastards that land on the moist spot of your eye. You'll try anything to get rid of them—snort, sneeze, shake your head, flap your ears, blink your eyes, flick your tail—but it's no use. Without humanlike arms or hands, it's nearly impossible to cover yourself with bug spray or build a nice front porch with screen doors and windows. About the only thing caribou can do is move out of town, so they leave the nice river valleys and picturesque mountain ridges of the northern interior and head up to the Beaufort Sea coast for a waterfront vacation—just you and tens of thousands of your sort-of-deer, sort-of-elk, sort-of-moose-like best friends. *Can anybody find Waldo?*

Then the greatest thing happens. Sometime around August, the temperature drops below freezing, and the little bugger that has been sucking juice out of your right eye for the better part of two months freezes solid and cracks in half the next time you blink. The blood bank is closed! It's time for the Porcupine caribou herd to bid adieu to the coast, hop on the Alcan, and head back to their winter homes around the Porcupine River Valley, just north of the Arctic Circle.

That's the migration of the caribou. Summer on the ocean. Winter in the valley. Mosquitoes up the nose. It's such a predictable pattern—so predictable that an entire human culture has relied on it for the better part of ten thousand years, making man the second most hated creature in the interior next to the mosquito. Ask any caribou and they'll tell you: The worst part about winter is those damn creatures that move quickly on snow-machines, stand erect on two legs, and sling lead at you from the guns they bought at the Fairbanks Kmart.

The most effective hunters in the Porcupine River Valley are Native Alaskans called the Gwich'in, which translates to mean the "people of the caribou." They hunt the animal, eat the animal, and wear the animal in a communal way that has sustained the tribe's life since well before the birth of Jack London, Jesus Christ, or even Senator Strom Thurmond. So if something or somebody or some Air Force messes with the caribou, you can bet the Gwich'in of Fort Yukon, Venetie, and Arctic Village are going to let you know about it.

Magic Rocks

"The concerns of the Gwich'in people are well documented," said Sarah James, a Gwich'in leader sitting to my right at a meeting in Fairbanks. "Ever since you guys put those nuclear plants up there, the caribou have not been coming. For more years than any of us have been around, we have been hunting those caribou, and we know when there is something wrong. So you made the problem. Now you have to fix it. You need to get the nuclear plants off of our land. That is Native land, my family's land, and my family's burial ground. You had no right to put it there in the first place without us knowing, and now it's on our land, and the caribou will not come, and the people are sick with cancer."

Nuclear? Cancer? Native burial ground?

In August and September 1992, just as the Porcupine caribou were headed back to their wintering grounds, a fire raged out of control in the tundra north of the Arctic Circle. Looking at a map, you could see that the only thing the fire could possibly affect was the Native villages of Fort Yukon, Venetie, and Arctic Village, and even those areas were dozens of miles from the fire. To most casual observers, including the Gwich'in in the nearby villages, it was just another summer fire. However, several hundred miles away, in a small antenna-covered building marked Det 460 back at Eielson Air Force Base, a group of nerdy Air Force personnel were in a tizzy. Unbeknownst to just about everybody in Alaska, the fire was encroaching on another legacy of the cold war, a secret seismic observatory capable of detecting nuclear blasts anywhere on the planet. Ironically, the observatory was on a site named "Burnt Mountain." *Huh, what a strange name for a mountain. Let's put some sensitive equipment on it.*

Back on Burnt Mountain, the fire had spread to within a hundred yards of one node of the observatory, destroying the data cables that relayed the site's activity back to the geeks at Det 460. Without that precious data signal, all of Det 460 was completely useless. Like fighter pilots sitting on alert, the geeks who monitored the seismic observatory sprang into action. They loaded helicopters with firefighting gear and requested the assistance of several outside agencies, including the Alaska Bureau of Land Management's smoke jumpers, who heroically jumped onto the front lines to fight the blaze. Perhaps some of the bravest firefighters in the country, the BLM smoke jumpers are normally prepared for everything, but it seemed they were woefully underdressed for this occasion. While they worked in their normal gear, the geeks from Det 460 were decked out in radiation suits.

Oh, don't worry about the lead suits, guys. We always wear these. There's no problem here. Just please extinguish the fire as soon as possible.

Hidden deep inside the little shacks on Burnt Mountain, in the center of a trash-can-size container, sits a *magic* material called strontium 90. A chunk of it about the size of a hockey puck is the fuel for a radioisotope thermoelectric generator—or, as most common, everyday people call it, an RTG. With no power lines available, the Air Force had to rely on some sort of generator to run the different nodes of the seismic array on Burnt Mountain. When the observatory was built in 1972, the power source of choice for remote, unmanned military sites was strontium 90—which we pathetically and shamefully described to Sarah James and others as a piece of rock that *magically* gives off heat. As the magic rock decays, the generator turns the heat into 6 to 15 watts of power that would fuel the Burnt Mountain seismic array to the year 2009 at no additional annual cost to the government. Now, as the fire raged, the big question on everyone's mind was "What happens when the fire hits the magic rocks?" Nobody knew for sure, but wondering about it certainly encouraged the smoke jumpers to work a little bit harder.

Alas, disaster was averted. The well-protected geeks and their unprotected hired help were able to steer the fire away from the observatory and its magic rocks. After burning thirty-five thousand acres of prime caribou real estate for about a month, the fire died out, and the reclusive personnel from Det 460 returned to their prickly, temperature-controlled building at Eielson, thankful that they were out of danger and comfortable behind their consoles of blips and flashing lights that told them whether the Russians or the Chinese or whoever were being good and not testing their nuclear devices that day. Everything was back to normal—and would stay that way, just as long as nobody opened their mouth.

NUCLEAR SECRET LAID BARE.
AIR FORCE GENERATORS EXPOSED BY WILDFIRE
TESTING SOUGHT AT SITE
NATIVES TELL AIR FORCE:
RADIOACTIVE UNITS MUST GO

—FAIRBANKS DAILY NEWS-MINER,
SEPTEMBER–OCTOBER 1992

The Omnipotent Air Force

The events at Burnt Mountain in 1992 caused a flurry of action by just about every environmental, Native, and government organization in Alaska. Most vocal were the Gwich'in of Fort Yukon, Venetie, and Arctic Village. Represented by Jonathan Solomon of the Gwich'in Steering Committee, the Natives demanded that the RTGs be removed. Det 460 and the Air Force wouldn't budge. The Burnt Mountain site is vital to national security, they argued, and the only realistic way to power the generators is with RTGs. To break the stalemate, Senators Frank Murkowski and Ted Stevens commissioned the Congressional Office of Technology Assessment to look into alternative power sources for the seismic array. The Air Force began its own study. After years of testing and research, the unanimous results from both studies were finally ready for release. By that time, I had landed at Eielson, and as the resident PR nerd I had the fortunate task of working with the Det 460 geeks to tell the Natives that their concerns were essentially unfounded and that we—the omnipotent Air Force—would keep using the RTGs and the strontium 90, thank you very much.

"I don't understand why we are all here," said Bob Childers, a non-Native lawyer who advised the Gwich'in Steering Committee. "You guys know what our concerns are. You have heard all of our testimony. You have talked to all the Natives. We want the RTGs out of here, and that's it." Childers and Sarah James were two of a dozen people from Native groups and government organizations that had attended an April meeting between the Air Force and concerned organizations in Fairbanks to discuss the best way to release the results of the studies to the Native communities near Burnt Mountain.

"Well, we just want to make sure that we're all on the same page," said the colonel in charge of Det 460. "In fact, what we really want to do is go out to the villages and talk to the people about their concerns and present them with the results of the study."

"What's the point?" James asked. "They will have nothing different to say."

"Well, we just think we should come on up anyway," the colonel said, and the man in the blue suit struck again. Despite all logic and reason, the blue suiter—a man perhaps better educated for fast food management—thinks he has a good idea, then turns a deaf ear to other suggestions and makes the stupidest decision on the planet.

NATIVES: "But there's no point in you coming to the villages. We represent them."

AIR FORCE: "How does June sound?"

NATIVES: "June sounds as bad as July and as bad as April and as bad as September. There is no need for you to come."

AIR FORCE (big smiles): "All right, then. June it is. We'll see you there!"

Men, make sure you pack your radiation suits. We don't want to take any chances.

How to Make Native Alaskans Glow in the Dark

The Air Force could not have picked a person less suited than I was to join the Det 460 airmen on a trip to Fort Yukon, Venetie, and Arctic Village to see if the Natives had changed their minds regarding the RTGs and their strategically caustic placement in the middle of Porcupine caribou country. I knew a couple of kids in high school who claimed they were a quarter or an eighth or a sixteenth Indian, but for virtually all of my formative years my life had been centered around Budweiser-swilling, Van Halen–listening, Camaro-driving white folks. The first *real* Native Americans I ever spoke to were the ones sitting around the table that April in Fairbanks explaining politely that they did not want us to visit them again, goddammit, and they weren't really speaking to *me*. They were talking to the colonel and the other senior people at the table. James and her gang were not interested in talking to a powerless cheechako from New York who viewed the film *Dances with Wolves* as the definitive history of the American Indian. The only thing I knew for sure (and every Indian movie got this one right) was that the Natives considered the whites in uniforms to be the bad guys. However, the colonel was not available, and technically I was the expert in community relations, so by the idiotic process of elimination I became the idiotically logical choice to lead the latest Air Force expedition.

In light of the Air Force's record with the Natives, my trip stood little chance of succeeding. Their minds somewhere off in the wild blue yonder, about fifty years ago several Air Force scientists came up with the theory that the thyroid gland played a key function in human acclimation to the cold. Wouldn't you know it—the Natives who had lived at 40 below zero for the last ten thousand years seemed to acclimate better than the Air Force pilots from Florida and California. *Has to be the thyroid,* said the man with the blue hat. But how could they know for sure? What technique was there to test that little gland? For some reason not entirely clear to me and my 1080 SAT score, the Air Force chose the radioactive medical tracer iodine 131. In 1956 and 1957, the smock-wearing scientists from the Air Force lab administered the tracer to 121 people—19 airmen from the Lower 48 and, just to be completely fair, 102 Alaskan Natives from enclaves including Fort Yukon and Arctic Village, where the residents received the highest doses of the irradiated dye. When the results came in, there was good news and bad news. The good news was that the thyroid does not play a major role in adaptation to the climate after all, and the top guns from Florida should adapt to the cold just as well as the Natives. The bad news was that the test participants might get sick with cancer or other maladies sometime down the road and then die.

Don't worry about it, though, said the man with the blue hat. *I didn't say you* would *get sick—I said you* might *get sick. That's a big difference.*

Follow-up studies ultimately proved that none of the participants was ever diagnosed with thyroid cancer, but that didn't really matter. If the cancer among the Natives—and they were certain they all had it or were about to get it—was not caused by the iodine tests, there were plenty of other cold war projects that might take the blame. A local favorite was the old "underground nuclear weapons testing excuse."

Formerly a home for Aleut Natives until the Russians depleted the island's sea otter supply, the Aleutian Island of Amchitka turned from a National Wildlife Refuge in 1913 to a fighter base in 1943 to a DEW radar site in the 1950s to a great place to blow up the largest nuclear weapon ever tested underground by the United States in 1971. At five megatons, the Cannikin nuclear test was 385 times more powerful than the blasts at Hiroshima and 37 times more powerful than the two previous underground blasts the government conducted on Amchitka in 1964 and 1969. Many thought the test was outrageous, but despite worldwide protests and the objections of an upstart environmental group called Greenpeace—created solely to stop the blast—the Cannikin mission was a go. The explosion registered 7.0 on the Richter scale and killed, by Greenpeace estimates, approximately 86.5 million sea creatures that lived in the waters off the Amchitka Island Wildlife Preserve (which is now famous for its thirty-three toxic waste sites, napalm bomb stockpiles, and other mounds of unexploded and slightly rusty military ordnance).

What was particularly upsetting to the Natives of interior Alaska about the Amchitka testing was the radioactive material, including some of the infamous strontium 90, that leaked out of the underground containment area and drifted in the air over Alaska. Eventually the radioactive particulate was absorbed into the lichens of the interior's tundra—which in turn were eaten by the caribou of the Porcupine herd—which in turn were eaten by the people of Fort Yukon, Venetie, and Arctic Village—who in turn seemed to be dying of cancer at much higher rates today than before the Manhattan Project. Now I, no doubt because of my thorough grasp of Native issues and Van Halen lyrics, was going to fly up to these villages in my U.S. AIR FORCE uniform and read to them from the U.S. AIR FORCE study:

> The continued use of the RTGs (and their strontium 90) is clearly the safest, most reliable, and most economical approach to supplying the Burnt Mountain Seismic Observatory and should continue until the end of their useful life (sometime around 2009).

I could always claim I was just following orders.

The Way It Is

The first stop on our Native Alaskan "listening tour" was Fort Yukon. Above the Arctic Circle, 145 miles northeast of Fairbanks, the small village of six hundred sits on the gravel banks of the Yukon River near its confluence with the Porcupine River. Since there are no roads to Fort Yukon, the gang from Det 460 and I made our way to the Native outpost in a chartered Cessna Cherokee from Wright Aviation. For about two thousand dollars, the pilot and his plane would ferry us to each village, then wait on the tarmac with the engines running in case the listening tour turned into Little Big Horn. Truth is, we had no idea on earth what to expect. Our contact for the trip, a Native environmental representative named Davey James (one of several Jameses we would deal with on this mission), told us he would not be able to meet us at Fort Yukon. Instead, we were supposed to link up with a village leader we had met back in Fairbanks. I failed several times to get anyone on the phone at Fort Yukon to confirm our visit. For all I knew, we might have been the only people who had any idea that we were coming.

Flying over Alaska in the summer was much different than my flights with Colonels Brammeier and Adams in April. There was still some snow in the valleys between the rolling mountains of the interior, but the majority of the flight was over a solid blanket of dark, virgin forest. There was no urban sprawl visible leaving Fairbanks, no isolated mansions for the wealthy, and no small towns with antique shops nestled under the trees, just a pristine forest whose only flaw was an alarmingly high number of mini forest fires and their telltale columns of smoke rising above the horizon. Our pilot logged in the coordinates of each blaze and reported them back to Fairbanks to ensure the smoke jumpers knew exactly what blaze was where. The first major change in the horizon was the Yukon River. Cutting perpendicular to our flight path, the river seemed like a well-paved highway in the middle of the bush. As we approached, the skyline of Fort Yukon came into view in the shape of two large radar towers that looked like giant drive-in movie screens. Next to the towers were two barracks buildings that used to house three hundred airmen who made sure that any Soviet bombers planning to attack Fairbanks were detected well in advance by the long-range radar there. By the time I visited, the site that praised itself as the "coldest Air Force station in the world" had been closed for years, outmoded due to new technology and new threats—and, on that particular day in June, temperatures in the mid-80s.

We landed on an airstrip outside the center of the town.

Before I could get out of the plane to wonder what to do next, a van pulled up alongside to welcome us to the village.

"Who are you guys?" the stocky Native woman driving the van asked.

"We're from Eielson Air Force Base. We're here for the meeting about Burnt Mountain," I said.

"No meeting here."

"Yeah, I'm supposed to link up with some people here. They should be expecting us," I said.

"No, there is nobody expecting you," she said.

"Well, what about our meeting? I mean—where do we—what should I—who else can I talk to?"

The Native woman recommended we load our gear into the van and head to the community center, where people might want to talk to us. The center sat just outside the main section of Fort Yukon, which—although populated—looked a lot like an Old West ghost town complete with dust and tumbleweeds. The handful of clapboard buildings that lined the streets were in need of repair, and the entire town seemed to be littered with an old car here or an old snowmachine there or an old refrigerator there. The place was rustic, and not necessarily in a kitschy Cracker Barrel kind of way.

"See, no meeting scheduled," the woman said, pointing at the bulletin board on the community center. "But maybe if you stick around, some people will come to see who is here."

With that advice, we sat down and waited for a meeting to take shape around us. After polishing off some bag lunches from Eielson, we got our first customer. Clarence Alexander, a former village chief and onetime head of the Council of Athabascan Tribal Government, came into the center.

"Are you here to take the RTGs away?" he asked.

"No, not exactly," I said. "We're here to make sure we have heard everyone's concerns regarding the RTGs. (*Big smile.*) Some environmental studies were conducted to see if it made sense to replace the items. (*Crunched brow, serious yet friendly expression.*) We want to show everyone the results of the study and get your comments before we make a final decision."

Alexander exhaled tiredly. Old and wrinkled and gray, he was tired of fighting this administrative battle and tired of years of living under the towering radar sites at Fort Yukon and tired of midlevel officials in blue suits telling him what was right or wrong for his village and his family and tired of my fancy charts and my uniform and my rank and my frank yet serious smile.

"I remember when you brought these things here. I remember when they paraded these things around the village so that we would know what they were. I remember the fire and the visits to the mountain, and I am not interested in talking any more about it. Why are you here? Why come to ask us what you already know—that we want the things out of here? There is no need to talk more about this."

Alexander taught me all I needed to know about the Gwich'in and the caribou and the RTGs. He told me about the days when there were more caribou than needed, when the animals would simply walk up to you, when there was no need to hunt far away, and how good it was and how well they all ate. Then he told me that the caribou never come back anymore because of the observatory on Burnt Mountain and the pipeline that cuts through the grazing land, and he told me about when the Air Force came to set up its cold war radar site in the 1950s and how that was the first year the caribou stayed away. He told me that the government people came and went, always saying the same things but doing nothing—just like me and the gang from Det 460 who came to Fort Yukon without telling anybody we were coming and then called him over to say nothing new.

Then Alexander got up and told us that no more people would be coming to the community center to see us that day. As far as I was concerned, that was great, since I was now horribly depressed and feeling guilty for being associated with the Air Force. With an

hour to kill before we were scheduled to depart Fort Yukon, I figured I would goose-step my way around the town and at least get
some good pictures of the place to add to my scrapbook: me
standing by the Yukon; me next to some flat-bottom river boats;
me in front of the Arctic Circle Baptist Church; me outside the
old radar station. After the tour, we loaded up into the village van
and headed back to the airport without fanfare.

Taxation Without Authorization

Permanent "Native Villages" are a relatively new invention in
Alaska. Prior to the gold rush in the early 1900s, most Native set-
tlements consisted of a handful of cabins or other shelters that
were only occupied during the coldest of the cold months. The
Natives were nomadic for the rest of the year as they followed the
harried caribou and other food sources from camp to camp in
much the same way the North American Plains Indians migrated
with the buffalo. With the gold rush came outside influence,
bringing a new culture of property to the Athabascans. The scattering of shelters that Natives kept in particular regions eventually coalesced into supply posts frequented by the gold-miner set,
and those areas ultimately became permanent villages in the
familiar sense with schools, water wells, community buildings, an
airstrip, and a 7-Eleven (*one of these days anyway*). Although they
now maintain year-round residence in one of these Native Villages, the Gwich'in of the interior still hunt the caribou. Instead
of moving their entire home for a lengthy journey, they simply
saddle up on a snowmachine and range out from the town.

Some might consider Fort Yukon a Native Village. A federally
recognized tribe is based there, and about 90 percent of the residents are Native. There is something very Western about the
place, though. It has two Christian churches. There is a large

rusting Air Force station. The state's lone member of the U.S. House of Representatives, Don Young, lives there. You almost get the feeling that if Fort Yukon had a few thousand more people it would look very much like Fairbanks (which has two 7-Elevens).

Venetie is different. About sixty miles north of Fort Yukon, Venetie is more than just a Native Village. Venetie is Indian Country. At least, it was until 1998, when the Supreme Court said it wasn't.

In the legal sense, "Indian Country" is a piece of federally supervised Native land in which the tribal governments retain much of their ancient sovereignty, can make laws, and can exert extensive regulatory powers. Most reservations in the Lower 48 are examples of Indian Country. However, there are no reservations in Alaska. Spurred by the discovery of oil on the frontier, Alaskan lawmakers passed the Alaskan Native Claims Settlement Act in 1971 in hopes of creating a solution better than reservations to preserve Native traditions and sovereignty while creating a system in which Natives could transition into a Western culture. The Act created twelve Native Corporations comprising two hundred Native Villages and forty-four million acres of Alaskan land drawn along traditional Native boundaries. Under the Act every Alaskan Native received one hundred shares of stock in the corporation that represented his or her village. If oil was discovered under the corporation's land, all Natives who owned stock in the company would stand to receive a large dividend. But while the Native Corporations retained their mineral rights, they exchanged any aboriginal claims to the land for a onetime payment of $962.5 million.

Except in Venetie. Ultimately refusing to sell out, the Gwich'in of Venetie and nearby Arctic Village used a provision of the act to take full ownership of the 1.8 million acres of land that the federal government had given them as a reservation in 1943. No Native Corporation. No cash exchange for aboriginal rights. Venetie, Arctic Village, and their surrounding land were governed instead by a joint tribal council that essentially made and enforced their own laws and standards. It was by most people's definition Indian Country, and in Indian Country a tribe is free to tax anyone who does business there. Accordingly, the Natives of Venetie levied a 5 percent business tax on a contractor who was building a state-funded school in their village in 1986. Like any sensible American, the law-abiding contractor did not pay the $161,000 tax bill, thus unwittingly initiating the first good Indian war in a hundred years.

Unfortunately for Hollywood, the battles in the Alaskan Indian Country War were not fought with tomahawks and flamboyant cavalry officers. Instead, the fights took place in courtrooms. In 1996, the U.S. Ninth Circuit Court of Appeals confirmed that Venetie was in fact Indian Country and could issue whatever taxes, land use regulations, environmental restrictions, and social laws it wanted to. Fork over the G's, Mr. Contractor. The Native Village of Venetie needs some sidewalks (and paved roads, and sewage, and electricity, and a recycling station, and a landfill, and a better public bathroom than the outhouse that sits across from the community center with the words MEN SHIT ROOM spray-painted on the door).

Fearing that the other 225 Native Villages would also apply to become Indian Country, making it difficult and expensive for companies to do business in Alaska, the state legislature set aside a million dollars and formed a coalition of western states to challenge the ruling in the U.S. Supreme Court. Indeed, in 1998, the Supreme Court said the Gwich'in tribal land could not possibly be Indian Country under U.S. law. To be Indian Country, Justice Clarence Thomas said, the tribal land had to have been set aside by the federal government for tribal use and be under federal supervision. Venetie, he said, met neither of those requirements. It was simply a big chunk of privately owned land the size of Delaware. The Court also said there was nothing stopping the Native Village of Venetie from applying for municipal status—in other words, becoming a "real" town. With that status, Venetie would be able to charge a business tax to future concerns. However, the Village would have to give up much of its Native culture and tradition to become an official municipality with a town board and elections and all that stuff, and that was simply too much for the Gwich'in to swallow, so despite its exclusively Indian population and Indian law, Venetie is not really Indian Country after all. It looked a lot like it to me, though.

Italian Influences on Native Alaskans

From the air, Venetie takes the shape of an upper-case *T*. The long section is formed by a narrow dirt runway that ends in the center of a scattering of buildings along the Chandalar River. Only one structure is recognizable from the air: the large red roof of the infamous school that sparked the Indian Country War. The rest of the buildings blend naturally with the dirt and the scrub spruce as if they had always been there. As our plane touched down on the runway, the natural feel of the place disappeared. Venetie was no postcard-perfect vision of a Native Village. Even more than Fort Yukon, Venetie seemed less a town and more a group of shacks in the middle of a junkyard. Without roads or landfills or heavy equipment to move the scraps of modern life, Venetie was drowning in rusted oil drums, discarded snowmachines, aircraft wreckage, ancient lengths of steel pipe, a collection of used televisions, and virtually everything else you might find on the sidewalks of a city street on Monday morning before the garbage trucks come. There are no garbage trucks in Venetie, so the old toys and baby cribs and bicycles sit where they were left last winter.

I do not want to give the impression that the Natives of Venetie are sloppy. Given the kind of municipal infrastructure most Americans have in the Lower 48, they might transform their village into a Rockwell painting in a matter of days. As things are, aside from burying all the waste in a giant hole, there is little they can do, and since the ground is frozen and there is probably no backhoe in working order in town, even digging is a near impossibility. The planes with all the goodies keep coming—new snowmachines every winter, new bikes every summer, new everything to replace all the old everything already there—but the pilots who link Venetie to the modern world don't get paid to take the garbage away, so it sits. (By the way, other Alaskans do little better than the Natives. The outlying areas of Fairbanks look like a never-ending salvage yard.)

Nobody met us when we landed at Venetie, but since the runway seemed to terminate in the middle of the village, it was easy to walk into the center of the town in search of our contact, the mysterious Davey James. A group of children, the first Native children I had seen in Alaska, came over to me as I walked. They were girls between the ages of about six and ten, and they were no different than any other girls in the entire world. They smiled a lot, they teased each other, and when I took their picture, one of them made rabbit ears behind another's head. The oldest of the group wore a baby-carrying backpack with an infant strapped in. Between bites of her cheese sandwich, she guided me through the maze of buildings in search of Davey James. Since there are no cars in Venetie, there are no roads in the town, just paths between structures that were sprinkled about the runway without benefit of a straightedge. All of them were built with one of three materials: logs, whipsawed timber, or milled wood that had been flown into the village. Most buildings had tin roofs. Electricity cables hung from house to house and from pole to pole. Despite my uniform, the occupants of the village took no notice as I walked through the area with my baby-carrying guide.

We finally linked up with James at the tribal government building. James had a chubbier face than the other Natives I met and wore a red baseball cap, a flannel shirt, and blue jeans. He welcomed me to the town and introduced me to the village second chief and tribal secretary, who said they hoped we would be able to resolve all the issues that day. Everyone was ready for the meeting, James said, but he thought it might go a little better if we went door to door to let people know we were ready to get started. When we reached the first house, I realized that it might take a while. It was dinnertime there, and no one was ready for any meeting. That being the case, James told me we should just sit down and join the dinner, which we did. I ate a large plate of pasta with a bolognese sauce that featured ground moose. It was fantastico. With the exception of the Native faces, I could have been in a Brooklyn kitchen. There was a lot of joking and laughter among the group, who welcomed me without an odd look. The room we ate in was a typical living room with a television, a crucifix, a wood stove, and a standard collection of wall-mounted family pictures including a young man in a U.S. Army uniform—a young man who had served as an Arctic Scout with the Alaska Army National Guard, James told me.

After tossing our paper plates into the garbage can (I wondered where they would be going next), James and I headed back on the door-knocking tour, finally ending up at the village community center, where my team happily greeted me, glad to know I hadn't been eaten by grizzlies over the past hour. Several community members came in behind me, and the stage was set for the Big Meeting. I started with my memorized speech.

> We came here for one reason today, to continue a process that, together, we began in 1992 to investigate alternative power sources for the Air Force's seismic observatory at Burnt Mountain. It is an investigation with one goal—to make sure we use the safest, most environmentally sound power source available. (*I really meant that.*)

As you know, the Air Force seismic observatory detects nuclear testing around the world. It is an important observatory, one that the United States and Alaska rely on to make sure no other nation can threaten us with nuclear war, and more than ensuring our safety from nuclear attack, the Air Force wants to make sure the observatory is safe to those who live near it, to the Gwich'in people of Interior Alaska. (*I really meant that, too.*)

Our purpose here today is to listen to your environmental concerns about alternative power sources for the observatory. Now, as one village member said in a meeting in April, "The concerns of the Gwich'in people are well documented," and they are. They include the migration habits of the porcupine caribou herd. They include the effects of another fire. Most of all, they include the safety and health of the people and animals that live here. The concerns of the Gwich'in people are well documented, but the Air Force is not willing to take a chance. We haven't met together like this for a few years, and we want to make sure we know what's on your mind today. (*I did not really mean that. I knew what was on all their minds but was forced to visit these villages anyway.*)

I continued the talk with a brief history of the Burnt Mountain issue and the study results that told the Natives their concerns were baseless. The Natives in the room talked among themselves, looked out the window, and otherwise ignored me as I spoke.

I quoted from the Air Force study, which said that the "continued use of the RTGs is clearly the safest, most reliable, and most economical approach to supplying the Burnt Mountain Seismic Observatory" and that the RTGs "should continue to be operated until the end of their useful life," around 2009. I reminded them that the independent investigation conducted by the U.S. Congress concluded that "continued use of the RTGs at Burnt Mountain bears low risk for the safety of maintenance workers and local populations and for the environment."

Despite support for the RTGs, though, both reports also suggested that we look into alternative power sources. The alternatives under consideration included gasoline- or propane-powered generators as well as wind and solar generators. While the wind and solar options appeared attractive at the outset, variations in both wind and sunlight meant that either option would have to be run with a gasoline or propane backup. The problem with such volatile fuel was in its transportation and maintenance. Both reports suggested the risk of crash for a fuel-laden aircraft was far greater and more damaging than any risk presented by the RTGs. In addition, it would cost an estimated five million dollars to make the conversion.

> We'll listen to your ideas and concerns. We'll write them down and make sure we look into them as we study the impact on the environment a new power source would have. And with that—we will make sure we address the concerns of the Gwich'in people.

I delivered the talk just the way I practiced, but I was severely unnerved by the silence and blank stares in the room when I finished.

"Does anybody have anything they would like to say?"

An elder named Gideon James stepped forward and asked the most logical question. "So are you going to take the RTGs out or not?"

"Well . . ." and I went on to tell them that we were still a long way from making that decision and that we were just on a listening tour at that time. Then, in a lecture that was virtually identical to Clarence Alexander's back at Fort Yukon, Gideon James questioned our motives, restated the well-known desire to have the

RTGs out, and discussed the effects cancer was having on all the Natives of the interior. In a tearful summation, the elder James blamed it all on me and my Air Force cronies. He finished by telling me that no more people would be coming to the community center to see us that day.

"Well, then," I said, "thank you all for coming. Please feel free to have some of the Air Force fiftieth anniversary pins that I brought along." Everyone came up and grabbed a handful of the commemorative pins, then left the room.

Double-Dealing with the Arctic Scouts

After the meeting, Davey James and a couple of other young men pulled me aside.

"If these RTGs are so important for the Air Force, surely you need someone to protect them," James said.

"Well, we can monitor any change in the facility from Eielson by remote controls," I said.

"But surely if there was damage to the site, it would be bad for the Air Force."

"Yeah, I guess, but the sites are in the middle of nowhere. There is no threat to them."

"But people can get there easily, especially in the winter. They can take snowmachines or dogsleds. And who knows what they could do to the site," James said.

I sensed that James had something to offer, so I decided to play along. "Okay, let's say the site is important and needs to be protected. How could we do that?"

"Burnt Mountain is on tribal land," James said. "We know that land well. We hunt caribou there. We go there in the summer to check our traplines. Maybe the Arctic Scouts could patrol Burnt Mountain every now and again to make sure it is safe."

As members of the Army National Guard, the Arctic Scouts could hypothetically be given additional federal funding to patrol the array at Burnt Mountain. If it took one week for the Native soldiers of Fort Yukon and Venetie and Arctic Village to patrol the site, the average soldier might earn an additional thousand dollars per patrol. James went on to suggest that the patrolling could be done by people from each village several times a year, boosting the average income of the self-sufficient Natives by a large percentage. That would mean more snowmachines, more bicycles—in fact, more of everything for the Gwich'in of the interior.

What about the elders, though? They wanted the RTGs out of there.

"You do not need to take the RTGs away," James said. "Not if we are patrolling them and keeping them safe from vandalism and fires. Then there is nothing to worry about."

So two positions among the Natives became clear. The elders like Clarence Alexander and Gideon James wanted the RTGs out regardless of the costs or risks of a more volatile fuel. To them, diesel or propane was more acceptable because they were familiar with it. To them, the RTGs and their magic rocks would always present a perceived danger. The second position was stated by Davey James and his younger generation. They didn't care what power source was there, they wanted something out of it. At other meetings they had requested that the Air Force run power cables from the RTGs to remote hunting cabins, and in our meeting at Venetie they essentially asked for money—albeit without actually asking for it.

The opposing positions presented the Air Force with a complex problem. Whatever course of action it chose, the Air Force would probably be wrong. What the hell, the Natives already hated the boys in blue, so I guess it didn't really matter what they did.

Kit Fox Down

We learned at Venetie that an elder at Arctic Village had died the night before. The entire village was in a state of mourning, and Davey James recommended we not fly there. To my relief, the geeks from Det 460 agreed, and we loaded up the plane at 6:30 P.M. for the return flight to Fairbanks. Since we had the plane for the entire day, we asked the pilot to fly us over Burnt Mountain so I could actually see the source of all the frustration.

If people wanted to find the equipment to vandalize it or damage it, they would have to know exactly where to look. Even then, it was like looking for a needle in Iowa. The RTG sites first appeared as specks on the ground and never really got any bigger. Sitting on the summit of bald hilltops, each site consisted of two tin buildings no bigger than a garden shed in any suburban backyard. Their roofs were painted with red-and-white stripes. Several firebreaks were visible where the trees had begun to grow down the side of the mountain.

We circled the RTG sites twice, then turned back for Fairbanks. The pilot again took note of forest fires, and the rest of us got lost in thoughts about being stranded in such a remote place alone. As if we were giving off bad karma, the radio crackled as someone made a distress call.

"Mayday, mayday . . . engine trouble . . . near Fairbanks . . . going down."

Someone was about to experience the nightmare I had just been imagining. The pilot called the tower to get coordinates and learned we were virtually next to the plane in trouble. We made a wide arc toward the location of the distress call. All of us stared out the window, looking on the ground and in the air and everywhere for a plane.

"I got one . . . I got a plane . . . a yellow one . . . two o'clock!"

I turned to look just in time to watch the small plane crash into a swamp and flip over on its back. The adrenaline surged through my body as I morbidly stared at the crash. I tried to wonder what was going on inside the plane. The water must have been filling in the cockpit. Any survivors might be trying to get out. I might have just seen someone crash—*and die.*

There was little we could do. We radioed the coordinates of the crash site and continued to circle the area, getting as low as the pilot dared. The downed plane was not going fast when it crashed, and the body of the aircraft seemed intact. Miraculously, a man crawled out the side of the wreck. Another one followed. They were hip deep in the swamp but appeared to be okay. Both scampered onto the top of the plane, which was actually the bottom since it had crashed upside down.

"Hey, that's Captain Anderson!" someone shouted. Tim Anderson was Eielson's environmental officer. He had built his plane, a Kit Fox, in his garage on weekends. Apparently, his first test flight was less than a success.

Anderson gave us a big thumbs-up to let us know he was okay. Relieved, we lingered in the area a few more minutes until we got word that a rescue team was on its way. In addition to the pararescuemen at Eielson Air Force Base, an Army rescue crew was always on call at Fort Wainwright. They swooped down in their dual-rotor Chinook and hoisted the wayward Air Force officer and his buddy to safety.

Anderson may have been an environmental support geek back at Eielson, but he now wore a higher rank. Just like a motorcycle rider is not really a biker until he smacks pavement, an aviator is not really a true Alaskan pilot until he crashes his first plane. Anderson became an Alaskan pilot that day. Better still, he was one of the few who crashed—*and lived to tell about it.*

Disappearing Magic Rocks

As the very ignorant but official community and Native affairs expert at Eielson, I recommended in my listening-tour report that the Air Force leave the RTGs in place and give the Natives a monetary stake in the operation through regular patrols of the Burnt Mountain seismic array. It was hard to ignore that the environmental studies conducted on alternative power sources unanimously stated that the RTGs were the safest power option. If the Natives had a financial interest in Burnt Mountain, they would be better educated about the RTGs and more likely to pass on their knowledge of the technology to their villages. The taxpayers would save millions by keeping the existing power sources in place. Also, for the first time in recent memory, the Natives and the Air Force would be partners in a given venture.

If the Air Force chose to leave the RTGs in place without giving the Natives a stake, the government ran the risk of galvanizing the Natives into one position—the immediate removal of the RTGs—which brought with it a possible threat of vandalism in the winter months. If the Air Force chose to replace the RTGs with an alternative power source, it would still have to deal with the Native request that the Arctic Scouts patrol and protect the RTGs.

While our meetings with the Natives in both Fairbanks and the villages were publicized in the announcements section of the *Fairbanks Daily News-Miner*, I chose not to call my friends in the media to encourage their attendance. I was unsure how the meetings would play, but my guess was that Native elders scolding the Air Force would make a better sound bite than me reading the positive results from the environmental studies. Instead, I met one-on-one with several local journalists and other community leaders after our visits to ask them for their opinion on how they thought it would play out in the public if the Air Force kept the RTGs. In this private forum, I was able to review the environmental information with the journalists and present them with the divergent views of the Native community. All the journalists I talked to thought it made the most sense to keep the RTGs in place. None of them thought we needed to pay the Natives, but they found the desire to make them partners a positive step for the relationship between the Air Force and the Native community. My intent in all these meetings was to educate the public and defuse any negative perceptions before the Air Force's final decision was announced. Leaving the RTGs might seem a controversial decision on the surface. When it happened, I wanted the media solidly in my corner.

The final decision was announced in the summer of 2001.

NUCLEAR DEVICES TO BE RELOCATED

. . . Now, almost a decade since leaders from seven Interior villages demanded their removal, the Air Force is planning to take the nuclear-powered generators out from Burnt Mountain.

"From what the Air Force told us . . . it's basically a situation where it is probably a very safe battery," Bob Childers told the *News-Miner.* "But with high consequences for a mistake— and people wanted them out of there."

After years of pondering alternatives to the 10 nuclear devices, the Air Force has now decided to replace them with diesel-solar hybrid generators. . . .

—SEAN COCKERHAM, *FAIRBANKS DAILY NEWS MINER*

By Air Force estimates, the cost of the replacement added to all the other costs surrounding the Burnt Mountain fire in 1992 would exceed ten million dollars. Since we're talking about the federal government, there is a good chance that price has at least tripled.

JULY

The Wild Life

MOOSE RANCHING ON THE LAST FRONTIER

Critics of hunting and fishing often say that it's unnecessary to kill wild animals when the meat is available at the supermarket. Of course, someone had to kill a cow or a pig or a tuna at some point for it to get to the market, but that's okay, the critics argue, because the animals were not killed for *sport*. A good old-fashioned farmyard butchering is much better.

Hey, Cousin Jethro, when was the last time you sharpened this thing? It's like cutting with a goshdarn butter knife.

Clearly, the critics have it all wrong. Hunting and fishing, provided it is for sustenance, is the way to go. If people want to eat meat, they should go out and get it themselves. That gives the animal a fighting chance, and with so many cheechakos prowling Alaska's forests and waters, the animal, at least in the north country, stands a great chance of surviving the engagement.

You never know, the animal might even win. Take, for example, the Alaska moose hunter who stumbles across a cow and her two calves. Unless that hunter has a very quick draw—and a bazooka—there is a good chance that the moose will win. The same goes for grizzly bear and polar bear and even caribou.

But what about fish? Is there any chance the fish will survive an encounter with a fat guy from Wisconsin with a fly rod? Absolutely. One look into the clear waters of the Russian River on the Kenai Peninsula reveals dozens of colorful streaks moving under the water. At first, the streaks look like fish, but they're not, exactly—they're colorful fishing lures stuck into the mouth or side of a salmon. The salmon in Alaskan waters are so tough, many just fight their way through.

Unfortunately, I don't think a farmed salmon has such a good chance. There's about a 99.9 percent chance that fish is going to get caught and grilled up at a Manhattan restaurant.

Losing a lure isn't the only risk associated with fishing. Fish in Alaska are caught in one of two places: in remote waters, where a bear or moose might trample the angler, or out on the open sea, where a sudden storm may capsize the boat. The fish would probably be ignorant of the entire ordeal, but if the guy from Wisconsin survives, he may never put on a pair of hip waders again (assuming he still had legs to do so).

So much for a low-carb diet.

But forcing people to hunt or fish if they want to eat meat won't work, will it? Thousands of ranches would go out of business. Commercial fisherman, many of whom take the blame for exhausting the world's fish supply, would go out of business. Worst of all, fast food chains would only be able to sell French fries and apple pies. Thousands of minimum-wage earners would be out of work. Without the Big Mac, America would become an entire nation of vegetarians.

Except in Alaska. People on the Last Frontier still possess the skills to hunt and feed themselves off the land—Natives and Alaskans both. Many do it already. Now, though, even they are losing their skills. New fast food joints seem to pop up every other month. More frozen ground beef is being shipped north. Pretty soon, Alaskans will hunt and fish for food as infrequently as their counterparts in the Lower 48.

The result: All the Alaskan favorites will be raised on a ranch or a farm and then, with white gloves, placed on the plate for you, and a moose, caribou, grizzly, or salmon wouldn't stand a chance, even against a cheechako.

The Right Stuff

The little red phone rings every morning around eight A.M. The airman at the command post wants to make sure you are there and listening. "Roger, I read you loud and clear," I say back to the airman on the other end of the phone. It rings again several more times that day, and more often than not, it's just the airman at the command post testing the little red phone, more formally known as the crash alert net—but it's not always a test.

About an hour later, the phone rings again. This time, it's far from routine. Your heart races. Your adrenaline rises. There is a problem. Somebody's life is on the line. As they say in the military, this is where our training pays off; this is where we earn our money.

RING! RING! RING! All nets stand by for a priority message. There is an aircraft inbound with mechanical problems. Aircraft type is A-10. Estimated time of arrival is three minutes.

Security policemen drop their doughnuts; fire trucks scramble; public affairs officers fumble through their bookcases to find the large dust-covered notebook titled *When the Shit Hits the Fan and Everybody Needs a PR Guy* and called the *Oh Shit* book for short. In the book is a series of instructions broken down by category: What to do when an aircraft crashes. Who to call when an airman blows himself up. Where to go in the case of a nuclear detonation. (As far away as one can get, it says.) Of course, there is nothing listed for a generic mechanical problem, but if the mechanical problem turns into a crash, the book is capable of guiding a monkey through the process of notifying the media and the community.

RING! RING! RING! The A-10 with mechanical problems is zero-one minutes out.

Stop the presses. Cancel all leave. If this thing crashes, the Air Force will suddenly look to its public affairs experts to make everything all right. We'll have to calm the people of Eielson and explain to the world that there is "nothing to see here." We will suddenly become the most important people in the Air Force. Forget the pilots. They're the ones who got us into this mess in the first place. No, public affairs officers are in charge now. Tex Brown will look to us to bail him out of this one. There will have to be news releases, media kits, and press conferences. We'll need to schedule a quick session of media training for the general. Everybody needs to work.

As the PAO on the scene, I spring into Captain Kirk mode. "George, I need fact sheets on the A-10. How fast does it fly? What color is it? Is it made of kryptonite or lead? Ken, find out everything there is to know about historical mechanical problems with the A-10. Start with the basics, like what the hell is an A-10 Warthog anyway. Carla, I need you to stand by to stand by to stand by. Okay everyone move! Not you, Carla. You just stand by."

RING! RING! RING! We have visual on the A-10. All nets stand by.

Managing the public relations that result from an aircraft crash is the equivalent of combat for public affairs officers. It doesn't matter if you have a journalism degree. It doesn't matter if you have gone to Airborne School. It doesn't matter if you have negotiated a peace settlement between Natives and the government. The only thing that matters is your performance when a plane comes hobbling back in with landing gear still up. Only then will you know if you have the right stuff.

If a news reporter rattles you, if you spell a name wrong in the release, or if you agree to an interview on *60 Minutes*—you lose big-time. On the other hand, if you field dozens of media calls with the coolness of a Yankees outfielder, if you distribute a Pulitzer Prize–wining press release, and if you coax Mike Wallace off the line—you win. You enter an elite fraternity of combat-tested PAOs. Your actions will be forever immortalized as a case study at the Defense Information School in Fort Meade, Maryland.

RING! RING! RING! All nets stand by for a priority message. This is the command post giving the all clear at 1424 hours. Repeat, all clear at 1424 hours.

A sigh of relief. No fire. No crash. All is well.

In a small morbid recess in the back of the rookie PAO's mind, though, there is some sadness at the good news. Bad news is what the military public affairs officer trains for, so when there's no bad news, the PAO essentially rides the pine. Imagine practicing all year with the team but never getting a chance to play the game for real. It can be depressing for the PAO who has never experienced tragedy. He's like the young infantry officer who has trained for and now wants nothing more than fierce combat. Then one day he gets what he wants on an ice-and-snow-covered hillside in the middle of nowhere. Now all he wants to do is go home and never see war again.

There had been two plane crashes near Eielson in the months before I arrived. In August, an F-15C on a Cope Thunder mission crashed into a remote section of the Yukon–Charley Rivers National Preserve 109 miles east of Eielson. The pilot, Captain Garth Doty, ejected after losing control of the aircraft. He was rescued an hour later by the PJs from Eielson. In October, an A-10 from the 355th Fighter Squadron crashed while flying a night mission near Delta Junction. The pilot, Captain Troy Dunn, also ejected and was rescued two hours later by a helicopter team from Fort Wainwright. Both pilots crashed—*and lived to tell about it.*

In those instances Captain Troeber and her team pulled out the dust-covered book and executed its steps to perfection. They released the news to the local media; they coordinated a media flight out to the F-15 crash site; they prepared the Eielson brass for interviews with reporters. They were veterans of public affairs "combat."

I was still a rookie when I arrived at the base. No planes crashed during my time at Keesler or in my first six months at Eielson. All of the airmen in the PA shop had proven their worth except me. Given the intense combat training taking place during Cope Thunder, I stood a good chance to lose my cherry.

When One's Plane Does Not Return

RING! RING! RING! All nets stand by for a priority message. An aircraft has crashed. Aircraft type is not known. Crash site is not known. Condition of pilot is not known. All members of the Disaster Control Group report to the command post immediately.

July 24. The crash phone rang at about 11:45 A.M. Captain Troeber took the call as some of the staff, including me, looked on. She tensed up as she listened, and we knew immediately that it was no drill. She put down the phone and told me to grab the *Oh Shit* book. "We're going to the command post."

We didn't have to go far; the command post was deep in the basement of our building. Our badges were inspected by M-16-wielding military policemen. Once we were cleared, we entered a room that was already crowded with airmen from every major organization on base—both fighter squadrons, Cope Thunder, the fire station, and the rescue squadron. A booth sat in the middle of the room. It was haven for the Disaster Control Group (DCG) commander. Lieutenant Colonel Bill Heinen sat inside the booth. The deputy commander of the 354th Support Group, Colonel Heinen controlled all the disaster assets such as fire trucks and medical teams. Even General Brown played second fiddle to Heinen during a recovery operation. Several other desks and tables surrounded the booth. The desk assigned to the PAO had its own telephone and computer terminal where we could spin our damage control. I had been into the room for exercises, but this was my first real-world function in the command post. We were not dressed for the occasion—because of a meeting, we wearing our formal blue uniforms instead of combat fatigues—and I immediately felt like the PR geek I was. At least I had an important job to do. Or so I thought.

As the head of media relations, the *Oh Shit* book said, I needed to release as much information about the crash as possible to the media within one hour. There was even a preformatted news release in the book. All I had to do was fill in the blanks with a grease pencil.

EIELSON AIR FORCE BASE, Alaska—A _____
(aircraft)

with _____ on board crashed at _____ today
(number)   (time)

_____ . The aircraft was conducting
(location)

_____ .
(type of training)

A board of officers will investigate the cause of the crash.

Just the basics. That's all I needed to release within one hour. The Department of Defense policy for releasing information to the public is "maximum disclosure, minimum delay." It does not matter if the information is embarrassing. It does not matter if it makes certain individuals look bad. Despite my desire to disclose as much as I could in as little time as possible, neither Heinen nor Tex thought I was the most important guy in the room. They were more concerned with the rescue operation. Did the pilot eject from the aircraft? Did he survive the ejection? Has the rescue team made contact with him yet?

But, sir, my news release—the commie pinko media is waiting!

I quickly learned that the best way to fill in the blanks was to stand next to Colonel Heinen and wait for people to give him updates. The aircraft was a Jaguar from the British Royal Air

Force taking part in a Cope Thunder mission. The pilot ejected and is alive. We have established radio contact on a PRC 90 survival radio. An MH-60 from the Alaska Air National Guard is en route to pick him up. The crash site is about twenty miles northeast of Eielson. The plot on the map shows it on the border between military and private land. The PJs just called. It looks like they have the pilot. He's okay.

Bingo! Here's the news release:

EIELSON AIR FORCE BASE, Alaska—A Royal Air Force Jaguar GR1 crashed today at 11:30 A.M. about twenty miles northeast of Eielson. The pilot ejected safely and was rescued by the 210th Rescue Squadron, Alaska Air National Guard.

The aircraft is based out of Coltishall, England, and was participating in a Cope Thunder exercise.

The cause of the crash is unknown.

I handed a typed copy to General Brown. He blessed the release, and I left the command post for my office. It was now about noon, well within my one-hour window, but no sooner did I get back to the office than the phone rang. It was a producer from *Dateline NBC* in Washington, D.C. They had already heard about the crash and wanted to know if the pilot would be available to appear on a "Dateline Survivors" segment. How the hell did they get word so fast? We hadn't even announced it yet! I told them I'd call them back. The phone was already ringing when I hung up. "This is Mr. Important from the Associated Press in Washington. We hear you guys lost a plane. What's going on? What happened to the pilot?"

Clearly the news media had a way around the public affairs establishment. "How did you guys find out about this so fast?" I asked. The man on the phone responded with a cocky Ivy League accent. "We're the Associated Press. We are the first to know." I politely informed him that *Dateline NBC* had already called.

Since the cat was out of the bag, I opted to skip the fax machine and call my Alaskan journalism buddies and read the release to them over the phone. To get the facts out fastest, I called the AP in Anchorage (screw the Ivy League guy in Washington). They immediately put the story on the wire for all other journalists to see. I then called Curtis Smith at the TV station, since they had a regular news update. John McWhorter at Alaska Public Radio was next. He would get it on the evening news. Then I called Brian O'Donoghue at the *News-Miner*, since he was the most thorough reporter. I faxed to the rest.

All the locals immediately set out for Eielson. The broadcasters wanted pictures, and O'Donoghue wanted some quotes. We designated a "pressroom" in the office and created news kits for each journalist. The kits contained the initial release, information about the Jaguar, a fact sheet about Cope Thunder and Eielson, and a history of crashes at the base. I briefed the media when they arrived, then headed out to meet Captain Troeber and set up a press conference. Colonel Heinen and the RAF wing commander, Chris Harper, were the main speakers at the conference. As a bonus, the 210th provided us with a home video of the rescue. The reporters loved it, even though O'Donoghue later described it as "herky jerky." It was now about 2:30 P.M., just three hours since the crash.

Harper was the highlight of the press conference. The man was an expert at the peculiar British skill of understatement. He made the entire affair sound like a rough day on the rugby pitch. "One always likes to see one's planes return from each mission," Harper said, "but if there has to be a loss, I'd far rather have it be an airplane than a pilot any day." *Good one, old chap!*

The news conference was not the only place where the Brits got to show off their skill with the English language. The RAF boys were legendary in downtown Fairbanks, adding a touch of class to a rough American rabble. Of course, the British pilots behaved more obnoxiously than any American serviceman would dream of—a drunk U.S. airman is despicable, but somehow a drunk British pilot is adorable—and they had plenty of opportunity. Along with their fighter jets, the Brits would bring an entire cargo plane loaded to the gills with booze for the much anticipated gin party on the flightline.

The lads got away with the gin party, but the U.S. Air Force and its political and legal correctness put the kibosh on another tradition. At the start of every RAF deployment, the Brits would buy a piano for use in the officers' club. Throughout the mission there would be tons of singing and playing. On the last night of the deployment, the RAF pilots would drag the piano out of the club and put it to the torch to mark the end of the trip. That sort of thing just does not happen on an American installation. The Brits wound up donating the piano to the officers' club, where it still sits today. *When did the colonists get so serious?*

The piano is not their only legacy at the club. Halfway through a verse of "Wild Rover," they somehow managed to get fifteen drunken pilots to stand on a tabletop. When the table ultimately broke, the pilots fell to the ground, dragging with them the fire sprinkler system they had been holding for balance. The pipes burst, and the club filled knee high with water. Had they been American pilots, someone would have been court-martialed. Since they were Brits, the whole incident was laughed off. Showing they were good sports, the offending RAF pilots bought a new table with an inscription from their fighter squadron.

As with the table in the bar, Harper was quick to clear his airmen from any fault during the Jaguar crash. "It was absolutely mechanical failure," he told the reporters just hours after the crash—and days before any British investigators landed in Alaska. Had an American commander made such a bold statement that quickly, the media and the brass would be all over him until he retired quietly to some ranch in South Dakota.

The American pilots, at the time, told a different story. They said the Brits had been flying extremely low since they arrived, spurning warnings from the planners at Cope Thunder. According to our guys, the RAF pilot flew his Jaguar so low that he hit the tops of the trees. After the first strike, he sort of bounced over the forest canopy like a rock skimming on water. On the third hit, the RAF airman ejected from the aircraft just before it sank below the tree line.

It didn't matter. O'Donoghue wasn't interested in the crash. His questions indicated that the real story lay with the British pilot struggling to survive in the Alaskan wilderness in the moments after the crash with only a tiny James Bond gun for protection against bears. "Was he scared when he landed on the ground? Did he see any grizzly bear or moose? What was going through his mind?"

"We're not sure what he saw," Harper said, "but we're looking forward to sharing some of his stories tonight at our hotel in Fairbanks." (Crashing—*and living to tell about it.*) Undoubtedly, they were also looking forward to drinking a lot of beer and pinching girls on the fannies and wearing kilts and making toasts to the queen and to the downed British pilot—that old bloke would have some fine stories to tell that night. He was not alone. Old Flynn, the new "combat"-tested PAO, would be able to join him knowing that he, too, had the right stuff (for a public affairs geek, anyway).

Military pilots don't always have the right stuff, though. Chris Harper and his jolly RAF aviators learned later that training for combat is not always so good-humored.

RING! RING! RING! All nets stand by for a priority message. We have lost contact with an aircraft. Aircraft type is GR1. A search has been initiated.

"The call comes in and your adrenaline surges," said Master Sergeant John Norgren, one of the most recent additions to Eielson's public affairs team. Even though Norgren had seen a lot of public affairs "combat," the veteran PAO still felt nervous excitement when the crash phone rang at Eielson at 12:40 P.M. July 25, 2001. The command post reported a loss in contact with another one of Chris Harper's Jaguars from RAF Coltishall. Norgren stood by. There was little he could do until the command post learned more. With the mountains around Alaska, pilots lose contact with their mother ship all the time.

The next call changed everything. The loss of contact turned into a loss of aircraft. The man on the crash phone initiated a recall to the command post at 1:00 P.M. Norgren grabbed the *Oh Shit* book and headed down to the command post. Back upstairs in the public affairs office, the first call comes in. Rod Boyce from the *Daily News-Miner* has been tipped off to the missing aircraft. He's looking for details, but the rescue operation is still unfolding; no details will come for another three hours.

Eielson Air Force Base, Alaska—A Royal Air Force Jaguar fighter aircraft, participating in a multinational military air exercise held in Alaska, was reported to be overdue to land at Eielson at about 12:20 P.M. today.

The pilot and aircraft are participating in Cooperative Cope Thunder. The pilot is the only person aboard the aircraft.

Other aircraft flying in the area at the time are searching for the missing Jaguar. Eielson aircraft are on standby if needed to continue the search for the jet.

Additional details will be provided as soon as they become available.

"There is adrenaline and excitement. Then they initiate the recall, and you learn that the plane is lost. There is no contact from the pilot, and you begin to worry about him. All of a sudden, it's sobering. The fatigue sets in. Then you learn the name of the pilot. Then you see pictures of him. Then you find out that he has died," Norgren recalled.

Eielson Air Force Base, Alaska—The Royal Air Force Jaguar
pilot who was killed in a crash July 25 has been identified as
Flight Lieutenant Jason Hayes, 28, from Aldershot, England.

Hayes joined the Royal Air Force in 1996 after studying
pharmacology at Dundee University. He was married.

Hayes was at Eielson participating in Cooperative Cope Thunder, a multinational military air exercise held in Alaska. The two-
week exercise, one of four held annually, gives pilots a chance to
fly eight to ten simulated combat flights.

Nine British investigators are scheduled to arrive at Eielson
Friday to conduct an investigation into the cause of the accident.

About a hundred people have died in airplane crashes at
Eielson since 1951. Less than half were pilots. Most were enlisted
crewmen and even innocent civilians who were in the path of
the wreckage. Not one of the people killed at Eielson was a
public affairs officer. It doesn't matter. When the *Oh Shit* book
is put away and the media interviews are over, every person at
the base has to cope with the loss of an airman who lived next
door.

A Better Bird Trap

The E-3 Sentry Airborne Warning and Control System (AWACS)
was perhaps the strangest-looking airplane assigned to Elmendorf Air Force Base in Anchorage. A modified Boeing 707, the
airplane sported a giant rotating radar disk that looked a lot like
a giant black-and-white cookie that you might find in a Brooklyn
deli. Scores of Elmendorf employees passing the runway on their
way to work admired the plane's gooney shape as it taxied down
the runway for the start of a seven-hour surveillance training mis-

sion. Captain Glenn "Skip" Rogers was in command of the flight, labeled as "Yukla 27," and its twenty-three other airmen. He lifted her off the ground at 7:46 A.M.

It was September 22, arguably one of the most beautiful times of year for Alaska. The grass was still green, the leaves on the birches were a warm gold, and the spires of the Chugach Mountains were covered in white. It was the time of year when you could catch an Alaskan staring at the world around him in quiet amazement. Above, a perfect **V** of clacking Canada geese flew over. It was time for their second migration of the year. They had flown north to start their families in the spring. Now, with a fresh set of feathers and perhaps a few squawking goslings, the geese were moving back south. Below them the ground was mostly a thicket of spruce broken only by a ribbon of water. *Too dangerous a place to set down.* It would be easy for a bird to be surprised by a predator lurking in the golden woods. They wanted a clear patch of grass, perhaps with a little water nearby. The large open areas of a military runway beckoned, a quiet, relaxing place.

The peacefulness of that September morning broke as the AWACS rumbled down the runway. Perhaps it scared the new families of geese resting in the grass, or maybe it was just time for the birds to leave. Either way, the geese—as common as pigeons in New York—lifted off ahead of the oncoming Sentry. Several collided with the plane as it nosed up into the air; some were ingested by the aircraft's giant turbine engines hanging from its left wing.

No power on engine two! Losing power on engine one! Need more altitude. Skip struggled to get the stalled plane higher in the air as it began to list to the left in a slow climbing turn. 250 feet . . . 260 . . . 265 . . . 268 . . . maybe, just maybe . . . 270 feet . . . 265 . . . 240 . . . 200 . . . No. No. No.

"We're goin' in, we're going down." His last transmission. 7:47 A.M. A fireball followed by a mushroom cloud of greasy black smoke spreads over Anchorage. At its height the explosion is visible for thirty miles.

"The aircrew did everything humanly possible to fly this aircraft out of an unflyable situation . . . [they] accomplished their emergency procedures flawlessly," said Colonel Tom Gresch, the accident investigator. It wasn't enough. All twenty-four crew members of Yukla 27 died in the crash, the first such loss of an E-3 Sentry.

The last line of every news release about a plane crash states that a "board of officers will investigate the cause of the crash." In the case of the F-15 that crashed the August before I arrived, the "board of officers" blamed the crash on the aircraft's pilot. Captain Garth Doty survived the crash, but with a report that stated "pilot error." On some days Doty probably wished he'd gone down with the bird instead of ejecting from it. In the case of the Eielson-based A-10 that crashed two months later, the board determined that pilot Troy Dunn, who ejected safely at two thousand feet, was not at fault. Rather, the accident was blamed on the ill-fated combination of dim instruments and the pilot's night vision goggles. That's how most reports went: Either the pilot messed up or the plane messed up, which means either the pilot loses his job or the pilot keeps his job (and very reason for living). However, when the crash involves twenty-four deaths, and the deceased pilot was clearly not at fault, is it enough to blame a few Canada geese? Or were there other hands involved? What about the guy who was in charge of keeping the birds away from the runway? Is there someone like that who should be blamed?

AIR FORCE REPRIMANDS 4 FOR CRASH

ELMENDORF COLONEL LOSES JOB

OVER FATAL AWACS DOWNING

ELMENDORF AIR FORCE BASE, ALASKA—The colonel in charge of Elemendorf's bird-control program has lost his job over the fatal crash of an AWACS jet brought down by geese last fall.

—ANCHORAGE DAILY NEWS

Colonel Wayne Heskew, the chairman of the bird hazard reduction working group, was reprimanded and relieved as vice commander at Elmendorf's 3rd Wing in the wake of the crash. Heskew disputed the decision; he thought the Air Force was just looking for someone to take the fall.

His counterpart at Eielson was Colonel John Craig, and Craig wasn't about to sit back and watch some stupid bird take down one of his planes and his career with it. *Let's see some action now!*

"The AWACS crash has had an impact on our Bird Aircraft Strike Hazard Program," Craig told Brian O'Donoghue in an interview along Eielson's runway. "It's focused us, like everyone else, on the entire bird threat."

I called O'Donoghue out to Eielson for a Canada goose roundup Craig's people had arranged with a graduate student from the University of Alaska. Since it was July, the large birds were molting and their goslings were too young to fly, affording a perfect opportunity for Eielson's people to herd a group of birds into a cage for transport away from the runway. It was a "textbook exercise," according to Captain Tim Anderson, the head of Eielson's environmental office and the guy we spotted after he crashed his Kit Fox earlier that summer.

Maybe it was, but it looked ridiculous—especially when the rounder-uppers were Craig and Lieutenant Colonel Scott Adams, who participated in the roundup from a safety perspective. Here were a couple of proud fighter pilots, one an F-16 jock, the other an A-10 warrior, hunched over trying to corral a group of geese into a cage. It was like herding cats! Even so, it became a primary focus that summer as Alaskans and airmen alike tried to recover from the AWACS crash with their own lives and careers intact.

Within days of the disciplinary actions against Heskew in Anchorage, Eielson sent people down to the local farmers co-op to pick up a couple of noisemaking propane cannons. They worked at first, then the birds got used to them. O'Donoghue even noted in his visit that "two large geese and a cluster of goslings were rooting through the grass directly beneath the cannon's muzzle." As summer approached, the more effective method was to simply let the grass grow longer, which made it more difficult for the geese to find food. One Eielson employee claimed the longer grass reduced the problem by 90 to 95 percent. Even so, strikes still occurred. Every month, Adams threw up a slide for General Brown that showed the number of bird strikes for a given period. There was always one or two. Most caused no damage, but in the post—AWACS-crash Air Force, Craig and Adams knew that even one was too many.

Did You Moose Me?

The Canada goose was certainly the bird of the hour that summer at Eielson, but as wildlife around the base went, the geese were not our only concern. The real runway hazard stood taller than a man and weighed more than a Yugo. As I drove down the road along the flightline, I saw three of them walk from the woods onto the runway where two Vipers were preparing to launch. A bird strike could cause some damage to a plane, but a moose strike would likely destroy the fighter beyond recognition. I picked up my cell phone and made a quick call to the tower to let them know Bullwinkle and the gang were taxiing on the south end of the runway. "Roger, sir, they're regulars."

These three particular moose, a cow and her two calves, were a fairly common site at Eielson. While they were fun to look at they always seemed to wind up in precisely the wrong place at the wrong time: by my truck when I was trying to go home, blocking the general's front door for hours at a time, or grazing by the entrance to the officers' club at four P.M. on Friday. (*The nerve!*) Something clearly had to be done, but there really is nothing that can be done. If you walk near them, they just might trample you.

It's not that they don't like people; quite the contrary. People make the nice roads for them to walk on. People plant the nice plants they like to feed on. People have killed a lot of the wolves that used to eat them. As a result of this great outpouring of moose love, the monsters are all over the place. If you catch them at just the wrong moment, especially if you somehow wind up between a mother and her calf—look out! You might as well jump into a giant meat grinder. A moose's hooves would achieve the same effect.

Try telling that to some of the tour groups that came to Eielson in the summer. They sat on their buses staring out the window, practically trying to will a moose to appear.

"Lieutenant," said a loud blond woman with a collegiate southern accent, "I don't care where you take us, but we are not leaving this tour bus until you find us a moose."

The woman was Janet Huckabee, the first lady of the State of Arkansas. She was leading a group of Arkansas dignitaries in Alaska to see their National Guard boys, the Flying Razorbacks, taking part in Cope Thunder. I politely explained to her that I needed to get them to an event at the officers' club, but she didn't seem to care. "Moose, Lieutenant, moose," Huckabee said to keep me focused. Of course, the one time I needed to find a moose, I couldn't locate one. There were none by the pipeline. There were none by the ski area. There were none on the side of the road by the fighter squadron. There were none near the runway. There were none in my parking lot. That was all the usual places, so Huckabee, whom I began to find slightly attractive in a former-high-school-cheerleader-bonfire-beer-party kind of way, finally relented. "All right, then. Take us to the officers' club if you have to, but you still owe me one moose, young man." *Hmmm . . . a married Arkansas politician . . . maybe I had a chance.*

Of course, it being a Friday around four P.M., there was one other place I should have checked: the entrance to the club, which is exactly where my three moose were standing—and keeping a large group of people from going inside. "Oh! Oh! Oh! Oh!

Oh!" my ex-cheerleader first lady said as she pressed her face against the window. "You did it, Lieutenant. I knew you could!" She flirtatiously (at least that's how I interpreted it) patted me on the shoulder as she hurried out of the bus. I shouted, "Don't go out there! You might get trampled!" Despite my warnings, the Razorbacks filed off the bus under the direction of the first lady and began taking pictures at dangerously close range. Fortunately, nobody got killed, and Ms. Huckabee and I reflected on the excitement over a couple of long-neck Budweisers.

A moose sighting is the biggest deal ever for a tourist in Alaska. You can always tell when someone has seen one. A chain reaction of rubbernecking begins. As you're driving down the highway, a row of cars will be pulled off the road. Ninety-nine times out of a hundred, they are looking at a moose. (The other time, the cars all pulled off because the guy in front of them did. Of course, he just wanted to take a whizz, and now he has ten cars and RVs lined up next to him, their occupants desperately looking for a set of antlers.)

Things were a little less predictable back at Harding Lake. Most of the moose stayed away from the lake for one reason or another. Then there was Lennie, a giant bull moose with massive antlers and a penchant for sneaking up on me. We first met one dark morning in my driveway that winter. The snow was squeaking under my feet as I walked out toward my truck to warm it up: squeak, squeak, squeak, squeak. I stopped walking, and the squeaks continued. When I turned to look for an axe murderer, I came face-to-face with the giant moose. I can't recall what the survival instructors said to do if you have this type of encounter, but my reactions seemed to work: I screamed like a girl and ran back into my cabin and stayed there until Lennie went away.

I didn't name the moose "Lennie" until later—after the giant animal repeatedly exhibited innocent yet slow-witted behavior that reminded me of the character in Steinbeck's *Of Mice and Men*. The first time was when he snuck up beside me on the

Richardson Highway just before the turn into Harding Lake. As if he were merging into traffic, Lennie pulled out onto the highway and began to trot up the road. Soon the moose was leading a line of cars. Every now and then he would look right, then left, as if checking for hazards. He never strayed from his lane. I followed behind him at ten or fifteen miles an hour until I turned off for my house.

I saw him several more times over the year; rather, he saw me and seemed to have been watching me for hours when I finally noticed him. He was always quite cordial until the morning he charged out of the woods and rammed my truck just behind the right-side door. All I saw was a flash of brown color out of the corner of my eye, then *wham!* The entire truck shifted in the direction of his charge, but Lennie seemed unfazed as I saw him trot off in my rearview mirror.

I never saw Lennie again after he rammed me. That is, I never saw Lennie again alive. Since my moose meat supplier did a lot of hunting in the vicinity of Harding Lake, there is a slight chance that I next saw Lennie on my grill (a small piece of him, anyway). With a little red wine marinade, he was delicious.

The Salmon Slayer

> As for the salmon, as seen this morning urging their way up the swift current—tens of thousands of them, side by side, with their backs out of the water in shallow places now that the tide was low—nothing that I could write might possibly give anything like a fair conception of the extravagance of their numbers. There was more salmon apparently, bulk for bulk, than water in the stream. The struggling multitudes, crowding one against another, could not get out of our way when we waded into the midst of them.
>
> —JOHN MUIR, *TRAVELS IN ALASKA*

As real men from the Alaskan and Arkansas fighter wings flew combat training missions over interior Alaska, this not-quite-real man was back at Eielson with the dignitaries from Arkansas. Joining Janet Huckabee was a group of business leaders and lawyers and politicians who were getting a free trip to Alaska courtesy of a program called ESGR, or Employer Support for the Guard and Reserve—although I doubt many of these people on the Arkansas A-list actually had employees who were in the Arkansas Air National Guard. Most of the Flying Razorbacks I met worked on chicken farms near Fort Smith or simply didn't work except for their part-time gig with the guard. As I understood the South from my time in Mississippi, working only a few hours a week is quite normal. Also normal was Huckabee's request that week to eat some fresh salmon.

The most popular tourist attraction in Alaska swims into the Great Land's waters every summer. They have spent a life on the open sea, and now—in their golden years—they return to their birthplace to drop their eggs and sperm, after which they die on the stream bottom, filling the water with the very nutrients that the baby salmon need to survive. It is one of the most remarkable examples of the circle of life. Unfortunately for them, there are a lot of bears and guys named Bubba from Michigan vying to break the circle for dinner.

Perhaps the most dangerous section of the gauntlet for the salmon is on the Kenai Peninsula. Just south of Anchorage, the peninsula and its Russian and Kenai rivers comprise the most popular salmon-catching area of Alaska, often the host venue for an event that rivals the WWF: combat fishing. In July, when every local yokel and beer-gutted fisherman from the Lower 48 descends on one of the sleepy little towns like Soldotna, the ensuing jousting and body-checking for a good fishing spot would bring a hockey player to tears.

Bubba from Michigan gets up before dawn, pulls on his hip waders, jumps in his seventy-nine-foot-long RV, and heads down to a bend in the river a pal told him about. He's all alone as he sends his first cast into the rushing blue water. He feels a near-miss on his line, and he smiles with the knowledge that he will be a salmon slayer that day. Then Bucky shows up. He's from upstate New York and also knows about the bend in the river. He nods and tips his John Deere baseball cap to Bubba before he sends his cast into the current. Then Duke and his three children, Bo, Luke, and Daisy, arrive. The kids have never been salmon fishing and are hoping to make a killing.

By the time the sun comes up, Bubba's peaceful existence on the Kenai River has been compromised by a plethora of red-necks—and even otherwise respectable doctors and lawyers from all over the Lower 48. People all around him have started to pull in the giant salmon, but he's still batting zero. For chrissake, the guy on his left who keeps bumping into him has already caught three! Bubba is still okay—until some moron named Herb acci-dentally throws a cast that hooks onto Bubba's Mack Truck base-ball cap. That's all she wrote. Poor Bubba throws his pole into the raging river. Then he goes to retrieve his dirty old cap and steps deeper into the river to grab it. Now he gets caught up in a dozen fishing lines, and he swears as the current begins to take him away from the safety of the shore. Oblivious to the struggle, Bo, Luke, and Daisy simultaneously cast their hooks into the river. Bubba grabs the lines to help pull himself back up, but that causes more trouble. Luke drops his pole and starts crying. Bo tells the fat man to let go of his pole. All of this pisses off Duke, who steps into the current to help old Bubba out. When the two get to the shoreline, Duke sneers at Bubba and screams, "Why don't you find your own place to fish, Jack?"

"But this was my place to start with!"

I avoided much of this scenario by hooking up with a local. My media friend Curtis grew up in Soldotna and introduced me to a guy named Darin Hagen. Having grown up on the banks of the Kenai, Darin was rumored to be the chief salmon slayer of the region. (At least that's how Curtis—who was desperately trying to hook up with Darin's sister Jody—described Darin whenever the fisherman was within earshot.) Of only average height and slight build, the twenty-something angler did not seem any more a gruff salmon slayer than Peter Pan. Darin was already attaching his fishing boat to his pickup as we pulled into the driveway. His dress was Alaskan business casual—a pair of jeans tucked into unlaced rubber boots and a green sweatshirt labeled TROUT UNLIMITED. His boat seemed average. His truck was unassuming. His smile made him look like a junior high student who had just won a spelling bee. I had expected someone a bit more Alaskan. It looked like we got a kid from Pennsylvania Dutch country instead.

It wasn't until we got to the boat launch on the Kenai River that I realized my first impressions might have been premature. Perhaps his demeanor was not the mark of an amateur but that of a true, quiet professional. Darin reached into the back of his truck and handed each of us a beautifully hand-crafted fishing pole. When not fishing, he made the rods and sold them to Alaskan fishermen who knew better. He then pulled on a pair of hip waders and neoprene gloves with the fingers cut off. With every step closer to the river, Darin seemed closer to his true comfort zone. Finally, he jumped into his boat, started the engine, and pulled a worn oil-coated canvas fishing hat onto his head.

He looked at us, smiled a more mature grin, and throttled the engine. "Let's do it," he said confidently.

Now, that's more like it! Armed with a three-day fishing license from Kmart and a borrowed pair of hip waders, I hopped proudly into the boat knowing that I, too, would be a salmon slayer that day.

The water on the Kenai River was colored opaque blue by glacial sediments. Fast and murderously cold, the river seemed it might swallow our flat-bottom skiff and dump us into the river.

Traveling upstream, it seemed to me, Darin's boat would have a tough time, but his trusty outboard came through, and soon we were cruising up the river. It had been raining on the Kenai Peninsula for the last three months, and this day was no exception. Rain droplets stung our faces as we zipped up the river. Tall spruce trees lined the banks, which for the most part were only a foot or two above the water level. A log cabin built up off the ground would appear every now and then, but the most common sight were the fishermen. They lined the banks every few yards as we zipped by. Darin knew of a better place, though—one accessible only by boat and by Alaskans who actually knew what they were doing. *All hail the slayer!*

After what seemed like five more miles we tied the boat off to a tree along the bank. The next closest angler was at least twenty-five yards away—practically marathon distance for the Kenai River at that time of year. Using his pole as a training aid, Darin gave some quick instructions. The trick to catching reds is to understand that you are not really catching them. They are too focused. They don't want your food. That's why we don't use bait. The trick, really, is to snag the suckers. (If anyone asks, you're not actually snagging them. That would be illegal.) You want to throw your cast upstream about seven to ten meters away from the shore, where the current is still weak enough for the salmon to get through. Then let the hook float down with the current. If you're lucky, the fish will just happen to swim, mouth open, into your hook.

Are you serious? We just hope a fish swallows our hook accidentally?

Yup. Of course, there is some technique to it. After a while you'll be able to feel it when your hook bumps into a fish. That's when you yank the line hard and drive the hook into the mouth, the fin, or wherever. Once you get a good snag (whoops, I mean bite), just pull the fish up. It's that easy. You are allowed six a day. We should catch that by dinnertime.

With that, we spread out across the shoreline and threw our first casts into the raging river. Curtis and Darin fished as if they were members of a ballet troupe. The line went out smoother than a golf swing; they shuffled their stance ever so slightly, then played the fishing line like a violin as they moved it laterally in hopes of bumping into a fish. I, on the other hand, had the grace of an NFL lineman. My casts somehow never cleared three feet, and sometimes they caught on a twig behind me. When I finally did get one out there, my hook was forever snagged on a rock or a tree or an unexploded Japanese bomb, for all I knew. I soon depleted my extra supply of hooks, then Curtis's. Darin, always the consummate professional, never laughed at me. He sighed, tilted his head, and encouraged me to keep at it. "There's a lot of fish out there. I know you'll get the first one."

As he said that, he suddenly jerked on the fishing line hard. The slack immediately ran out, and a giant salmon broke the water as it fought to free the hook snagged into the side of its mouth. Darin took two steps deeper into the river and began to reel the shiny fish in. Curtis placed his custom-made pole aside and walked calmly over to the boat, where he grabbed a net. He sidled up next to Darin, who now seemed to be guiding the fish rather than fighting it. As the fish neared, Curtis dipped the net in and pulled the fish from the water. Despite its flipping and flopping, I could see that the salmon approached two feet in length. Darin took the net from Curtis and placed the fish down on the rocky shore. Call me a wimp, but I felt bad for the fish as it struggled to breathe in the suffocating air. The fish didn't suffer long. Darin grabbed a large rock and bashed its head until it stopped moving. Moments later, he pulled out a knife and filleted the fish right on the bow of the boat.

The fish had no doubt swum tens of thousands of miles, dodged commercial fisherman who guarded the entrances to the mighty rivers, and deftly maneuvered past hundreds of grizzlies.

Then it made its one mistake. It swam too close to Darin—teacher of cheechakos, maker of poles, slayer of salmon.

As he predicted, Darin caught his six-fish limit in no time. Curtis lagged slightly with only four salmon. I . . . well, I guess I was still a cheechako.

The salmon slayer had not shown off all his skills yet. Back at his house, the man who had violently clubbed the life out of the salmon displayed a heretofore unseen tenderness as he placed the pink meat on the grill. Then, with a secret recipe that he absolutely refused to share—it involved a smoker and some brown sugar—Darin made candied salmon, arguably the most delicious appetizer I have ever had.

"Where the heck did Curtis go?" Darin asked. "He always disappears when we come here." Of course, you and I know that, having proved himself a man on the banks of the Kenai, the slick TV reporter was showing off his skills to the comely blonde with a pretty smile and a love of salmon-slayer stories.

None of that sort of thing awaited this cheechako. I had failed yet another test of manhood on the banks of the Kenai and had to settle for the engaging first lady of Arkansas and her Budweiser-swilling friends back in Fairbanks. She had seen a moose; now she wanted fresh salmon, but as far inland as Fairbanks, the quality of fresh salmon can be somewhat sketchy. Having survived salmon slayers and colonies of grizzly bear, the few salmon that make it as far inland as Fairbanks are often tougher than a leather-clad Harley-Davidson rider named Helga. Even so, I was able to give the Arkansas royalty the next best thing: the Alaska Salmon Bake at Alaskaland. For just twenty dollars each, we were able to gorge ourselves on salmon and baked beans and long-neck Budweisers until the moose came home.

AUGUST

Conduct Unbecoming an Officer
and an Alaskan

ALASKAN GROWN

Potatoes don't cost much in Idaho. Peaches are cheap in Georgia. Corn is practically free in Nebraska. Why, then, does it cost Alaskans and people from the Lower 48 the same amount of cash to fill their gas tanks?

Alaska provides 20 percent of all oil used by the United States, far greater than any other state in the union. Yet the people who drill and deliver the precious resource to their fellow countrymen appear to be getting screwed.

There are multiple refineries in Alaska that make gasoline. The refinery in North Pole, for example, taps directly into the Trans-Alaska Pipeline and processes fifteen thousand barrels of oil a day. One might deduce, then, that gas prices next to the Santa Claus House are close to a dollar a gallon, but Alaska seems to operate against virtually every economic model in the world. Gasoline in the small interior town costs between $1.50 and $2.00 a gallon—the same price as in New York City, where gas prices are inflated by heavy local taxes.

It doesn't add up, and it doesn't seem fair.

Alaskans already pay extensively to live in the Great Land. According to the American Chamber of Commerce Research Association, the cost of living in cities like Anchorage and Fairbanks is more than 20 percent above the national average. In remote areas like Kodiak, it's almost 30 percent higher. A half gallon of milk costs $2.28 in Fairbanks but only $1.52 in Oklahoma City. A doctor's visit costs $92 in Fairbanks but only $59 in Orlando. An average house costs $264K in Anchorage but only $188K in Dallas. The high cost of living touches everything in Alaska. Even a McDonald's Quarter Pounder with Cheese is $2.89 in Fairbanks but only $2.09 in Dayton.

Fairbanks and Anchorage are listed among the twenty most expensive cities in the nation, yet unlike in pricey cities like New York and San Francisco that boast large wages and compatible household incomes, Alaskans get paid about the same as Americans in other major cities. Even the average household incomes in cities like Des Moines and Washington, D.C., which are not on the most expensive list, are more than ten and twenty thousand dollars greater than that of Anchorage, which rates at fifty thousand dollars.

It doesn't add up, and it doesn't seem fair—until you consider some of the benefits.

To counter the disparity between the cost of living and the average income, the state touts the Alaska Permanent Fund, a $24 billion fund designed to allow Alaskans to share in oil revenues. Distributed annually since 1976, the Permanent Fund Dividend (PFD) paid each Alaskan resident almost two-thousand dollars in 2002. The PFD (or, as some call it, the Personal Flotation Device) has long been a thing of excitement to both Alaskans and would-be cheechakos. *Alaska is so great they actually pay you to live there!*

The PFD more than makes up for high gas prices. Depending on how far they drive, the PFD may completely pay for some Alaskans' annual fuel bill. Perhaps even more significant than the PFD, Alaskans pay no income or sales tax, so fifty thousand dollars in Fairbanks is worth a lot more than it is in Philadelphia. Maybe the people in Alaska are not getting screwed after all. Who wouldn't prefer a two-thousand-dollar cash payment and no income tax to cheap potatoes?

An easy choice, right? Before you answer, consider that, using good farming practices, the potato should be grown in Idaho and the corn in Nebraska and the peach in Georgia for a long, long time. Unfortunately Alaskan oil does not match up. One day soon, the oil reserves will dry up, and the state will need to levy taxes or take from the Permanent Fund to cover the budget deficit. Alaskans will be left holding the bag—a high cost of living income and sales taxes, and no PFD to help out.

Fortunately, there is good news, too. Alaskans have always found a way to make a go of a bad situation. After the United States expends the remaining Alaskan oil, the resulting greenhouse gases may well warm the Alaskan climate enough to grow peaches in Anchorage. You can bet the peaches will be cheaper in Alaska than in the extreme temperatures of the desert once lovingly referred to as Georgia.

Ain't Nobody Seen Me Do It

I stood in the Weaver shooting stance, right leg slightly forward, fingers interlocked around the handle of the 9mm pistol. One magazine with seven rounds was loaded in the weapon. Another seven-round magazine rested on the ledge next to me. The target was in the shape of a man's torso with concentric circles emanating from the middle of the chest area. On the command to fire, I had to shoot the first seven rounds in the small circles on the target, reload, and fire the remainder of my rounds. The targets were only fifteen meters away. Even so, several factors conspired against my landing all of my rounds. There was a slight wind. The sun was shining in the corner of my eye. I wasn't wearing my glasses. I had forgotten to wear my lucky underwear. I was not a New York City police officer.

"Fire!"

I took in a long breath, exhaled, and squeezed the trigger slowly after all the air was out of my lungs. The first round jumped out of the gun with a kick. A few more squeezes, and the rest were out. After what seemed an eternity, I found the button that ejected the spent magazine, reloaded, and went back to work, always watching my breathing, always aiming at the center of the target, and always making sure I was not squeezing too hard with one hand or the other.

"Cease fire! Cease fire!"

My last rounds. We were instructed to lock the bolt of the weapon to the rear. After the instructors inspected our weapons, we moved downrange to have a look at the targets. I needed to land thirty-six of the forty rounds in the circles to get an expert rating, but I could see trouble brewing as I approached the target. All of my rounds seemed to have hit below and to the left of where I was aiming. Some were near the middle of the target. The rest made a nice trail that moved diagonally off the paper. Needless to say, I was no expert. I did qualify—just barely.

How depressing. What Alaskan can't shoot? More humbling, though, what military officer can't shoot? If you believe what you see in movies, all military officers should be expert marksmen— able to shoot one-handed and canted to the side. I really should have been able to pop all forty rounds into that target. Instead I dribbled off the paper and into a pile of rocks on the ground. The range instructor strolled up disapprovingly to put a score on my target.

There was good news, too. I was not the worst. Three instructors crowded around a target to the far left of the range. A captain from the JAG office was there. He was a lawyer, but not in the tradition of the sharpshooting Atticus Finch of *To Kill a Mockingbird*. Quite the contrary: of the forty rounds that the captain shot, not one bullet had struck the target. Granted, Air Force officers are normally only required to shoot once every two years—but to miss with every shot?

The instructors looked at each other. "Aiming for the pipeline," one of them decided.

As if it weren't bad enough to give Air Force officers handheld firearms in the first place, the clever planners at Eielson Air Force

Base had placed the rifle range right next to the Trans-Alaska oil pipeline, separated from it by only an earthen berm. It wasn't impossible to imagine that a skinny Air Force lawyer who had never shot a gun before joining the military could have inadvertently sent some rounds into the shiny steel of the pipeline, causing an environmental nightmare. State hunting regulations prohibit the use of firearms within five miles of the pipeline, but nobody said anything about an Air Force shooting range.

I pulled up to the pipeline after leaving the range. No oil was spilling, and I guess it was crazy to think a bullet could have strayed from the range. In truth, though, many bullets have hit the pipeline over the years, about fifty according to the Alyeska Pipeline Service Company, the consortium of oil interests that manages the pipeline. In each instance, the four-foot-wide pipeline's skin of galvanized steel and insulation protected the pipeline from penetration. However, if you drink just enough beer, threaten to shoot your brother, and then aim your hunting rifle at the pipeline instead, there's a really good chance you'll puncture the sucker.

On October 4, 2001, a thirty-seven-year-old man with eight prior felony convictions allegedly did just that. Despite claiming to police that "ain't nobody seen [him] do it," Daniel Carson Lewis was convicted in March 2002 on a weapons charge in connection with the vandalism. According to authorities, his drunken marksmanship resulted in the spill of 285,000 gallons of crude oil fifty miles northwest of Fairbanks. Soaking two acres of spruce forest, the spill cost about twenty million dollars to clean up—but it could have been worse.

At least Lewis showed restraint by only *shooting* the pipeline. Others have actually tried to blow up the pipeline. In 1977, just as the first oil began flowing through it, three men detonated several dynamite charges against the pipe. My guess is that they were probably drunk, too, since they failed to do any real damage. In contrast, someone who tried it sober a year later succeeded in blowing a hole that spilled nearly 635,000 gallons just north of Fairbanks. No one was ever arrested for that blast, but in 2000 a Canadian man was arrested for plotting to blow up the pipeline in an effort to profit from an anticipated rise in oil prices. The sharpshooting Lewis is practically a saint compared to those guys—and a pretty good marksman, too, unless, of course, he was actually aiming for his brother. (Whatever the case, he is certainly a better marksman than thief. After he was arrested for shooting the pipeline, Lewis's DNA was matched to DNA found at the scene of a burglary in September 2001, and the ten-time loser was convicted. I guess it didn't matter that ain't nobody seen him do it that time.)

Crossing three mountain ranges and eight hundred rivers and streams, the pipeline is the most impressive engineering feat in Alaska. At Eielson, the pipeline rests on supports about four feet above the permanently frozen ground. Since the oil flowing through the pipeline gives off heat, the supports also carry tall, skinny radiators that suck the heat away from the pipe to ensure the ground stays frozen. Having traveled almost half of its journey by the time it gets to Eielson, the pipeline dips underground for the start of the second half of its trip from Prudhoe Bay along the Arctic coast down to Valdez in the south. In all, 375 miles of the pipeline's route are underground. During its construction between 1974 and 1977, critics argued that the system would cause grave ecological problems from constant spills and interruption of caribou migration routes. Now that it has pumped more than thirteen billion gallons, those fears have been largely allayed. Before Lewis shot a hole in the pipeline, Alyeska estimated that only .0000025 percent of the oil pumped through the system had leaked. Had it not been for cold beer, who knows? Maybe nothing would have ever leaked.

Americans can be proud of the pipeline. Economically, it's a modern-day version of the Erie Canal. Ecologically, it has surprised even the harshest critics. However, despite the pipeline's successful record, it is often associated with the worst oil spill in U.S. history.

The Trans-Alaska Pipeline terminates in the port city of Valdez in south-central Alaska, where tankers load the crude for transport around the world. While leaving the port in the early hours of March 24, 1989, the 987-foot *Exxon Valdez* tanker ran aground on Bligh Reef in Prince William Sound, spilling 10.8 million gallons of black crude oil that spread like a shroud over the waters of the sound. The oil touched 1,300 miles of coastline and coated hundreds of thousands of animals. Thousands of recovery workers and ships and aircraft responded to Valdez to work on the spill. There was little they could do in the short-term. The pictures of oil-covered birds dead or dying on the black shore shocked the world, but they could not fully capture the scale of the disaster. More than 300,000 birds, 2,800 sea otters, and 300 seals were believed killed by the spill. The sound's whales, salmon, and several other fish species were decimated. The families that made a living from the sound's waters lost everything.

The government blamed it all on Exxon and the captain of the *Valdez,* Joseph Hazelwood, who was allegedly belowdecks intoxicated. In a settlement reached with the State of Alaska and the U.S. government, Exxon agreed to pay more than a billion dollars in punitive and restorative fines. Hazelwood was acquitted of all charges except the "negligent discharge of oil." The skipper, who had a history of alcoholism, was sentenced to perform a thousand hours of community service. I repeat, had it not been for beer, who knows?

Just Drill it!

Oil was first discovered in Alaska in 1957 on the Kenai Peninsula in the south-central region of the state. By 1964, the peninsula wells had yielded thirty thousand barrels, wetting the lips of major oil companies, who immediately flew to the farthest reaches of the frontier in search of crude. They found the mother lode in 1968 at Prudhoe Bay on the Arctic Ocean. Prudhoe Bay and other sources on Alaska's North Slope have yielded more than thirteen billion gallons of oil since operations began. Today Alaskan crude accounts for about 20 percent of the U.S. total demand. However, the North Slope wells are slowing down. Production peaked in 1988 at more than two million gallons a day. By the year 2000, production fell to half that. Scientists believe that the North Slope will produce about five billion more gallons before running dry sometime near 2020. This is not a surprise. In fact, early estimates predicted Prudhoe Bay would yield much less.

Unfortunately, prior knowledge does not make it any easier for the state of Alaska and its people, who rely heavily on oil revenues. More than 80 percent of the state's revenue and tax income comes from oil production. When oil production began declining in 1988, the state began to experience its first budget shortfalls. To make up for the shortfalls, it has tapped into its constitutional budget reserve. At the current rate, the reserve will be dry in 2004, leaving a large budget deficit, so Alaskan lawmakers are looking at ways to come up with more revenue by cutting the budget, adding a sales tax, adding an income tax, or cutting the Alaska Permanent Fund. Whatever the final decision, and it is likely to be a combination of these tactics, the group most affected is Alaskan residents, who already live in one of the most expensive places in the world. They have yet another solution, and their rallying cry is *"Just drill it!"*

It, of course, is the Arctic National Wildlife Refuge, a reserve of arctic tundra about the size of South Carolina. Reports by the U.S. Department of the Interior indicate there might be nine to sixteen billion barrels of oil sitting under the northern coast of the refuge. Then again, there might not; there might be less than one billion barrels.

Alaskans are an optimistic people, To them, drilling for oil in the Arctic National Wildlife Refuge (ANWR) is the best answer to their fast-approaching economic crisis. At the moment, though, Congress won't let them. The Alaska National Interest Lands and Conservation Act (ANILCA) of 1980 expanded the size of the refuge and placed a restriction on drilling. While 92 percent of ANWR was permanently closed to drilling, the act permitted limited exploration of the 1.5-million-acre northern coast. Some amount of oil has been identified; to drill it takes additional congressional approval. That approval seemed imminent in the late 1980s, but the *Exxon Valdez* oil spill destroyed any immediate hopes Alaskans had for drilling. The Clinton administration blocked drilling throughout the 1990s. Then drilling in ANWR became a key tenet of President George W. Bush's energy plan. With a Republican majority in Congress, many Alaskans view drilling as a done deal.

Some of my old friends from Fort Yukon and the Native Village of Venetie are also at the center of the argument. The area of ANWR under consideration for drilling happens to be the same area where the Porcupine caribou herd spends its summers making little caribou babies and cowering from mosquitoes. Any negative impact on the Porcupine herd would reverberate through the Gwich'in communities of the interior, but the needs of the many in Alaska seem to outweigh the needs of the few. Alaska's only U.S. congressman hails from the Gwich'in community of Fort Yukon, but he—like 75 percent of all Alaskans—solidly supports drilling. The majority would argue that there will be no negative impact on the Porcupine herd. If one can believe the oil industry's claim that the caribou herd that lives near Prudhoe Bay has grown by more than 600 percent in the last twenty years, then one can reasonably argue that the Gwich'in will eat more caribou than ever before.

There are dozens of arguments for and against drilling in ANWR—and thousands of public relations flacks spinning the facts in their favor. I suspect the truth is somewhere in the middle. Will ANWR ever be drilled? The U.S. Geological Survey estimates that the entire planet holds up to 2.1 trillion barrels of oil, enough to sustain current worldwide consumption rates for only sixty-three to ninety-five years. When the world's holes start to dry up, it could be awfully hard to resist the juicy reserves that are currently off limits—unless, of course, the oil industry comes up with an alternative fuel source. Perhaps Alaska can even corner the U.S. market for the next natural resource. *Anybody know how many BTUs are generated by a single burning moose nugget?*

Impersonation of Fat Retired Americans

There was little talk about the *Exxon Valdez* oil spill when I reported to Alaska. In fact, when anyone spoke of Valdez, it was usually related to fishing the port's waters in Prince William Sound. "What about the oil spill?" I asked. "That's ancient history," a person from Fairbanks might say. So, having caught no salmon in July, I had nothing to lose in accepting an offer from Reggie Dawkins, the senior noncommissioned officer of the public affairs office, to go halibut fishing with his friends at Valdez in August.

Named for the minister of the Spanish navy at the time, the port of Valdez was discovered in 1790 by a Spanish naval mission to probe the new Russian colony in Alaska. Content that the Russians were not encroaching on Spain's holdings along the Pacific coast of what is now California, the Spanish never established a permanent colony at the Alaskan port. However, they did hammer into the ground a sign with the name "Valdez" etched on it, and that name stuck. Valdez was ultimately settled by both

Natives and other Alaskans and grew into a major fishing community. Then it was completely destroyed by the most powerful earthquake in U.S. history. Centered in Prince William Sound, the "Good Friday" quake of 1964 measured 9.2 on the Richter scale and killed 115 Alaskans in the south-central region of the state. The people of Valdez rebuilt the town four miles from the original site, where better soil would protect them from the other quakes. Good thing. On average, one quake measuring at least 5.0 on the Richter scale hits Valdez a year.

We set out for the infamous town in a borrowed recreational vehicle that had more square feet than most New York City apartments. It was simply obnoxious—two bedrooms, two baths, a full kitchen, and an entertainment center straight off the Sony Style showroom at 550 Madison Avenue. I sat in the RV with a scowl. Tourists drive RVs, and not just any tourists; old tourists named Bud and Bette drive RVs. RVs are their gas-guzzling second homes, and they drive them to Alaska every summer like the returning salmon. The RVs clog up the highways. They fill up all the parking spots. They emit noxious clouds of smoke. Worst of all, they attract the absolute worst drivers. You need a special license to drive a bus. RVs are the same size, but anyone, even retirees who have to wear those really large black sunglasses so they can see, can drive them—and back them up into parked cars and career them down the wrong side of the road.

Now I had to ride in one and admit that I was not an Alaskan but just a tourist who couldn't catch a salmon and probably couldn't catch a halibut. Then I discovered a new philosophy: Don't knock it till you try it!

Recreational vehicles may be the most obnoxious things on wheels, but they sure as hell beat taking a Yugo. Six of us loaded into the RV for the eight-hour drive, and not one of us got a leg cramp or had to suffer through any of the others' mysterious bodily odors. We could change rooms, stretch out our legs, use the bathroom, and even enjoy the wonderful cooking of Reggie's

Italian-born wife, Danny. The drive from Fairbanks to Valdez in the rolling palace was the most pleasurable cruise I have ever been on.

We turned south from Harding Lake, giving me my first look at the Richardson Highway since I arrived at Eielson in the dark and ice in December. For all practical purposes, it was the first time I was seeing this part of Alaska. The highway handrailed the Tanana River for the first leg of the trip, sometimes running right against it. The river appeared shallow in most spots and unsure as to which direction it actually wanted to flow. Sometimes the river would break into half a dozen little streams that crisscrossed each other, creating little spruce-tree-covered islands that only birds could reach easily. In other areas, the river's network of streams would all come together, creating a wide and powerful river like the Hudson or Ohio or Missouri. All the while, the river valley spread for miles to the south and west of the road, affording for the entire first half of the drive a beautiful view of the Alaska Range, whose mountains grew in size with every mile. At Delta Junction, the Richardson Highway makes a sharp right turn along a small river that points toward the mountains. The next town, Paxson, is almost a hundred miles from the junction. Along this stretch the relative flatness that characterizes Fairbanks disappears in a crescendo of mountain peaks. The wide Tanana Valley gone, we struggled to see the summits from the narrow pass we drove along.

"Oh my God!" Reggie shouted from the front. "Is that a bear?"

I turned to see what Reggie was looking at. Sure enough, a small grizzly bear was cantering across the road fifty meters in front of us. We slowed a bit at the site where the bear entered the brush along the roads, but he was gone. That is how I saw my first grizzly bear in Alaska. Although the animal looked a little thin, I was content to see it from fifty meters away and from inside a sort of armored personnel carrier.

The final leg of the journey began after the intersection with the Glenn Highway in Glennallen. A right turn would have sent us to Anchorage. A left turn would have sent us north to Tok. We continued straight into the Chugach Mountains and a series of passes riddled with sharp turns, sudden vistas, and a seemingly unnavigable patch of fog. The sun disappeared on this final stretch of the highway and would not return until after we got back to Fairbanks two days later. Our destination sat at the base of the near-vertical Chugach Mountains. Valdez is not only a seaport; its mountainous backyard makes it the home of the World Extreme Skiing Championship.

We drove straight through the town and pulled our mountain cruiser into an RV park right on the water. Despite all the talk about fishing and skiing and earthquakes, I was still fixated on the oil spill and its images. I wanted to see for myself how the water looked today. While Reggie and Danny began preparing dinner, I left the RV for the nearest dock. The fog was low over the harbor, but I had no problem seeing out on the water for a few dozen meters. As I suspected, the water was not clean. An empty plastic milk bottle, some fish parts, and an empty cigarette pack bobbed up and down in the water around the dock. It sort of looked like the Hudson River. I didn't see any oil or telltale rainbow slicks on the water, though, just the refuse of a handful of lazy people—most likely the guests of the RV park.

According to the *Exxon Valdez* Oil Spill Trustee Council, a federal-state group that oversees the restoration of the affected areas, about 85 percent of all the oil spilled has evaporated, biodegraded, or been recovered. Most of the remainder is locked into the sediment of Prince William Sound. About 2 percent of the oil is still evident on the beaches. We would find out for ourselves the next day whether or not the fish and wildlife had recovered, too.

Pavlov's Fish

We awoke early the second morning and headed down to the fog-shrouded marina where the dozens of local fishing charters picked up their passengers. Reggie had reserved our boat and its captain, Ed (no last name was offered), while back at Eielson. He met us at the marina entrance. Looking every bit the salty skipper, Ed accepted our hundred dollars per person (cash only). He stuffed the wad of money into the pocket of his grease-stained and shredded khaki shorts. Ed looked to be in his fifties, with gray hair and a white beard, deep wrinkles and leather skin and long crows' feet around his squinted blue eyes. His white T-shirt had faded to yellow where it wasn't stained with oil and grease. He carried a little cooler.

"Don't forget to enter the derby," he said and walked away from us toward his boat. That was practically the last complete sentence he spoke to any of us.

The Valdez Halibut Derby was a contest that all tourists excitedly entered for a few dollars a ticket. The winner was the person who came back to the marina with the largest halibut. Fish weighing more than three hundred pounds have been caught in Prince William's deep water, but while the big fish might win you a few bucks, the halibut we were looking for weighed between twenty-five and thirty-five pounds. These younger fish were said to have the best flavor.

We loaded the thirty-something-foot fishing boat and pulled out of the marina by eight A.M. Ed didn't tell anyone how far we were going, so I climbed the stairs up to the place he drove the boat from. Despite his dirty, rough appearance, I noticed Ed was wearing brand-new white sneakers.

"Where are we headed?" I asked politely.

He didn't answer.

"Excuse me, Ed, about how far out are we going?"

Still no answer.

All right, then . . . I climbed back down the stairs and reported my findings to Reggie and the rest of the group, who laughed heartily.

"Do you know this guy?" I asked. "Is this like his M.O.? The old grizzled skipper that only takes tourists out because he needs to eat?"

"Hell, I don't know," Reggie said. "Don't sweat it. When he stops the boat, we'll fish. Enjoy the ride."

As usual, Reggie's advice was good. Not a fisherman by any stretch of the imagination, I derived more pleasure from sight-seeing, and as the fog began to lift, I was surprised to see a marine show that looked like a Jacques Cousteau documentary. The steep slopes of the Chugach Mountains rose in three directions. Ice blue waves slapped against the boat, spraying us with cool salty water. Wildlife of all shapes and sizes cluttered the waters like so many people at a weekend farmer's market. Eagles and hawks skimmed across the tide looking for prey. Sea otters floated lazily on their backs. Fish of all kinds were flipping and flopping out of the water. Three seals peered curiously from their perch on a buoy. A pair of whales arced in and out of the water about a hundred meters from our boat. Hundreds of thousands of marine animals perished in the wake of the *Exxon Valdez* oil spill, but it appeared that they were back in full force. In fact, they are not. Of the nearly thirty species and marine resources tracked by the *Exxon Valdez* Oil Spill Trustee Council, only nine were listed as "fully recovered" by 2001, including bald eagles, river otters, a family of killer whales, and two types of salmon. Several other resources are still listed as "not recovering," including certain seals, pigeons, and ducks. Harbor seals in the Gulf of Alaska have declined 80 percent. Halibut, due largely to their migratory cycles and deep water habitat, were less affected by the spill.

Ed continued to maneuver the boat farther and farther away from the port. While still surrounded by large mountains and small islands, I began to feel slightly vulnerable. *What if the boat breaks down out here? What if someone falls into the cold water? What if a tsunami swamps us?* When small icebergs spawned from the glaciers began to appear on the water, I got really nervous.

"Hey, Ed," I called from the rear of the boat up to the new white sneaks. "About how far out are we going?"

Sensing my frustration, Ed finally answered. "Bit farther."

"Do you have like a secret place where we will catch a ton of fish?"

"Might," he replied curtly.

Then again, he might not. When we finally stopped, nothing happened when we dipped our baited hooks into the sound. It was one thing for me not to catch any fish, but everyone? Surely there was something wrong.

Fishing for halibut seemed a pretty simple affair. We loaded some small dead fish onto the hook, then lowered the bait several fathoms until we felt the lead weight on the line hit the bottom. The baited hook was supported by a float and sat several inches off the ocean floor. The halibut is a bottom feeder. The plan was to stick a big hunk of food right where he would be looking for it. However, these halibut must have been Pavlov's rare fish that have actually learned that a hunk of meat with a string attached to it is bad news. Either that or we were in a bad spot.

"Gonna move," Ed said after twenty minutes of the shutout.

By lunchtime we were still sans halibut and moving, it seemed, to completely random locations, but who could doubt our stoic captain? He talked and looked every part the Hemingway hero. Surely he knew the right place. We all watched him on his perch turning the ship one way, then the other, scanning the far reaches of the water, and squinting through his all-seeing eyes for that one place where his customers could cash in on the bounty of Prince William Sound. Despite a lack of success, we didn't doubt Captain Ed for a minute.

"Here," he said and cut the engines.

Our loyalty was rewarded. Ed personally made sure all our bait was loaded properly, then pulled a can of WD-40 lubricant from a compartment. "This'll get 'em," he said as he soaked our bait with the shimmering oil.

What the hell, I figured. *There's almost eleven million gallons of oil in here anyway. Why not add a little squirt of WD-40?*

Moments after casting, a fish grabbed my bait. Instinctively, I looked to my sergeant for guidance.

"Can't help you now. I got one on, too."

In fact, everybody seemed to be getting hits. Whatever group of fish we found knew nothing of Pavlov. I know it's dark down there, but didn't they see their buddies getting yanked out of the water?

I hadn't caught anything larger than a three-inch sunfish in my entire life. The fish I now had on the line was certainly bigger. Fortunately, the reel I was using came complete with an electric motor. I simply pressed a button and watched as the pole bent more and more, the fish caught in my tractor beam. The pole bent so much I began to think that it might snap.

So did Ed—and that was his rod, goshdarn it. He bumped me out of the way and took the pole. "Don't nobody better lose a pole, goddamm it!" he hollered. Ed continued bringing my fish in. "Grab that net," he said, pointing to a corner of the boat.

You can never be sure what you will pull out of the water in Alaska. In April 2002, a fisherman from Sitka found a twelve-foot-long giant Pacific squid attached to his halibut. The rare giant squid can grow up to sixty feet. Apparently the monster wrapped itself around the halibut, eating the fish during its long ride to the surface. My net would have been little help in that instance, but I was prepared for the worst.

I moved next to Ed with the net just as the fish came into view through the water. With a sunfish as my reference point, I imme-diately concluded that I had caught a shark. No squid was attached, but the fish looked giant under the water, moving slowly back and forth as if the fight had been taken out of it. The minute the fish broke the surface, though, it began a mad struggle to get off the hook and back to the safety of the dark waters.

"Get 'im," Ed said as he guided the half-submerged fish to the side of the boat.

I dipped the net into the water, pulled it over the fish, and felt the full weight of the halibut as I pulled it up into the boat. It took two hands. Once it was on board, Ed bent over and took the hook out of the fish's mouth, grabbed it by the tail, and tossed it into a cooler. There was no ritualistic smashing of the fish's head as there had been on the Kenai River, and Ed did not reach for a knife to carve the fish up. He simply tossed it into a cooler without fanfare.

"Okay, who else has got one?" he said.

I had mixed feelings about the halibut. I was happy I caught it, but I thought it was pretty lame that Ed had taken the pole from me to land the fish. I was glad to know that I would be able to bring some meat home with me, but I felt sympathy for the fish sitting in the cooler left to suffocate. We killed the salmon immediately after we caught it. I'm sure the salmon did not appreciate that, but I'll bet he preferred it to suffocating in the cooler of Ed's boat. Then again, how much sympathy can you feel for a fish dumb enough to eat a hunk of oil-soaked meat with a string attached to it?

I did take some consolation in the fact that my halibut was not alone. Two of his buddies joined him moments later.

Shut Up and Color

With three fish weighing thirty pounds in the cooler, it seemed that our stoic captain had come through. Like the salmon slayer from Kenai, the charter boat captain from Valdez guaranteed that we would leave with some fish. At the quick rate we caught the first three, we were sure to go home with enough fish to stock our freezers for the rest of the year. Then, for reasons we did not understand, Ed ordered another move of the boat. Again, we did not protest. He had already brought us to one good killing ground. We could only assume that he had another one—a better one—in mind. Sure enough, he stopped the boat after about fifteen minutes of expert piloting. This time, no matter how much WD-40 we put on the bait, we couldn't catch a thing. Not even a nibble.

"What's the deal?" I asked Reggie.

"You got me. I thought we were doing just fine back where we were."

"Should we ask him to go back there?"

"That makes sense to me," Reggie said, "but he is the expert."

I looked up at Ed as he snacked on a sandwich from his cooler. Minutes before, he had been helping us wrestle a couple of fish into the boat. Now he looked like he couldn't be bothered.

Well, he found the fish last time. He must know the best place to go. Maybe the fish we encountered before were swimming in this direction and he wanted to cut them off. Maybe if we wait just a little bit longer we will catch the mother lode. Just look at him. How could you doubt those looks? The guy might as well have a peg leg and a hook for a hand.

So none of us said anything, and an hour later Ed leaned over his railing to notify us that we were going in. "Let's wrap it up," he said.

That's it? But we only have three fish. There are six of us! We need more time. We need to go back to that place!

Reggie must have had similar thoughts. "You know, it would be nice if we all could catch one on our own today," he said to Ed.

"Yup. But looks like they ain't biting," Ed said.

"We were doing fine at that last spot. Can't we go back there?"

"No time. I got another group back at Valdez."

"Well, maybe we can hit a place on the way in," Reggie suggested desperately.

"No time left. I gotta get back. I got another group," Ed said. He rose and headed to his controls, ending the negotiation. "There's good days and bad days," he said. "Today was a bad day."

We returned to Valdez in silence. The three fish were divided evenly among us at the marina, and we headed back to our RV for dinner. Grilled with olive oil and lemon, the halibut we ate was spectacular. None of us could really appreciate it, though. We were mad at Ed and his decision to move us from the one spot where we were actually catching fish, and we were mad at ourselves. None of us wanted to leave the sweet spot we found in the sound, but none of us wanted to override Ed, the perceived expert. He made a bad decision, and none of us said a word. We just pulled in our lines obediently and moved out of the kill zone. We believed in him and his wrinkles and his salt-treated face and his grease-stained shirt, and because of it, we got a raw deal. We could have got much more fish from the market for the money we spent on the charter.

"At least we got to see some nice scenery," I said to nobody in particular.

"Who cares about the scenery? We came for halibut," Reggie replied. "Heck, with Ed as captain we were lucky we even got three. It was as if he purposely moved us so we wouldn't catch any more."

"Why would he do that?" I asked.

"Who knows? Maybe he plans to go back to that spot by himself. Maybe he's an environmentalist. Maybe he doesn't like military guys. Maybe he's just stupid."

The idea that the charter captain might have purposely screwed us gained momentum in all our minds. By the end of the night we were convinced that there was some great plot against us. Why else would he have moved us from the good spot? Maybe we should have said something—but why? It was his job to find us the fish, not take them away from us. I expressed my displeasure in our great captain and our blind obedience in my next "Cheechako" column.

MUTINY OVER HALIBUT

The charter played out like an episode of *Wild Kingdom*. Sea otters floated lazily on their backs. Pink salmon were flipping and flopping out of the water. A menacing shark prowled the shallows near the boat. Three sea lions peered curiously from their perch on a buoy. A killer whale waved at us with his tail before completing a series of airborne half twists.

But we hadn't rented a charter boat to watch Marlin Perkins. We rented a charter boat to catch some halibut. In retrospect, we should have settled for Marlin Perkins. Or, better yet, we could have mutinied.

Captain Ed lives most of the year in the bush, but every summer he ventures to Valdez, where his job is to protect halibut by misguiding his customers. At least, that's what I think, because the minute his charter boat started to pull in some fish, we moved. Then we moved again, and again. Then we pretty much gave up. The day's total for six people paying a hundred dollars each: three halibut, the largest weighing a slight thirty pounds.

Webster's defines mutiny as "open rebellion against lawful authority." There's not much question that a boat captain is the lawful authority on his own boat. It's kind of like making rules inside your car or truck, like no French fries allowed or no looking at your sister. There are no written laws to this effect; these are natural laws. But when is it okay to mutiny on a charter? How much is too much?

A declaration of independence: "When in the course of human events it becomes necessary for one people to dissolve the fishing bonds which have connected them with a charter, a decent respect to the opinions of mankind requires that they should declare the causes which impel them to the separation.

"We hold these truths to be self-evident, that if you rent a stinking charter you should catch some fish. What good is life, liberty, and the pursuit of happiness when all a C-note gets you is a thirty-pound halibut? Whenever a skipper becomes destructive to happy fishing, it is the right of the people to rebel and institute a new skipper."

Oh, yeah, we talked a big game—but not until after he left. At the time, we figured, "He's the skipper; he must know what he's doing." Wrong! While he deserved the benefit of the doubt, he didn't deserve unquestioned authority.

Had we the audacity to ask questions, we might have more halibut in the freezer now. Then again, we might not have any—but not for a lack of trying.

As chief of public affairs at Eielson, Captain Troeber was required to review all my columns before they ran in the base newspaper to make sure that they didn't contain curse words or make fun of the Air Force or General Brown or whatever. She was away that week, so the duty to review the column and all the other newspaper articles for propriety fell on me. I reread my column several times to be sure that it was okay. My main goal in writing the column was to tell the story and make my readers aware of the dangers of blind obedience. Questioning your superiors is a touchy subject in the military, mostly because the person doing the questioning is right and the superior is wrong and unable to take criticism, but if soldiers, sailors, airmen, and Marines don't question orders from time to time, the military could wind up invading Canada after the Toronto Blue Jays beat the Houston Astros. So I gave my blessing to my column and sent it off to the printer. What's the worst anyone could do to me—shave my head and make me join the military?

Despite a lot of "atta boys" for the column over the past seven months, many officers on base did not find it appropriate. After one column that made reference to my trying to purchase fake ID in Times Square with a friend when we were teenagers (which

I was forced to do after they raised the drinking age to twenty-one), the commander of Eielson's support squadron gave me a written reprimand. "As an officer in the USAF, you must be careful of the picture you paint. You are an officer held to a high standard of behavior and discipline. Your past is the past. But with respect to our Core Values of Integrity, Service, and Excellence, how do our enlisted folks perceive an officer who openly admits to previous illegal or unethical conduct . . ." blah, blah, blah. It's not like I was in the infantry. I was just a PR geek who never even learned to fire an M-16.

Many of the newspaper's articles were also distributed across the base e-mail system. This really upset one by-the-book captain. "Perhaps you would be interested to know that my [noncommissioned officers] brought your silly little column to my attention and were perplexed that such unprofessional and meaningless verbiage could find its way into official government computer systems. They will be pleased to know that an officer was the author."

Granted, Alaska is a militarized state with a very serious mission, but give me a break! I was writing a humor column, not military doctrine. The critics didn't bother me much, but they drove Troeber nuts. It seemed to her that everything I wrote would offend somebody and that she was left "cleaning up the mess." She later told me that the column made her life miserable at times because it forced her to smooth over relations with the offended party, but I still cajoled her into continuing the column. As long as I stayed away from military topics, how could we get in trouble?

Unfortunately, I had no idea the charter we took in Valdez was booked through Eielson's own morale, welfare, and recreation department. Nor did I know that the boat was owned by the Air Force. I certainly had no idea that Captain Ed was an Air Force employee. Maybe if that bozo talked a little more, I would have.

"You're in for it, mister," Troeber said as she stormed passed me the morning the column ran in the paper. "I've got a brand-new colonel at Eielson calling me, for chrissake, and I will be damned if the first time I hear from a colonel is when he's yelling at me about your stupid column!"

Apparently the charter operation fell under the colonel's command. Ed worked from Valdez for the 354th Services Squadron, an Eielson organization, and the squadron and its colonel were ticked off about my writing.

"I never wrote that it was an Air Force charter," I told Troeber.

"*They* know you were on *their* boat," she spouted.

"So what?" I said. "Two people on all of Eielson know it was an Air Force boat. Big deal. Nobody else on base knows it was an Air Force boat and an Air Force captain. The only reason they're mad is because they know I'm right. Their operation stinks."

"Well, you need to apologize to them," Troeber said.

"Fine, where's their office? I'll tell them I'm sorry."

"No." Troeber paused. "You need to write another column about the fishing trip. You need to apologize to the charter captain in that column, and you need to write about how good the trip was."

"Are you joking?" I asked.

"Do I look like I'm joking?"

"Sort of," I replied.

"Damn it, Lieutenant, I am not joking!"

"Okay, but who do I apologize to in the column? I never identified who owned the charter or mentioned Ed's full name. If you force me to write an apology, I will need to identify everybody. Right now only two people know that I wrote about a bad Air Force charter operation. If you make me write an apology, everyone on Eielson will know exactly whose charter I went on, and they will then all know that the charter sucks and that Ed is a boob."

"Write the apology," she said. "That's an order."

Some people in the military are ordered to charge machine gun nests. Me? Well, I guess I'm just lucky.

NO OFFENSE INTENDED, BUT HALIBUT FALLS FLAT

Anytime I write a column about the Great Land, I run the risk of offending someone. Last week I did.

Ed is a charter captain for the 354th Services Squadron's charter operation at Valdez. On the surface, I accused Ed of protecting the halibut population by running the charter where we couldn't catch any. That was sarcasm based on the fact I only caught one fish; it was not my intention to criticize Ed or the operation in any way.

My real intention was to chastise those among us who won't question authority. "Had we the audacity to ask questions, we might have more halibut in the freezer now," I wrote.

Fishing is always a gamble. I was simply playing up the fact we didn't catch any fish, which was merely due to bad luck, not a poor charter service. The 354th Services Squadron takes pride in the recreation services offered in Valdez. It is a great service for the men, women, and families of Eielson Air Force Base. Ed and the other people in the operation work for us. Indeed, I had a great weekend in Valdez. When we left, I swore I'd do it again and take advantage of the opportunities Services' offers.

"What's up with the column????" Mark Bevilacqua asked me over e-mail. "I was ready for a good laugh—and I read the 'apology.' Who spanked you down anyway?"

I guess a little humility is good for the soul, but I wasn't humble for very long. I let my stubborn Irish pride get the best of me when Troeber told me that the only way I would be permitted to continue writing the column was to write exclusively about "happy Air Force things."

I politely declined. Angry and feeling vengeful, I headed out to the shooting range next to the pipeline.

Make me write about happy Air Force things, huh? Well, how's this for happy Air Force things? "Crazed officer shoots pipeline with .50-caliber machine gun: Claims that 'ain't nobody seem him do it.'"

September

Primordial Savages

Column Inches

Alaska's a pretty exciting place, but there's not always enough happening at an Air Force base to merit a lot of column inches. When
I refused to write about only "happy Air Force things," effectively
ending my weekly column, Troeber suddenly found a big hole in
Eielson's newspaper that needed to be filled, so two weeks after
the demise of "Cheechako," I received something of a reprieve.

"I know the regular column is over," Troeber said, "but you are
still going to write for the newspaper, right?"

"About happy Air Force things?" I asked with a shrug.

"Yeah, that and other really important things."

"Such as?"

"Well, you know . . . stuff people should know about."

As my boss, Troeber could probably have ordered me to write
about whatever she wanted, but after a couple of weeks of not
writing, I was happy to have a chance to get back in the paper.
There is really no end to what one can say about moose nuggets.

AUTHENTIC ALASKAN ECONOMIC THEORY

More than twenty thousand Alaskans are self-employed, almost
7 percent of the workforce. A drive along any highway or a visit
to any town reveals what most of those masses actually do for
themselves. They walk through the woods, look for caribou

antlers, and sell them for $49.99 at Anyone's Alaskan Trinket Shop.

It's not just the antlers, either. They sell deadfall branches as "authentic walking sticks." They make wooden bear-paw cutouts. For twice the money, they'll turn a salmon carving into a clock. They sell T-shirts with fish on them that say JUST FOR THE HALIBUT. They sell framed copies of a moose picture they took in their backyard. They make scores of plates and towels and pajaMAS and posters that say ALASKA or THE GREAT LAND or THE LAST FRONTIER with a picture of a moose or a grizzly or the northern lights or the Big Dipper.

The really fancy stores don't just sell moose crap coated with polyurethane, they sell moose nugget earrings and necklaces and money clips. Around Christmas, they'll sell a shiny little moose nugget with a Santa Claus hat on it. For a few extra dollars, they'll even gift wrap it in a little baby blue box.

Since the first cheechakos came to Alaska in the 1700s, the Great Land for most has been about making a Great Fortune. Alaskans have made most of their money over the years on fur, on salmon, on gold, on copper, on timber, on oil, and on the massive service industry that supported the fortune seekers.

Still, in coming to Alaska to make a buck, many realized there was a lot more to the frontier than a budget surplus. There was the weather, the water, the sun, the lights, the mountains, the wildlife, the wilderness, the space, and the seclusion.

To enjoy all the state has to offer, though, Alaskans still had to make money. Only a few of the risk takers who came to the state made fortunes. Most had to figure out something else.

When Alaska changed license plate designs, the self-employed sold their old yellow plates for twenty dollars each. Since that was a big hit, they pulled down their old Tesoro Alaska gas station hat and their Fairbanks Golden Days pin from 1976 and their old high school hockey jersey—bloodstains and all. Together, they sold on eBay for almost fifty dollars.

They carved forks out of bones. They cut giant grizzly bears out of tree trunks. They painted the Big Dipper on animal bones.

They salvaged every piece of rusty metal from the junkyard and labeled each as an original Alaskan gold pan. For six dollars more, they will etch your name on it. On Christmas, they will even fill it with real Alaskan snow for ten more dollars.

The Alaska Department of Labor says that the Great Land's industries that rely on natural resource development and extraction, as well as those selling Alaska's beauty, drive the labor market on the Last Frontier. If that's true, the twenty thousand self-employed residents may be onto the most significant economic plan ever to hit the north.

By combining the Great Land's rotten wood and discarded antlers with the millions of tourists who come to the state each year, they may have finally come up with Alaska's only rush-proof economic solution—a solution that reinforces that old Alaskan adage. "One moose's turd is another man's treasure."

The Call of the Weekend Hobby

Dave Swanson turned off the gym-bag-size gold dredge pump, lunatic hope in his eyes, frenzied anticipation in his movements. The pump sucked water and gravel from the side of the stream through a three-inch-wide tube that channeled the rock-and-soil-filled slurry to a "sluice box," where the heaviest bits of rock sediment were separated and caught for further examination. Gold was the heaviest bit of rock that might get caught. When the water stopped rushing over the box, Dave joined his partner, Frank Baxter, who was already kneeling over the contraption. They stroked the finer pieces of gravel with their cold-reddened fingers, searching for a nugget . . . then a flake . . . and then just dust, but there was no gold. Again.

Both men sat back on their legs. Their shoulders sagged. It was near midnight, and they were tired of digging. Their breath clouded the chilled September air through the light rain that had been falling on them all day. The tundra water flowed cold all around them and on them and through the little rips in their rubberized boots. Still, they weren't totally discouraged.

"Maybe we'll find some color tomorrow," Dave told me.

Dave was a weapons safety officer I met during my day-to-day activities at Eielson. Frank was a retired Air Force master sergeant who lived in North Pole. The amateur gold miners had invited me along on one of their last weekend mining trips of the summer, but they didn't promise I would find any of the yellow stuff. While both men reveled in the thrill of finding gold, neither of them planned to quit his day job. In two years of recreational mining in the interior, they had barely found enough gold to pay for their hobby, but they had an infinite amount of hope that one day the endless hours of backbreaking labor in near-freezing water might show a little reward.

Their confidence was inspiring. I caught the fever about three seconds after they asked me to go.

"Are you kidding?" I replied rhetorically. "Do I want to go gold mining? Do I want to sweat on the banks of an Alaskan stream in hopes of finding a fortune? Do I want to do the most Alaskan of all Alaskan things that there have ever been in Alaska?"

Nothing in history defines the Last Frontier more than the great gold rushes: stories from the Yukon; adventures to the Klondike; riches beyond the wildest dreams. September was my tenth month in Alaska. I had been dog mushing and hiking and fishing. I had eaten moose and halibut and salmon. I had even played rugby on a frozen river. None of that could ever compare to the chance to go gold mining, the chance to follow in the very footsteps of gold-seeking dreamers from all over the world. More than a hundred thousand people tried to make their way through Alaska to the gold fields of the Klondike after the 1898 discovery of gold there. This was my chance to do the same thing, sort of. There was no gold fever in Alaska anymore, but still . . . the chance to look for gold was irresistible.

"Sure," I said to Dave. "I'll go."

The first major gold strike in Alaska took place in 1880 where Juneau is today. The Juneau strike was followed by discoveries near Dawson and Circle in the interior in 1886 and 1893 respectively. Nothing generated more excitement, though, than the strike at Rabbit Creek on the Klondike River in 1896. While the discovery was actually in Canada, fortune seekers had to pass through Alaska to get there—a very different Alaska than I had seen near Fairbanks. The towns that sprang up at Dyea and Skagway were lawless frontier towns. Jack London, whose writing popularized the gold rushes more than anything else, ventured to the Klondike through Dyea. His description of the town, as seen through the eyes of the dog Buck in *Call of the Wild*, would be enough to discourage even some of the hardiest souls.

Buck's first day on the Dyea beach was like a nightmare. Every hour was filled with shock and surprise. He had been suddenly jerked from the heart of civilization and flung into the heart of things primordial. No lazy, sun-kissed life was this, with nothing to do but loaf and be bored. Here was neither peace, nor rest, nor a moment's safety. All was confusion and action, and every moment life and limb were in peril. There was imperative need to be constantly alert; for these dogs and men were not town dogs and men. They were savages, all of them, who knew no law but the law of club and fang.

The gold rush towns of Alaska were no place for naturalists or explorers. The prospectors were not impressed by the beauty of the mountains and the majesty of the glaciers. Beginning in 1880, Alaska became a place for risk takers and fortune seekers. The word "cheechako" took on a new meaning during the gold rush. It let you know that you were on trial for your very life. If you made it past the con artists and the knife-wielding back-alley thugs, and if you were able to secure the thousand pounds of provisions the Canadian Mounties required of you to enter their country, you then got your first good chance to die on the steep steps of the Chilkoot Trail. Sixty-three cheechakos died in an avalanche there in 1898. There were thunderous streams to navigate, extreme weather to endure, and always a grizzly or two blocking your way. If you made it past all of that—and more than half washed out—then you had the chance to pan for some actual gold. Good luck finding any. The gold was usually gone by the time you got there. That's when cheechakos like Jack London turned around and headed home. They survived scores of challenges, but they left a year later, still cheechakos, still broke (albeit with some good stories). If you stayed, though, if you had the strength of character to admit loss and try it all again someplace else, well, then you became a sourdough, one of the wise old Alaskans who always knew more than the new guy. It was the sourdoughs who left Canada for the dark interior of Alaska. They found gold at Nome on the western coast later that same great year of 1898, and in 1902 they found it just twelve miles north of Fairbanks. That strike, no doubt because of the indomitable spirit of the sourdoughs, is still producing.

The big companies have the gold market cornered in the interior now, but if you are a cheechako and still hunger for that taste of Alaska—that chance to prove yourself as a sourdough in your own right—there is certainly no reason you shouldn't give it a shot. Just don't expect to get rich.

"On a good trip it [gold] pays for food and gas, and there may be a little extra left, but you can't put a price on the recreational part of it. I guess mining is more about getting away for the weekend than making money," Frank said.

The call of the wild still beckons, just not as loud. The primordial savages have been replaced by a couple of married guys who just want to get out of the house for the weekend.

"Where we're going is pretty far out there," Dave told me in my office the day before we left.

"Where exactly is it?" I asked.

"I don't want to tell you *here*," he whispered. "There's too many people around. It's secret." He was dead serious.

Either that or he was afraid I wouldn't come when I found out how far we were driving. The "secret" mining location was three hours from Eielson, north of Fairbanks on the road to Prudhoe Bay. The forests that surrounded the roads gave way to the featureless tundra of the arctic. Miles from where the pavement stopped on the road, we turned off on a trail that led up into rolling tundra-covered hills that gave me a feeling of manliness to drive over. After following vehicle ruts for five miles and over two thousand-foot-tall hills, we crossed a little stream and pulled up to a larger stream, where we would set up shop. (If they are not presently, all commercials for SUVs should be filmed on this trail—although Dave might not tell the advertising department how to get there.)

"So this is the secret place?" I asked when we got out of the truck.

"Yup," Frank nodded proudly. "We won't see another person for the next two days."

Twenty minutes later another truck came down off the hill, crossed the little stream, and parked two hundred meters past our secret location. It turned out that our site was not *really* secret. It was listed in gold-mining books and is on state land.

The truck was driven by Bob Warren, a major from Cope Thunder. He and his daughter, Heather, chose the same location for their weekend getaway.

"What's this? Bring Your Daughter to Work Day?" Dave said.

So much for the guys' weekend away. *Could it get any less primordial?*

We awoke the next morning to the sound of more visitors to the secret location. A parade of four-wheelers laden with rifles and supplies rumbled down the trail. They were hunters trying to get a head start on the first day of moose season, and they kept coming all weekend, hundreds of them it seemed, each one with more gear and more rifles than the next guy. My moose friend Lennie wouldn't have stood a chance. With antlers like his, he would be the prized kill of the season.

We began the day working the same gravel bar the veteran amateurs selected the day before. Mining for gold is backbreaking work. The goal is to dredge a stream bank, sift through all the sediment, then redeposit the rock and soil somewhere else. No matter how much "waterproof" gear you're wearing, there is just no way to stay dry. Then, when you have busted your back for hours in a stream north of the Arctic Circle—and when you find nothing at all for your troubles—there are just two things you can do to relieve the anger and frustration: drink a lot of beer (anger), then shoot at your empty beer cans with a .44 magnum (frustration). Dave and Frank were well prepared for all possibilities.

After several hours, we had dug a crater at the end of a naturally formed gravel bar. It was the first sign that anyone had mined on the stream in that area. The rest of the area looked more like a moonscape than a serene getaway. Craters where miners had dredged and redeposited and dredged and redeposited dotted the secret stream. Not surprisingly, we found nothing that morning and decided to move.

The ideal place to look for gold is a "natural sluice box" such as the inside bend in a stream. It takes water moving at a certain speed to carry the heavy gold sediment. We wanted to look in places where the water slowed enough to drop the mineral. Dave and Frank had found three ounces at a location farther down the stream the year before, so we headed there. Before long, our dredge was sucking the gravel from the inside bend of a channel where it looked like the stream had not run in hundreds of years. We let material pour out over the sluice for several minutes before we shut the pump off and looked at the box.

"Watch there be nothing," Dave commented, hoping he'd be wrong. He was.

"Yup—see—there's one!" Excitement rose in Frank's voice. "Watch how it doesn't float."

"I see one piece. *Two pieces.* THREE PIECES!"

Dave scurried off to get a vial to put the gold in.

I couldn't believe it. Before the discovery I had sort of thought that the entire thing was a joke, as if Dave and Frank were more like Loch Ness Monster watchers than gold miners. There it was, though: proof of life in the sluice box.

"How much is it worth?" I asked.

"Well, let's see," Frank said, making mental calculations. "Based on the latest price for gold, I would guess that it's worth about one cent."

Once cent? A penny for all our troubles? Where's the beer and the gun!

"The ones we like are the ones you can pick up with your fingers," Dave explained. We were using tweezers.

Dave and Frank were fueled by the discovery of the gold flakes and redoubled their efforts in the stream, but I wanted nuggets, not flakes. Slightly deflated, I decided to take a walk around our claim. The stream and its eroded banks and surrounding hills looked like any terrain features in the Lower 48, but instead of being covered with woods and underbrush, the surrounding frozen "wilderness" was covered only by a thick carpet of tundra—a foot-thick web of lichens and moss and Smurf-size shrubs. Walking on the tundra was like walking on a mattress. My feet never went through the carpet. The tundra acted in unison and gave way under each step until it finally seemed to hit something solid. It was one of the most intriguing and beautiful places I had seen. I felt bad walking along the tundra, though, because I had heard that each step on the stuff can destroy it for years, much like damage to a coral reef. Still, despite the secret location of our claim, I suspected that I was not the first person to walk on the ground surrounding the stream. We had already seen the family from Eielson and the armada of four-wheelers, but the biggest clue that our claim had been well picked over and the tundra well walked over was the rusting hulks of cranes, giant mechanical shovels, and an assortment of barrels and cogs and even a couple of wood stoves. The land we were on was owned by the State of Alaska and presumably under the management of its Department of Natural Resources, but clearly the state was using the preferred big business technique of natural bioremediation to clean up the industrial wasteland that sat along the stream and the tundra.

I left the secret mining location after two days of backbreaking labor with a vial of tiny gold flakes and a little dust for my troubles, but it was still Alaskan gold—the same gold that drove the masses to the Great Land for the past 120 years. Far from being discouraged by my meager findings, I was totally energized. Tourists of all shapes and sizes try their hand at gold mining when they come to Alaska, but they usually go to a business that seeds the soil with bits of gold that people can then pan out. Pretty pathetic, I thought, but I went mining for *real.* I ventured over giant hills (okay, I was driving) and crossed raging streams (well, it was only a few inches deep), and I faced down legions of savage hunters as they encroached on our camp (actually, they just drove by). I had set out to do the most Alaskan of Alaskan things to do in Alaska—and I had done it. That was worth a lot more than the three cents' worth of gold I took home.

Locked and Loaded Ink Pens

The settlement of Alaska by outsiders has been the result of several major "rushes." There were major rushes for fur, for gold, and for oil. Of those money-driven rushes, the gold rush is perhaps the best known and most storied, but the longest-lasting rush, and the one that has brought the most people from the outside, is the military rush. Alaska's strategic value was recognized as early as the state's purchase in 1867. Since then the U.S. armed forces have governed the state, explored the state, built communications systems and transportation routes for the state, evicted the enemy from the state, and erected defenses for the state. Under the military rush, the population of Alaska has increased from thirty thousand in 1867 to six hundred thousand today. Even now more than one-tenth of Alaska's residents serve in or work for the military. Instead of looking for riches, most of those sixty thousand people work for just a small paycheck and a handful of medals. They have transformed the Last Frontier into an offensive platform for operations all over the world. Tex Brown liked to say that Alaska was three thousand miles to anywhere. It takes about the same time to reach New York and Washington as it does Tokyo and Moscow. Today, Alaska and Eielson Air Force Base are just a short flight to virtually every hot spot in the Northern Hemisphere.

Alaska's most powerful offensive punch came from the 354th Fighter Wing at Eielson. "Our job is to deploy combat-ready forces—anytime, anyplace," Tex said at every opportunity: to South Korea, to the Middle East, to Taiwan if necessary. If the "balloon went up" (military-speak for when the shit hits the fan), Alaska's fighters might be the first to arrive at the scene. Two score F-16s and A-10s and their pilots don't go very far without gas, though. The Alaska Air National Guard and their giant KC-135 refueling jets escort the fighters to the combat theater, but even that's not enough. Each fighter requires a maintenance team of up to five airmen to keep the bird aloft. Each of those airmen requires a place to eat and sleep. That requires hundreds more Eielson people to cook food and erect shower stalls and drive tired airmen from the flightline to the mess tent and back. Having doctors and nurses on board to treat anyone who had to eat the military food is a given. All of those airmen then need financial help so they can get paid and legal help so they can prepare wills. And every single one of those people, every single pilot and mechanic and cook, needs a nerdy guy from the public affairs office to write stories about air strikes and rebuilt fighters and Tuesday night's steak sandwich dinner. If the balloon ever went up, virtually everyone in uniform at Eielson would pack his or her bags and fly to the combat theater to actually go to war— even if the weapon was a pen, which everyone knows is mightier than the sword. Anytime, anyplace.

The 354th Fighter Wing and its people work together in Alaska to accomplish one mission: to deploy to a combat theater, fly jets, drop bombs, and kill all the bad guys. Tex called us the "Iceman Team." (Some of the female airmen didn't appreciate the gender-specific label, but they lived with it just as long as Tex did not request that the Dallas Cowboy cheerleaders come to Eielson to entertain the troops—again.)

Most of the time, the Iceman Team was not dropping bombs and killing people for real. Instead, the team spent most of its days practicing combat missions over the skies and on the ground of the frontier with some of the best facilities and most advanced simulation technology available. Units training at Eielson utilize seventeen permanent military operating areas that include more than sixty-six thousand miles of airspace, half a million acres of ground training areas, three bombing ranges totaling more than ninety thousand acres, twenty-eight radar threat simulators, and 235 separate "targets" including vehicle convoys, building complexes, and two airfields complete with runways, taxiways, simulated hangars, and dummy aircraft.

"The ranges around Eielson make it a uniquely great place to train because of the varied environment," said Lieutenant Colonel Scott Adams, Eielson's safety officer and an A-10 pilot. "On one range you could envision yourself working in terrain like western Europe or Korea, while the other range featured flat terrain much like the alluvial deserts of the Southwest—except covered with tundra. The range maintenance people in the civil engineer and [Cope Thunder] squadrons did an exceptional job creating useful and realistic target displays on both ranges. The fact that live ordnance could be used on either range for a good part of the year made excellent training for maintenance and munitions personnel as well as pilots. The size of the airspace created an environment that supported opposed multiship missions very well."

Eielson's A-10 and F-16 pilots trained with one goal in mind: to stay combat-mission ready. The operations group that oversees the training ensures that the pilots train with the correct mix of air-to-ground and air-to-air sorties. Tasked to provide close air support for ground combat troops, the A-10 squadron naturally spent more time focusing on air-to-ground targets, but the F-16 is a multirole aircraft tasked to fight enemy aircraft and ground targets. New or less experienced pilots are required to fly at least ten tactical training sorties per month. More experienced pilots are only required to fly eight per month. Even eight per month is an exponentially larger number than many of their potential enemies fly—who may be lucky to get eight per year. Then there is Cope Thunder. Since the 354th Fighter Wing hosts the multiservice, multination training exercise, the pilots from Eielson get a chance to practice more than most. Cope Thunder scenarios present pilots with highly complex situations all flown on instrumented ranges that allow the mission director to watch the "combat" in real time. Better still, when the pilot lands he can review his performance from taped computer and video footage. Cope Thunder exists solely for the purpose of improving pilot performance and proficiency. The scenarios in the exercises are more challenging than anything they might ever see in their career.

The training for the fighter wing is not restricted to the cockpit. Only a handful of the military personnel at Eielson actually flew jets. Most worked in support roles. Training for combat also stressed the maintenance personnel and the ground munitions loaders and the air traffic controllers. The rest of the fighter wing received most of their wartime training during one of the 354th's combat employment readiness exercises (CERE).

A CERE tested Eielson's ability to accomplish its mission: to deploy combat-ready forces—anytime, anyplace. In the event of a real war, one of the 354th Fighter Wing's missions is to deploy in its entirety from Alaska to the combat theater. If a conflict erupted on the Korean Peninsula, for example, the 354th might be ordered to leave Alaska and find a new home at some other air base in the Pacific; the planners at Eielson call that place Base X. Flying fighter jets to Base X is a fairly straightforward process. The pilots pack their bags; the jets take off, refuel a couple of times, and land at the new base. However, the wing must prepare for the worst—a scenario in which Base X is simply a concrete runway in the middle of the desert or jungle. Then what? The fighter jets are actually some of the last aircraft to leave. Somebody needs to get to Base X first to make sure that the runway is operational and that maintenance people are ready to receive aircraft and that somebody has at least gone into the air traffic control tower to turn the lights on. In a wing-wide war deployment, that advance party might begin movement as early as ten hours from the receipt of their mission. They fly aboard transport aircraft from the Air Force's Air Mobility Command that will continue to rotate in and out of Eielson until all her people are on the ground. Behind the advance party are more support personnel, such as air-base defenders and cooks and engineers. Spare aircraft parts might move third. Finally, when Base X is operational, the fighters will launch. Even then it's not complete. The accountants and public affairs people and hundreds of other noncritical support airmen have to leave. Despite the seeming complexity of the movement, officers at the wing say the entire process will take only three days. They should know. Not only do they practice the movement in the CERE, the fighter wing actually deploys to a real Base X as much as twice a year.

In just seventy-two hours of a wing-wide deployment, Eielson Air Force Base would be a ghost town with only civilian employees and a handful of people in uniform to mind the shop and refuel other transient aircraft that are on the way to the war. Oh—and let's not forget, a lot of spouses and children who were just separated on virtually no notice.

A full wing-wide deployment, though, is quite rare. Several years ago the Air Force adopted the Air Expeditionary Force (AEF), a new wartime concept to "organize, train, equip, deploy, and sustain itself in the dynamic 21st century global security environment." Under this concept, the Air Force provides rapidly responsive, tailored-to-need aerospace forces, ready to conduct military operations across the full spectrum of military missions. Using the AEF, the Air Force no longer waits until a crisis erupts to select a response force. The Air Force identifies the responders years out. The AEF includes more than 150 combat aircraft of all types and up to fifteen thousand people to support them. The units don't always know where they're going or what they'll be doing. They simply train for all contingencies and then wait for the call—a sort of quick reaction force for the global theater.

The 354th Fighter Wing and its F-16 and A-10 squadrons took over the AEF requirement for the Asian theater soon after the United States attacked Taliban and al-Qaeda forces in Afghanistan in 2001.

Danger Close

Almost a year before the September 11 attacks, more than five hundred airmen from Eielson were given word that in December 2001 they would be assigned to the AEF rotation that was currently supporting Operation Southern Watch in Kuwait and over the no-fly zones of Iraq. For the airmen at Eielson, the ninety-day deployment to Kuwait was nothing out of the ordinary. They and their families prepared as every military family has prepared for hundreds of years. After the attacks, the deployment took on new meaning. Eielson's airmen knew they were scheduled to go to the Middle East; they just weren't sure what they'd be doing. Would they be flying missions against Iraq? Would they be supporting the operations in Afghanistan? Most did stay in Kuwait supporting the ongoing mission there, but soon after their arrival, the 18th Fighter Squadron "Blue Foxes" and ten of their F-16s were formally tasked to conduct combat operations over Afghanistan. Thanks in large part to their training in Alaska, the Blue Foxes were ready.

"The training airspace in Alaska significantly contributed to our ability to conduct the full spectrum of training required by our pilots," Lieutenant Colonel Burt Bartley, commander of the Blue Foxes, told me after their return from the war zone.

To prepare for possible combat in Afghanistan, Bartley and his Alaskan fighter pilots trained to fight around the clock. With no enemy jets in the air and American troops on the ground, the Blue Foxes concentrated their training on close air support (CAS)—the ability to shoot guns and drop bombs on a dandelion while flying at more than five hundred miles per hour. Each F-16 pilot from Eielson who would deploy to Afghanistan was qualified and practiced in CAS operations, which are often made difficult by the high speed of the F-16. With night vision goggles strapped on, they even trained to hit the dandelion in the middle of the night.

"We take the mission of CAS very seriously and are keenly aware of the risk to friendly forces when operating in close proximity to ground troops," Bartley said.

To round out defensive training for the Blue Foxes, Eielson planners turned on their mechanical threat systems that simulated al-Qaeda terrorists shooting surface-to-air missiles at the fighter. Training on Alaska's ranges was excellent and, according to Bartley, gave his troops the skills they needed to do serious damage in Afghanistan if they needed to.

They did. On March 2, 2002, U.S. forces attacked a Taliban and al-Qaeda stronghold south of Kabul in the Shah-i-Kot valley. Operation Anaconda was planned as a simple mission to flush out any enemy resistance in the mountainous region but turned into a complex and vicious infantry battle that in its opening hours claimed the lives of eight Americans and wounded sixty more. Helicopters were shot down. Soldiers were ambushed. One American was even captured and killed as U.S. forces watched from their reconnaissance planes. It didn't matter where on the ground the special operations forces from the Army, Navy, and Air Force found themselves. The moment they tried to move, they came under fire from the enemy, who was holed up in fighting positions that offered good cover and concealment. According to official U.S. Army accounts of the battle, the special ops forces called for close air support within the first thirty minutes. Battle managers flying high over Afghanistan called in Eielson's Blue Foxes. At first, the guys on the ground asked the jets to strafe the enemy with their 20mm machine guns, bringing the pilots extremely close to the fight, but after the bullets ran out, the F-16s only had massive five-hundred pound bombs. Dropping bombs near ground troops is a delicate matter. Pilots usually make sure nobody is within 1,300-feet of their intended target. Anything within that 1,300-foot radius is subject to bomb fragments or even a direct hit. Guys who fight on the ground call it "danger close." With special operations troops a mere two hundred feet away from the target, "danger close" took on a whole new meaning. Despite the risk, the special operations forces asked the Blue Foxes to drop their bombs on the target.

"Hearing all the good guys on the ground pinned down by enemy fire and knowing there's only so much you can do about it was tough," Captain Chris Bacon, an F-16 pilot with the Blue Foxes, told the *Goldpanner* when he returned to Eielson later. "We went in and dropped bombs to help those guys out as best we could."

To make sure they hit the right targets, Bartley's pilots talked to Air Force forward air controllers on the ground who were practiced at the art of calling for close air support in support of ground troops. Fighting alongside Army Rangers and Navy SEALs, the controllers used laser target designators to get the exact location of the enemy position, then radioed the target's map coordinates directly to the fighter. When the pilot received the information, he punched coordinates into his F-16, which had its own global positioning system, and then let loose one of his bombs—a laser-guided GBU-12 five-hundred-pound bomb that would zero in on the target coordinates from as much as three or four miles out. Although inside the danger zone, the U.S. troops had one thing going for them when the bombs landed: They knew when they were coming and when to duck. The bad guys didn't.

After the F-16s got into the fight, no more Americans were killed, but a lot of al-Qaeda and Taliban were. The bullets and bombs dropped by the Blue Foxes helped the ground forces move on the enemy and ultimately destroy them. Between Anaconda and other smaller battles in Afghanistan, the Alaskan-based fighter squadron shot a lot of brass and guided 120 bombs to their targets on "a few of their 232 missions."

"It was [emotionally] very hard to see people out in the open trying to get away from you," Bacon told the *Goldpanner.*

The requests from the ground controllers weren't always designed to kill the enemy. "In many cases we flew missions over ground forces just to provide presence in the air," said Bartley. "I remember one [forward air controller] that asked for and received air cover during one cold dark night in the hills near Kowst. He stated over the radio that he did not need us to service any targets, he simply wanted the forces on both sides of the battle to hear aircraft overhead. This made the friendlies feel safe in order for them to get a little sleep. Obviously his intent was just the opposite for the Taliban and al-Qaeda forces."

The Blue Foxes and five hundred other airmen from Eielson returned safely to Alaska by March 22. It was the first time most of the pilots "had dropped bombs in anger," Bartley said. Even though only a few of the airmen had their finger on the trigger, all five hundred who supported the deployment, as well as the special operations forces who stayed behind on the ground during the fight, were integral in making the mission a success. During their AEF deployment Eielson's F-16s alone flew 818 sorties for almost 3,200 total hours, four times the peacetime rate. More than 2,000 of the flying hours were spent in operations over Afghanistan.

Bartley credited their success to preparation. They trained so hard in Alaska that they were ready for anything in combat. "Cope Thunder Exercises definitely helped the Blue Foxes prepare for combat," Bartley said. "The scenarios in Cope Thunder allow the pilots to train in much more difficult scenarios than we should have to face in combat. Any fighter pilot will admit that they learn something every time they go fly."

The same could probably be said for the Air Force men and women who supported the pilots on the ground. The jet maintainers got to work on a plane after a major fight. The cooks got to create new culinary delights to celebrate the successful combat. The doctors and nurses learned to treat new illnesses created by the party food. Every nerdy guy from the public affairs office got something more exciting to write about than gold mining and moose nuggets.

OCTOBER

The Return of Winter

REAL ALASKAN OR NORTHERN COUCH POTATO?

Cheechakos are often shocked by their first winter. It's too cold and too dark to do just about anything except lie in bed and find out what it means to be a manic depressive. By their second winter in Alaska, cheechakos *might* begin to realize that Alaska in the winter is not so bad. In fact, they realize it's not much different than Florida in the summer.

Floridians often start their cars and crank the A/C just as Alaskans start their cars to let them warm up. Tourists avoid Florida's heat in the summer just as they avoid Alaska's cold in the winter. Florida locals stay inside to enjoy the air-conditioning just as Alaskans stay inside to enjoy the heat.

About the only real difference is guilt. How could Floridians stay inside in the air-conditioning when there's an ocean beckoning them to come and swim? Or a marlin begging to be caught? Or an orange waiting to be picked? That adds up to a lot of guilt. There's none of that in Alaska.

There's nothing wrong with staying warm inside when it's pitch-dark and below zero outside. The water is all frozen. The fish are all under ice. The car needs to be plugged into a socket when it's not being driven. There's nothing to do outside in those temperatures. So why feel guilty about sitting at home and watching TV all day?

Television programming even seems to lend itself to an Alaskan winter. All the shows are in their new season, and the four-hour time difference from the East Coast means Alaskans can watch more of the really good programming without staying up late. The *Tonight Show* starts at 7:30 P.M. Sundays are even better. The first football game starts about the same time you wake up, and the night game, which usually ends near midnight on the East Coast, is over before nine.

So cheechakos *might* feel that the winter months are not so bad and that they can survive their second season. Notice, though, that I said they *might* think that. If they do, a real Alaskan will recognize immediately that they are still cheechakos.

If a newcomer had actually made the transition from cheechako to real Alaskan, he would realize something entirely different. He would realize that despite a commendable lack of pink flamingo lawn decorations, Alaska in the winter is, in fact, similar to Florida in the summer—and if he wastes it by spending all his time inside he should feel just as guilty as Floridians who huddle around the air conditioner.

Yes, the water is frozen, but there are hot springs just north of Fairbanks that you can swim in even when it's 50 below. Yes, the fish are under the ice, but with an ice auger and a little shelter, you can fish for trout all day long. Yes, the car will freeze if it's not plugged in, but you can run it every now and then—or even let it freeze completely. It will thaw pretty quickly if you slide a hot little charcoal grill underneath.

There are plenty of things to do outside during an Alaskan winter: cross-country skiing, dogsledding, snowmachining, ice skating—you name it. One way to identify real Alaskans is by the activities they do when it starts to get a little cold and dark, but don't assume that all the people outside in winter are real Alaskans. Some cheechakos try their hand at winter activities, too. The real test of whether the person snowmachining is a true Alaskan is to look at your watch.

If it's after 5:00 P.M., the person you're looking at is probably a cheechako. *Real* Alaskans know that the new episode of their favorite sitcom starts at 9:00 P.M. on the East Coast but can be seen on a satellite dish at 5:00 P.M. in Alaska, and they don't feel the slightest bit guilty about watching it from the warmth of their living room.

The Two Things to Do in October

The fallen leaves were still blowing on the ground when the first snow fell in Alaska that winter. The wispy white flakes that sparked excitement in my heart as a child on the East Coast brought instead a sense of sadness and a feeling of loss. Gone were the sun-filled days of the interior's summer. Gone was the warmth and the embrace of the outdoors. No more Saturday afternoon rugby games. No more drives up to the top of Murphy Dome to enjoy the moments of twilight and dawn between the sunset and sunrise. No more parties that seemed to last for days. The most remarkable summer of my life was officially over. All I had to look forward to was the darkness and the bone-chilling cold of interior Alaska. The comforter on my bed was of very little comfort, but I clung to it in hopes that it was all a bad dream. The cold temperature on my exposed face indicated otherwise. We used to joke that the Alaskan summer was great—both days of it. That joke seemed as accurate as ever now that the snow was falling.

There are only two seasons in the interior: summer and winter. Summer begins the first day of breakup and ends when the first snow falls in September or October. There is no time in between for spring and fall. There is no time for April showers and May flowers. There is no time for walks among the mottled leaves of Central Park. There is only nine months of hibernation followed by three months of celebration (and most of the three-month celebration is done wearing a jacket). No matter how cold the late days of summer might be, Alaskans will push their sunshine celebration until the last possible minute—until the first snow falls on them while they are water-skiing in the middle of

Harding Lake. Then, very reluctantly, Alaskans will hang up their skis and wet suits for winter.

Even though there is no fall season to help you prep for the cold months, Mother Nature will often give an Alaskan a couple of days to react. More often than not, the first flurries of the season hit in late September but melt in the sun's waning radiation, giving Alaskans a week or so to winterize their homes before the real snow—before October, that is, because October snow does not radiate away. When October snow hits the ground, it stays right where it is until breakup.

Therefore, despite my desire to hide under the warmth of my blankets, I got out of bed, dressed, and called Curtis and Kevin. There was a lot of work to do at Harding Lake. We had to put new insulation around the doors. We had to chop wood and stack it in the shed. We had to put away the water skis and tubes and life jackets. We had to put the boat on the trailer and cover it. Worst of all, we had to take the dock out of the lake, which was already showing ice crystals around its shore. I definitely needed help.

It's funny how things work out. I had no problem getting Curtis and Kevin out to the lake to help me put the dock and the boat *in* the water. Taking it out of the water was another issue. After two hours of waiting, it became apparent that both of my good friends were exercising their "out clause."

"Yeah, sure. I'll help you take the dock out. I can get there after I finish painting my garage."

"But you don't have a garage."

"Right . . . what I meant to say was that I'll get there after I finish this book I'm reading."

"Good. But you are coming, right?"

"Yeah. Just after I finish painting."

"I thought you were finishing up a book."

"Yeah, right. I'll be over right after that. You get started now, and I'll be there later."

There is a lot of work to get done in those short days between the September snow and the October snow. Despite the encroaching winter, there was quite a reward waiting for me at the end of my chores. Sleep. Lots of it.

After months of Fort Yukon politics and Cope Thunder complaints and Harding Lake parties and Valdez fishing adventures, the darkness of winter turns out to be not so bad. I worked at Eielson from 7:30 A.M. to 4:00 P.M. my first Monday in October. With the major exercises and community events completed for the year, I was able to leave work early and be home by 4:45. I had a fire lit in the wood stove by 5:00 P.M., and I covered myself with blankets on the couch. I was asleep in ten minutes and did not wake until 6:00 A.M. I got more than twelve hours of sleep my first night in October—about the same as I got in four days during the summer. The rest was wonderful, but best of all, I realized that I had not missed a damn thing. The lake was frozen. It was dark outside. Everyone else was asleep, too. The hibernation had begun.

However, after a few weeks of short workdays and long nights of sleeping, I began to realize that hibernating through the *entire* winter might not be the way to go. When I arrived in Mississippi, I quickly surmised that I would be able to see all that there was to see in six months. I was wrong. It only took two. After ten months in Alaska, it became clear that it would take years to see the entire state. A typical tour for an Air Force officer is three years. I was concerned that I wouldn't see half of the state in that time, so my first few weeks of guilt-free hibernation gave way to feeling that I should be out doing things. Surely not all action takes place in the summer. There had to be a whole new winter wonderland to discover in Alaska's interior.

"So what are we doing tonight?" I asked Kevin Groff on the phone. He had been in the state for more than a year and was likely to know what there was to do.

"Well, I guess we could grab a bite to eat and go to the movies," he said.

"No. I want to do something *Alaskan*."

"Well, in the middle of winter getting a bite to eat and going to the movies is a pretty Alaskan thing to do. Come on, let's go to the movies. What do you say?"

"No way. There must be something *Alaskan* to do. Maybe there's a dogsled race or something. What are *real* Alaskans doing right now?"

"They're probably sleeping or at the movies," Kevin said. "There's a new Jackie Chan flick in town. You know he does all his own stunts."

How can any self-respecting male pass that up?

So Kevin and I headed off to Fairbanks to do what he said was a very "Alaskan" thing to do in the winter: go to the movies. There was nothing else to do in October, he said, because people were still recovering from the summer. Believe it or not, it looked like Kevin was right. There was hardly an open parking spot in the lot. Everyone, it seemed, was at the movies. On closer inspection, many of the moviegoers had the telltale short hair of military personnel. Where were all the Alaskans?

I enjoyed the film, but I had really wanted to do something "Alaskan." I blamed myself. Calling an Air Force guy originally from Virginia is probably not the best route to take when you're looking for some local flavor. Curtis, who had spent virtually every day of his life in Alaska, would have been a much better person to call.

"Hey, Curtis," I said to him on the phone the next day, "I should have called you last night. I was looking for something to do. Unfortunately, I called Groff and not you. What were you up to last night?"

"It was too dark when I got home from work. I just went to sleep."

"Oh . . . okay," I said. "Well, now that you're all rested, do you want to do something tonight? Is there anything going on?"

"Well, it's discount night at the movies. You want to catch the new Jackie Chan flick? Pretty much everyone I know is going."

Going to the movies during a Fairbanks winter is a double

negative. Not only does it cost money, it costs a lot of calories. A jumbo bucket of buttered popcorn has enough calories to support an Arctic Survival School student for two weeks. So what? Nobody notices love handles under a parka, a fleece, two flannels, and an undershirt, and if a guy finally gets lucky, both he and his partner are likely to keep half their clothes on. Lingerie in Alaska is essentially anything warm with zippers. If you're in the military, though, you can't just let yourself go and refill that jumbo bucket of buttered corn. They have weight standards in the service—even in the Air Force, where drill instructors are not allowed to drop an airman for pushups—but trying to maintain a trim figure in the middle of a frontier winter is a challenge. The snow made it hard for me to run outside. I didn't know how to ice-skate. I didn't own cross-country skis. If you want any more excuses, I can list a page worth of them. It takes a level of motivation and a certain amount of equipment to exercise outside during an Alaskan winter. I was not willing to make the mental or financial investment. Instead, I opted for the well-heated gym at Eielson Air Force Base, where Groff and I spent an hour pretending to lift weights. If my exercise regimen did not work, I could simply buy a couple of new, larger uniforms. They cost about the same as cross-country skis but were much more practical.

Curtis had another philosophy on winter sports: *Why suffer if someone else was doing it better for you?* As a graduate of the University of Alaska–Fairbanks, Curtis did take some interest in sports. He couldn't play hockey to save his life, but Curtis was a rabid fan of the UAF Nanook hockey team, which faced off for its first games in October. With nothing else going on that month, going to the Nooks games with Curtis that October became the perfect "Alaskan" thing to do (even though the fights were not as good as those in the Jackie Chan film).

Like any good fan, Curtis had a love-hate passion for the Nanooks. In the 1980s, Curtis felt pity for the team, the only one, it seemed, in collegiate hockey that wore the experimental waist-to-ankle Cooperalls instead of the standard knee-length Breezers. In the early 1990s, he cheered for the team's new coach, Don Lucia, after his Nooks began beating up on the powerhouses of college hockey that had been looking for an easy win. The Nooks had a few good years in the early 1990s but began a downhill slide by the time Curtis got the chance to cover them as a sports reporter in Fairbanks.

"The Nanooks waited for me to become the local sports guy before they started to suck on a national level," he said. "I got so sick of running sound bites like 'Holy cow, we just need to do a better job of putting the puck in the net' or 'If that puck had bounced a bit differently in a couple of games, it would have turned our season around.' For the record: No, it would not have. They were horrific."

Even a horrific team can get worse. On October 7, sophomore defenseman and Fairbanks native Erik Drygas lost his skate edge in practice and fell head first into the boards, fracturing his fifth cervical vertebra. The player was partially paralyzed and could only move his extremities in a limited manner. Curtis was the first to report the story, which quickly grabbed national media attention. The players were unaccustomed to intense media scrutiny and very shaken up by the accident. Drygas was one of their own, and the Nanooks didn't like anyone from outside the fraternity—especially a reporter—talking about the accident and its impact on the team. When Curtis arrived at practice the next day, the team treated the journalist "like a leper." Curtis was sympathetic. He visited the player in the hospital, and while the team members at Drygas's bedside quietly scowled, the injured player was "remarkably calm and polite." A class act.

Drygas remained paralyzed but continued his hockey career as head coach at West Valley High in Fairbanks, the same school he was recruited from to play at UAF. His team finished first in its league and competed for the state championship in 2002. The Nanook insider is now also the official radio color commentator for the UAF hockey team. Drygas is revered as a hero in Fairbanks. His number 21 jersey was retired and hangs in Carlson arena.

Even though they dropped every game that month, there was something heroic and undeniably appealing about the Nanooks. That year, seven of the starters were Fairbanks locals. Eleven total were Alaskans. Division I college teams almost never boast that much local talent. More than even the baseball Goldpanners, the University of Alaska Nanook hockey club was the hometown team.

As part of his ongoing effort to convert me to a hockey fan, Curtis introduced me to what he called the "best old-time hockey movie ever made." *Slap Shot* features a financially broken team of questionable quality and its shady coach (Paul Newman) who tries to save them. Newman is great in the movie, but his character is completely upstaged by the nerdy yet savage Hanson brothers. With heavy-metal long hair, dark GI-style glasses, and foil wrapped around their fingers, the Hanson brothers were the natural choice for Curtis and me to imitate at the biggest Halloween party in the interior. The celebration and best-costume contest took place at the Howling Dog Saloon, a seasonal honky-tonk in the gold-mining town of Fox, about fifteen minutes north of Fairbanks. The bar included an outdoor volleyball sand court and amazing pizza from a guy born in Brooklyn, but the centerpiece and most notable feature of the saloon was a stage covered by "holy carpet." Somehow, the bar owners had recovered the red carpet that President Reagan and Pope John Paul II made a joint appearance on at Fairbanks International Airport in 1984. In my opinion, the rug could not have found a better home. Just about every type of constituent from interior Alaska found his or her way to the Howling Dog Saloon in the summer to pay respects to the holy carpet. On that Halloween night, the Hanson brothers arrived, too. (Well, two of them did. Groff was supposed be the third brother. He backed out at the last minute—something about "spending time with his wife." Whatever.)

Curtis and I stood in a line of costumed revelers, waiting for our chance to be judged by applause in front of the eclectic crowd at the Dog. We had received dozens of compliments all night from hockey-savvy Fairbanksans, but the real test was a group of about fifteen Nanook hockey players. They had already expressed their hatred of Curtis during the early Drygas coverage, but the team was beginning to warm to the journalist and his upbeat coverage of their dreadful season. The costume might prove to them finally that Curtis was not so much of an outsider. When he and I took center stage on the holy carpet like the president and the pope, the crowd went nuts, and nobody cheered louder than the Nanook players. Dressed as Jake Hanson, Curtis had finally bridged the gap between outsider and insider. Credit should also go to the atmosphere of the bar. At the season finale of the Howling Dog Saloon, roughnecks, pilots, soldiers, hockey players, and even journalists were all the same—which is to say, they were all pretty much drunk.

Self-Medicating in the Interior

Drinking beer—and lots of it—seemed common in the circles of people I knew in Alaska my first year. The rugby players drank a lot. Many young servicemen drank a lot. The Royal Air Force drank more than a lot. Other young residents seemed to drink a lot. There were exceptions, of course. Some of the people I knew drank only in strict moderation, but for the most part, the people I knew in Alaska drank like they were at a party. It did not seem to me that people were drinking because they had a dependency. It just seemed to be part of the Alaskan and military culture of "work hard, play hard." Of course, that does not make it okay.

Mixing alcohol with an environment as extreme as Alaska's can only result in trouble, and I wasn't long in the state before I saw the results firsthand. I noted at the ice rugby game during my first week in Alaska that people drank more on the frontier than they did in the Lower 48. Very few players on my collegiate or men's club teams on the outside drank at the rate of some of the ruggers on the inside. Because of that, the headline in the *News-Miner* the next morning was not a significant surprise.

SNOWMACHINER KILLED IN
COLLISION WITH TRUCK

Like many of the ruggers, Dan Johnson drove his snowmachine to the ice rugby game at Pike's Landing. While driving home on the Chena River after the post-game party, Johnson collided with a pickup truck that was parked on the river. Police estimated the thirty-two-year-old rugger was riding between forty and sixty miles per hour. He was killed instantly.

I don't know how much Johnson drank the afternoon after the rugby game. Many argued later that it didn't matter. While there are no laws against parking in the middle of the Chena River, it is generally understood that the river is used as a frozen highway in the winter. It would have been very dark on the river, and a snowmachine driver who had not been drinking at all might have met with the same results. Either way, it was one of the more tragic stories I encountered in Alaska. It wasn't the only one.

The crash phone rang early one morning with an atypical message. Instead of a plane crash, the command post was alerting us to a suicide attempt. An airman who was depressed turned to the bottle for relief, but that only made the depression worse. The airman parked his car near the pipeline, channeled the exhaust into the car, and waited with the engine running. The security police found him and broke the car's glass before it was too late.

The consequences of excessive drinking were not confined to the people I encountered. Nearly 14 percent of the Alaskan population is dependent on alcohol or drugs—twice the national average—and the consequences are telling. According to the Alaska Advisory Board on Alcoholism and Drug Abuse, the forty-ninth state has the highest alcohol-related death rate in the country—11.2 percent compared to 5 percent nationwide. Alaska has the highest incidence of fetal alcohol syndrome (FAS) in the country—four times the national average. Alcohol is implicated in 83 percent of child abuse investigations, 63 percent of sexual assaults, and 60 percent of domestic violence reports.

The problem is acute in the rural sections of Alaska, where deaths are seven times the national average. Ernie Turner, the director of the Alaska Division of Alcoholism and Drug Abuse, described in testimony to the Senate Committee on Indian Affairs in October 2000 the ravages alcohol had on one Native family in western Alaska:

> A young man with a wife and three children leaves his village to go to Nome to buy supplies for the whaling season. His mother has given him money for an outboard engine that will drive the family omiak, a skin boat, during the hunt. Also in his packsack are several ivory carvings that he hopes to sell for money to buy food and other supplies for his family. When he wakes up in the hospital he doesn't remember much of the first night in town or the three days that followed. He does recall that after the ivory shop did not buy his carvings he went to a bar to look for potential buyers. Now he has none of his mother's money. His carvings and the rest of his possessions including his return ticket home are missing. Physically and emotionally he feels terrible.
>
> His family will make do on supplies donated by relatives. His physical injuries will heal in time. His family will accept him back. He can carve more ivory. His mother will still acknowledge him as the lead male elder in the extended family.
>
> But he returned to the village ashamed and desolate. His

emotional pain became an excuse for drinking more alcohol. While drunk he got angry and beat his wife. Eventually she left him, leading to more guilt, more pain, and more alcohol. He got drunk one more time and fatally shot himself with a high-caliber rifle. Then it was his children who felt pain, guilt, and anger. Then it was his children who began to drink.

According to Turner, Alaska Natives make up about 17 percent of the population of the state but 38 percent of those who die by suicide and 31 percent of those who die by homicide.

The problem of alcoholism in Alaska is not a secret, and it appears that the federal and state government as well as tribal organizations are creating legislation and programs to deal with the problem. Studies show that the costs associated with alcohol abuse approach $450 million a year. Creating laws and culturally sensitive programs could lower that number and, more important, help the Alaskans who are affected by the disease. In his testimony, Turner, a recovering alcoholic, cites a growing number of people who have recovered from alcoholism or avoided it outright. Even the story about the ivory carver who took his own life ended in hope: The man's oldest son stopped drinking, went to training, and began work as a counselor. Still, everyone who has an opinion acknowledges that there is more work to do. For the sake of those affected, I hope so.

Alcoholism and its resulting depression and suicide seem to come with the cold, dark, and loneliness of the Last Frontier. Witnessing the effects of the disease was the only significant negative aspect of my life as a cheechako.

NOVEMBER

Alaskan for a Day

WHEN A CHEECHAKO BECOMES AN ALASKAN

Newcomers in Alaska have been called "cheechakos" since the gold rush. The moniker is almost used as a warning to *real* Alaskans. *You're going hiking with that guy? He's a cheechako. You better bring extra everything for him.* To Alaskans, calling a person from the Lower 48 a cheechako is almost a defense mechanism. Can you really rely on a person who thinks a dogsled is something you push your pet around in?

"He was a newcomer in the land, a che-cha-quo, and this was his first winter," Jack London wrote in his short story "To Build a Fire." London's cheechako doesn't think of the cold weather as anything more than an inconvenience. A temperature of –50 "did not lead him to meditate upon his frailty as a creature of temperature." Of course, London's hero froze to death moments later. A cheechako often thinks he can gut it out. An Alaskan knows when he's beat.

But when does a cheechako finally become an Alaskan? Historically speaking, newcomers remained cheechakos until they survived their first winter, but the harsh winter isn't all it's cracked up to be anymore. Modern technology has warmed the homes, cars and planes have replaced dogsleds, and fast food has replaced subsistence hunting.

It takes a newcomer a year to officially become a legal resident in Alaska, but if the challenge of winter is gone, what, then, is the challenge of an entire year? Just because you can collect a check from the Permanent Fund does not make you an Alaskan. Thousands of military personnel who have not lived in Alaska for years are still considered residents—but do they know how to defrost a frozen engine?

Alaskans are often described by their physical attributes—big, bearded, bold men. Granted, there are many big, bearded, bold men in Alaska, but that's no different than places like Samoa or Finland or Cuba. Has Castro secretly been an Alaskan all this time?

Maybe it's the physical attributes *plus* the lifestyle. That must define an Alaskan: the big, bearded, bold, meat-and-potato-eating, dog-mushing, Carhartt-and bunny-boot-wearing, tobacco-chewing, moose- and grizzly-shooting, ice-fishing, four-wheeler-and-pickup-driving, beer-drinking man. But not all Alaskans fit the stereotype. In the new millennium there are as many rough Alaskan men sipping cappuccino, visiting the tanning salon, and reading interior decorating magazines as there are at the gun shop. And let's not forget that the Alaskan population is not all male. Around mining camps and military bases there is at least one woman for every thirty-two men.

So what really makes an Alaskan?

The truth is, I don't know.

You Can Take the Boy out of New York, but...

I had promised my editor, Staff Sergeant George Hayward, that I would write a feature that answered the question I had contemplated for the last year: When does a cheechako really become an Alaskan? But I was stuck.

November marked both my twelfth month in Alaska and the beginning of my second winter. According to gold rush tradition, I was no longer a cheechako and could now boast that I was finally an Alaskan. Without the challenges of the gold rush days, without the thieves and claim jumpers, and without the daily need for an outhouse, the old gold rush tradition that made a cheechako an Alaskan after just one year seemed bunk. I knew dozens of people in the Air Force who didn't seem any more Alaskan than Ricky Martin. My boss at Eielson, Captain Sandy Troeber, rarely experienced Alaska outside of her official duties. Others, like my good rugby and Air Force friend Mark Bevilacqua, didn't want anything to do with the Great Land. Even Kevin Groff, who played on the rugby team and had been in country almost two years longer than I had, seemed more southern good-old-boy than Alaskan sourdough. And what about General Tex Brown? *First, let me remind you that Alaska was never an independent republic like Texas. Second, although Alaska may be bigger than the Lone Star State in size, it cannot match Texas in heart or beauty, and certainly not in cattle.*

In contrast, there were other Air Force members who seemed Alaskan within moments of their arrival in country, no one more so than F-16 pilot Doug "Stoli" Nikolai. He was an outdoorsman, he was an excellent ice rugby player, and he counted dozens of longtime Fairbanksans as friends. Alaskans didn't introduce Stoli as a fighter pilot or an Air Force captain. They simply introduced him as Doug or Stoli or the best rugby player in Alaska. You would probably have had to follow him to work Monday morning to realize that the guy trained to drop bombs and kill people for a living. While I spent many weekends hiking with zoomies like Groff and Bevilacqua, Stoli spent his weekends surrounded by bearded locals whose skill at snowmachine driving was equaled only by their skill at drinking beer. Except for his folksy Fargo accent, an Alaskan would be hard pressed to guess that Stoli was from one of those Lower 48 states up there by the Great Lakes ya' know.

So if time in country was *not* the major factor in determining whether one was a cheechako or an Alaskan, then what was? More important, did I rate? I still couldn't grow a full beard. I didn't know how to hunt. My fishing trips looked more like episodes of *The Three Stooges*. I had once even had my big four-wheel-drive vehicle pulled out of a ditch by a two-wheel-drive pickup with Lower 48 plates!

Stoli, on the other hand, was able to do all those Alaskan things well. He caught salmon without worry. He hunted grizzly and moose. If the government would let him, he could have grown a beard that rivaled Ted Kaczynski's.

Then again, Groff, whom I didn't really view as an Alaskan, could do all those things, too—and with an entire can of Redman chew between his cheek and gum. So perhaps I still had a chance. I had learned to tolerate outhouses over the past eleven months. Perhaps I had also learned to become an Alaskan, but how could I know for sure?

I asked some Alaskans what they thought the criteria were. Everyone agreed that a cheechako does not automatically become an Alaskan after one year. As bush resident Kurt Smith said, "That is from the old days when a person had to deal with sixty below and mosquitoes living in a cabin." It just does not apply anymore. However, none of them could point to any other rule of thumb. It's hard to describe, they said. It's hard to put into words. It's more of a state of mind, you know? Curtis's news director, Charles Fedullo, tried a little harder. He spouted off a list of criteria that a cheechako might use to determine whether or not he's an Alaskan:

- When sunny 32-degree weather leads to shorts and a T-shirt, sitting on a deck, and knowing spring has sprung.
- When an eight-hour drive to catch some salmon is a day trip and a five-pounder is so small you throw it back.
- When petite women in Carhartts driving big trucks are more appealing than the *Sports Illustrated* swimsuit issue.
- When driving a truck from village to village on a river rather than a road is not a big deal.

- When you see the governor or one of Alaska's U.S. senators having a cup of coffee and you decide to tell him or her how to solve the state's financial problems or the unrest in the Middle East—and he or she seems genuinely interested.

It's more than just a checklist, according to Curtis. He described becoming an Alaskan as "an evolution of spirit," and that characterization seemed to hold a lot of water with the others. The evolution came for Stoli on a snowmachine trip with other Fairbanks ruggers to Kurt Smith's cabin in the Wrangell Mountains. He said he simply fell in love with the wide-open spaces, the isolation, and the sheer beauty of the country. From that point on, Stoli knew for sure that he was an Alaskan. As for Fedullo, who came to Alaska from Philadelphia, he knew he had become an Alaskan when he returned to Alaska from the "outside" and saw "the stunning white mountains surrounding Anchorage, the rugged, harsh, alluring beauty of Denali, and the shimmering sunlight on the waters of Southeast." When he watched the geese fly south while sitting on a river in the interior, he knew he was home.

"You know the tranquility people all over the world search for is yours. You know the treasure of unbridled opportunity has found you, and you know that if you leave Alaska it will always be a part of you. Its beauty surrounds you, its frontier spirit and independence envelop you, and you know that someday you may leave, but nowhere else will ever be home," Fedullo said.

Journalists can be a bit schmaltzy (Fedullo's own words). Guys who live in the bush without electricity or running water get to the point a little faster, and in the opinion of Kurt Smith, one becomes an Alaskan only after "one has been tested."

The Test

Exactly what sort of test Kurt Smith had in mind as a criterion to become an Alaskan was not clear. Did I have to survive a bear attack? Spend three nights outside in subzero cold with only pajamas? Or simply run the Iditarod? Ice rugby in December seemed to me a pretty good test, and almost freezing to death near Granite Tors in May might also have been a candidate, but I think one of the more difficult tests I encountered in Alaska came right inside my own Bronco that November.

I'll call them Joe and Sarah, and neither of them shut up. Every discussion with Joe ended in a comparative study of the relative strengths of comic book heroes. Discussions with Sarah just never ended.

> **SARAH:** Oh my God, did you guys hear about Jewel? She was like living in a van before she got her record deal. How amazing is that?
>
> **JOE:** Spiderman! Are you kidding? He wouldn't last a minute against Superman.
>
> **SARAH:** And her songs are so nice. Have you listened to the words? They're amazing. She's like a poet and a singer, and she plays guitar, too.
>
> **JOE:** Now, if you want to put the entire Fantastic Four against Superman, you might have a shot.
>
> **SARAH:** Speaking of Batman, wouldn't it stink to have to wear that rubber suit on the movie set? It must have gotten so hot. It's amazing what they do in Hollywood. Did you guys watch *ET* last night? Wasn't it amazing? Did you see Tom Cruise? Isn't he like so hot?

In my quest for something *Alaskan* to do that winter, Curtis had invited me along on a weekend trip to the "Blixt cabin," a rebuilt cabin that a trapper named Fred Blixt built in 1935 in the White Mountains. The state Bureau of Land Management owned the cabin and rented it to the public for twenty dollars a night. Curtis's friend Jack Ruben had secured a reservation at the place a few months before in hopes of a romantic weekend with his new girlfriend, the ever-talkative Sarah. While the two got along well in the carnal sense, Jack realized by November that he couldn't stand the girl during the other twenty-three and a half hours of the day. Still, to Jack, the thirty good minutes were worth keeping the relationship alive, so to share the pain, Jack invited Curtis and another friend, Joe, along. Not wanting to be totally outnumbered, Sarah then invited one of her friends, Amber. The six of us met at Curtis's apartment in Fairbanks and all squeezed into my Bronco for the three-hour drive. Lacking a good radio signal that far north, we were forced to listen to the motor-mouths.

It was dark by the time we mercifully arrived at the Blixt cabin that Friday night. The log structure sat on top of a hill at the end of a snow-covered driveway just off the Elliott Highway. When we got out of the Bronco, we realized the temperature had dropped considerably. Since the insides of my nose were frozen, I scientifically guessed that it was colder than 20 below. That in itself was not a big deal, but since there was no electricity at the cabin, it meant that I would have to run the Bronco every now and then to make sure the engine did not freeze. (If Joe and Sarah kept up with their talking, I also eyed the Bronco as an alternate sleeping location.) The log cabin itself was a simple affair. It measured twelve by twenty feet. There was a small deck outside the door. Inside there was a wooden table, a wood stove, a bed, and a loft. Curtis, Amber, Joe, and I tossed our gear up to the loft. If there had been room for five in the loft, Jack probably would have thrown his gear upstairs, too. Instead, he had to share the downstairs bed with his talkative sort-of-girlfriend, Sarah. Fearful of having to engage her in dialogue one-on-one, Jack convinced all of us to stay up late that first night for cocktails and Trivial Pursuit. With a fire raging in the stove (we had to open the cabin door to stay cool), we answered questions about JFK and traded toasts until early morning, and with a little help from Uncle Bud, I managed to survive the first night of the test.

"All right, everybody up," Curtis shouted after what seemed like just a few moments of sleep. "Breakfast is ready, and the Nanooks take to the ice in two hours. I have bacon, eggs and pancakes. Who wants what?"

Nobody responded verbally, but the extraloud tossing and turning translated into something like "Bite me!"

Curtis had magically resurrected himself without damage from the previous night and created a dazzling breakfast on the hot plate of the cabin's wood stove. He had reminded us several times the previous day that the UAF hockey team would be on the road playing hockey powerhouse Michigan State University the next day, but I didn't appreciate what a big deal this was to him until he pulled a small radio out of his bag.

"Everyone up!" he ordered. "Beating the Spartans anytime is huge, but beating them at home is unthinkable. Today, we will three-peat."

"But I thought the Nooks, like, suck this year?" Sarah grumbled from her sleeping bag.

"Maybe so, but not in Michigan. Now eat so we can find a place where we can catch the UAF signal. I can't get a thing in this cabin."

"What, are you planning to listen to the game somewhere outside?" I asked.

"Where else?"

So the day's adventure was scheduled. The month before I had yearned for something totally *Alaskan* to do. Curtis showed me the Howling Dog Saloon. Now he was upping the stakes—catching a hockey broadcast on a hilltop somewhere near the Arctic Circle. Surely this would qualify as an Alaskan experience, ranking with ice rugby and dog mushing and gold mining. More important, it just might get me away from the marathon talkers in the cabin.

"I'll take two pancakes and bacon," I said as I crawled out of my sleeping bag. Fortunately for us, everyone else went back to sleep.

A Modern-Day Sourdough

"Just a little higher," Curtis hollered back to me. "I almost have a good signal."

He kept the radio next to his ear as he fiddled with the dial in an effort to tune in the UAF radio station that would carry the Spartans-Nooks game live. We trudged along a deer path that traced a route ever higher on the hill behind the Blixt cabin. I had fallen slightly behind the newsman as I struggled in my complete Air Force arctic gear with a case of beer on my shoulder. You might not think that you can warm up by moving when its −20, but you can. I was dripping with sweat by the time we broke through the spruce forests onto a bald peak high above the cabin.

"I got it!" Curtis shouted from the top of the hill. "I definitely have it . . . wait a minute . . . no way . . . the Nooks are up one-nothing! Oh my God!"

The Nanooks held the worst record in their division but had managed to score the first goal against the top-ranked Spartans in the opening minutes of the game. Curtis was in a state of euphoria as I neared the top of the hill.

"Well, then," I said, wiping sweat from my brow, "that must call for an ice-cold beer."

"Good call, Flynner," Curtis said.

I handed him a bottle of Redhook ESB with my gloved hand. In this particular game day celebration, Curtis and I faced a unique challenge when it came to our stash of beer—*how the heck to keep it warm!*

"It's frozen," Curtis said. "Give me one from the bottom."

With the hockey game in the background, Curtis and I set out to find wood for a fire that would keep our beer from freezing. When all was said and done, we had the most unusual campfire I had ever seen. Bottles of beer protruded from the rim of the fire like petals on a flower. *The things they don't teach at Arctic Survival School!*

We were completely set up by the end of the first period. We had selected the site because of its radio reception, but our location also offered a vista that couldn't be beat. Our hilltop gave way to spruce about forty feet down the slope. Smoke from the cabin's chimney drifted through branches even lower. From our vantage point, we could see down a small valley for miles. Except for the smoke from our chimney, there were no other signs of life in any direction—not that we would have noticed. We cheered boisterously from our solitude with each pass of the puck and shot on the goal. The valley reverberated with the cheers of two Nooks fans.

Then, mostly because we were sitting on the snow, we started to get cold. A year earlier, I might have pretended that the cold didn't bother me, that I was too tough to be bothered with a frozen backside, that I was stronger than the average guy and capable of withstanding the cold Alaskan afternoon. Perhaps I would have considered this another Alaskan strongman "test." For some reason, though, I looked at Curtis and admitted the unthinkable. "Hey, I'm a little cold. I bet we would be a lot better off if we weren't sitting in the snow."

"What are you saying?" Curtis replied. "Do you want to go back to the cabin?"

"No, not at all. I just think it would be warmer if we weren't sitting in the snow."

Curtis, who later admitted that he was cold, too, saw my revelation and admission of the cold as a watershed moment.

"Cheechakos are an excellent target for ribbing, but it has little to do with their toughness," he said. "After all, they made a choice to come to Alaska, and that alone is a bold move, but surviving Alaska is another story. There have been many Paul Bunyan types who approached the Last Frontier as a land that needed to be tamed, but many of *them* were tamed young and have headstones to prove it. You don't force your will on Alaska; you take what it gives you. It could mean staying at base camp when the weather on Denali turns sour or water-skiing on Harding Lake until the sun goes down—*in late June, it never will.* To be an Alaskan, your life depends on how fast you adapt."

Jack London's cheechako in "To Build a Fire" tried to tame the Alaskan weather when he opted to lead his dog team from one location to another in extreme cold weather instead of staying at the roadhouse until the temperature broke. He confidently drove on and ultimately froze to death after he failed to build a fire, but he had failed his "test" long before he froze to death. He failed the moment he chose to force his will on Alaska.

Of course, none of that was on my mind that day on the hill. The only thing I wanted to do that day was spend the rest of the afternoon on top of that cold mountain enjoying the hockey game, so I decided to go back to the cabin to get something to sit on so we wouldn't freeze in the snow. In that simple act of common sense, Curtis believed, I had finally evolved spiritually from the status of a cheechako to that of an Alaskan.

"When Flynn returned to the hill with a bench he lugged up from the Blixt cabin, it was clear he had come full circle," Curtis said later. "Sitting in the snow makes for great journal entries, but freezing your ass off is for cheechakos."

I had again worked up a sweat by carrying the spruce bench up to the top of the hill, but it was worth it. I grabbed a beer from the fire and sat on the warm wood as the sun began to glow red above the southern horizon. Curtis sat down next to me, placing the radio on the bench between us. We both sat in silence watching the sun drop, seemingly in time with the waning minutes of the hockey game on the radio. My body was warm, and the Nanooks were ahead. Facing yet another upset at home, the Spartan fans fell silent so that for a moment the only sound coming over the radio was the clack-clack of skates hitting the ice in Michigan.

Eielson Air Force Base and Tex Brown and my ridiculously large vehicle payments all faded away until all that was left was the sun's warm rays on my frost-nipped face and always the clacking skates of the Nooks, the Nooks, the Nooks. For that wonderful moment on a hilltop in the White Mountains on a bench listening to a Nanook game, as the sun dipped below the ridgeline, I also believed in my heart that I had finally become an Alaskan.

WHEN A CHEECHAKO
BECOMES AN ALASKAN (CONT.)

So what really makes an Alaskan? In a word—attitude.

Only a "can-do" attitude makes the Alaskan. Real Alaskans strive to make the best of conditions not too favorable for human life. If the river freezes, use it as a highway. If the ground won't support a road, fly there. If it's dark outside all day, sleep more. If the sun keeps you up in the summer, go hiking. If you're cold, for Pete's sake, put on a jacket!

On the other hand, having a "can-do" attitude is not quite enough for a cheechako. For cheechakos to become Alaskans, they actually have to know how to *do* all of those things for themselves, and they have to be able to do them *by* themselves, to survive the daily "tests" of the Great Land: to drive a dogsled, to kill their own dinner, to survive outside in subzero cold, and to live without indoor plumbing. Cheechakos have to be able to do all those things to become Alaskans. Perhaps most important, they have to love every minute of it, and they have to pray for nothing more than a chance to do it all again the next day.

DECEMBER

Permanent Skin Damage

○ ○ ○ ○ ○ ○ ○ ○ ○ ○ ○ ○ ○ ○ ○ ○ ○ ○ ○ ○

Things to Do When it's Only 30 Degrees Below Zero

Fairbanks in December is miserable for a cheechako. It's too cold and dark to ski or make a snowman or go out to dinner. It's too cold and dark to kiss or rub noses or hold mittens. It's definitely too cold and dark to decorate the house with lights and wreaths and plastic reindeer. Fairbanks in December is just about too cold and dark to do anything, for a cheechako. That's exactly how it's supposed to be.

Alaska has never been the kind of place where someone from New York can just show up and settle as if nothing ever changed, as if he or she had been there all along. You have to earn your keep in Alaska—especially in Fairbanks and the interior. You have to learn to understand the place and all of its cold and all of its oddities. Most important, you have to earn the trust of the people, who, on the surface, probably seem insane.

They are not. They just do things a little differently. Instead of going out to eat in Greenwich Village, Alaskans grill up the shoulder of a moose they shot in September. Instead of making a snowman, Alaskans carve sculptures out of blocks of ice. Instead of playing a nice game of softball in Central Park, Alaskans play tackle rugby on a frozen river when it's 30 below zero.

Well, maybe not all Alaskans. When I arrived in the state a year earlier, I supposed all locals were like the thick-jawed, hard-drinking, tough-as-nails guys (and one girl) I played ice rugby with on the Chena River. After meeting dozens of Alaskans like news-anchor Curtis Smith and reporter Brian O'Donoghue and salmon slayer Darin Hagen, I realized not all Alaskans were like the people I met at the rugby game. As I suspected when I first arrived in the state, *those guys really are insane,* and it has little to do with them being Alaskans. They're like any number of lunatics worldwide who took up rugby because it was slightly more fun than banging their heads against concrete walls. Rugby players are essentially crazy wherever they live. In Alaska, it just happens to be easier to play the game on a well-packed frozen river covered with three feet of powdery snow. For a lunatic rugger, playing when it's 30 below zero is just a bonus, but while you might need to have a screw loose to play rugby on a frozen river in Fairbanks, you certainly do not need to be insane to live in the interior—although it doesn't hurt.

I never met a Fairbanks rugby player who seemed unfit for the interior. On the contrary, they seemed to embody the spirit on the inside of Alaska: rugged and rowdy and yet, somehow, still really nice. How, then, could I not return to Pike's Landing for another game of ice rugby? After all, the weather report said the temperature might climb as high as 25 below.

J. D. Williams, the player I first met the year before, was already seated at the bar when I arrived for my second ice match. He still looked as menacing as ever, but I had grown much more comfortable around the gruff Alaskan. I grabbed a seat next to J. D. and ordered a beer; although it was early, I hoped to get a few in before the game started. (I was comfortable around J. D., but it didn't make getting tackled by him any more pleasant.) My friends from the Air Force—Stoli, Groff, and Bevilacqua—arrived later. To my surprise, some of the new Air Force guys we had recruited the night before at the officers' club showed up, too. We all enjoyed a good pregame celebration before we finally opened our rugby bags and started getting dressed for the match.

I watched with fond memory as the rookies piled layer on top of layer until they looked like something approaching the Michelin Man. I had done the same thing a year ago—before I had been tested. For my second game, I dressed in the same uniform I wore in June: shorts and a jersey. Stoli, of course, wore the same thing. As we headed out the door to the ice, one of the rookies asked with a surprised look if that was all we were wearing.

"Hey, rook, when you've been in Alaska a while you'll learn to deal with the cold, too."

Call it Alaskan. Call it tough. Call it insane. The truth is, my legs almost froze completely solid that day. I didn't get feeling back for a couple of weeks, and when it did come back it felt like I was being bitten repeatedly by a raccoon. Call it the myth of ice rugby.

I had supposed the year before that all *real* Alaskans went barelegged on the ice. Again I was wrong. Dog musher/rugger Kurt Smith, who had come out of the bush for the big game, dressed warmly for the match, as did several other *real* Alaskans. Each of them had played in shorts at some point in his career and then wisely decided to never do it again. They were "normal rugby players," and even they considered guys like Stoli, who repeatedly went with just shorts, as completely insane.

"You'll lose feeling for good next year," Stoli said after the game. "Then it never hurts to get tackled. How else do you think I'm the best rugby player in Alaska?"

There are dozens of myths about the Great Land—the toughness of the Alaskan man, the viciousness of the Kodiak bear, and the beauty of the frontier. Some are true. Some are not. I met some extremely tough men and women in Alaska. I also met some wimps who seemed more Alaskan than the tough guys. I never encountered a Kodiak or grizzly or black bear in Alaska (and I'm really happy about that), but I did my best to outsmart or outrun hordes of Alaskan mosquitoes. I came face-to-face with Alaska's famed beauty at every step—while dogsledding across the interior or flying over ANWR or simply staring at the northern lights. I also stumbled over a lot of litter and industrial waste.

In most cases, the truth behind Alaskan myths isn't too far from the surface. There is one Alaskan truth, however, that I had never even considered until my Alaskan tour of duty with the Air Force came to an end. It is a truth about the effect that all the other myths have on the people who live in the Great Land—the effect of the cold, the darkness, the beauty, the size, the isolation, the danger, the failures, and the victories. When taken together, the myths of the Last Frontier make Alaskans the closest, friendliest, and most honest people I have experienced anywhere in the country. To be one of them, even as an Air Force guy on a tour of duty, was to be a member of a strong community that interacted like a family.

Things to Do with Frozen Hair

I left Alaska after my tour at Eielson ended. I left the Air Force soon after and moved back to New York—to a slightly grimy pre-war high-rise on the Upper East Side of Manhattan. What a change it was. There were more people in my building than in the town of Salcha and more people in my neighborhood than in the entire state of Alaska. I didn't cook anymore, let alone kill or catch my food. Somebody from around the corner came to pick up and wash my laundry. My Bronco, my beloved truck that had gotten me out of scores of deep ditches and snowdrifts, was gone, since I couldn't afford six hundred dollars a month to park it in a garage. About the only thing that reminded me of Alaska was the rugby field at East River Park. It hurt just as much to get tackled on the pebble-and-glass-strewn dirt pitch as it did on the ice, but nobody in New York drank before the game to make it feel better. *The wimps waited until after!*

Kurt Smith moved to the bush because he couldn't tolerate the rat race in Fairbanks. He wouldn't stand a chance in New York, he told me later. "All the people, everywhere you turn, everybody going someplace and looking at their watches. No way, man." I have felt that way countless times since leaving the frontier.

On the other hand, New York seemed to be particularly strong where Alaska was weakest—pizza and women. Neither was very good in the interior, but both were exceptional back in New York. I found my favorite pizza in Brooklyn and my favorite woman in Greenwich Village. Lori Ann moved from Seattle to New York shortly after her last visit to Alaska in June. We moved in together after I arrived and immediately longed for the spacious cabin I had lived in at Harding Lake. We settled in a nine-hundred-square-foot railroad-style apartment that exhausted more than half of my meager salary as a corporate PR flack. Our neighbors screamed and shouted and left their trash in the hallway by our door. Our only views were the faces of people looking back at us from the windows of their own cramped railroad apartments. Sadly, there were no more moose. However, if rats are your thing, New York is truly the cat's meow.

"What are you guys waiting for?" Curtis says to me every time we talk. "Get your behinds back up to Alaska. We'll leave the light on for you."

I did make it back for a short official visit after Curtis landed his biggest catch on the Kenai Peninsula—Jody, the salmon slayer's sister. The two got a chance to get to know each other after Curtis moved from the interior to Anchorage for a job with the local NBC affiliate. With the slayer back on the peninsula, nothing could possibly get in the way of a nuptial. Although a New Yorker again, I managed to land a lead role as best man at their wedding. "Just as long as you can make a toast better than you can catch a salmon," Curtis said. *Not much better, as it turned out.*

Kevin Groff, his wife, Jennifer, their two children, their two dogs, and their two cats also showed up for the wedding. He had been transferred to Elmendorf Air Force Base in Anchorage, where his wife already worked. Despite the fact that they owned a house north of town, their days in the Great Land were numbered. The Groffs had to leave the reception early and drive back to Anchorage to finish packing for their next tour of duty, in San Antonio, Texas.

A couple of months after the wedding, Curtis, Kevin, and I got back together, this time in New York for my wedding to Lori. Curtis and Kevin were my groomsmen, but another friend from Alaska was not. Mark Bevilacqua, whom I almost froze to death with on Granite Tors, also came to the wedding. Perhaps he was put off by not being in the wedding party. Perhaps it was love at first sight. Whatever the case, the rugby-playing airman charmed my sister into moving back with him to Arizona, where he had settled after leaving the Air Force. He claims his intentions are honorable.

It took me a little more time to get back in touch with Doug "Stoli" Nikolai. I didn't speak with him again until I sat down to write about Alaska. Stoli was always the prime example of an outsider who became an Alaskan, but even he had to leave the Great Land. Although his Air Force travels have taken him around the world, one conversation with him made it clear that his soul was still far north. He owns a little piece of land on a river in the shadow of Denali, and as he described the bend in the river and the salmon that swam through it, I was certain that he was getting choked up. He stopped in the middle of his explanation. After a long pause, he changed subjects and started talking about outhouse racing and snowmachining and the people and the animals and this crazy day at the Chena hot springs when it was 50 below and the guys shaped the women's frozen hair into beer holders. "Now, that was something you'll only do in Alaska," he said.

Stoli was near the coast of Florida when we talked, but I believe he would have traded places with an Eskimo adrift on an ice float in a New York minute. Despite his leaving the state, I have no doubt that the best (and craziest) rugby player in Alaska is still very much an Alaskan.

I retained my Alaskan identity, too—although probably only for a week. It didn't take many cab rides and hip East Village bars and upscale TriBeCa restaurants to turn me back into a cheechako. If I had woken up in an Alaska winter one morning after a few months of Manhattan living, I probably would have died of shock.

Even so, Lori and I talk about Alaska all the time. With a new-born son, we wonder if it would be wrong to deprive a small boy of the fresh air and beauty of Alaska. We wonder if it's more dangerous to live in New York City or to use communal outhouses. We wonder if he would prefer Yankees games at fifty dollars a ticket or Alaska Goldpanners games at five dollars a ticket. (If we have to sell urethane-covered moose nuggets to make a living, tickets better not cost more than five dollars.) And always, there is the call of the wild.

"What are you guys still doing in New York?" Curtis asks on the phone. "The hot dogs give you cancer. The cab drivers are rude. The Jets and the Giants stink. Rudy Giuliani is no longer mayor. Get out of there! *Les Miserables* and *Cats* are coming to Anchorage this summer!"

As long as New York continues to make the best pizza and bagels in the world, it's going to be a hard decision. City or country? New York or Alaska? Rats in the subway or moose blocking your front door?

Sometimes, usually on weekends in the mountains—er, hills—of upstate New York, I take my Bronco out of storage, play a song from the younger world, close my eyes, point my nose north, and smell a fresh breeze off the coast of Valdez or a spruce tree near

Fairbanks or a campfire on a hilltop in the White Mountains. As the wilds of the Great Land come to me, I break out into a smile. For that wonderful moment in the hills of upstate New York, I become like, and yet unlike, an Alaskan all over again.

Acknowledgments

I wish to thank the warriors of Air Force public affairs, especially Major Valerie Trefts, Master Sergeant John Norgren, Technical Sergeant Elton Price, Staff Sergeant Adam Stump, Major Mike Haller, Major Sandra Troeber, and my first editor at *The Goldpanner*, George Hayward. Thanks also to Captain Daniel Sullivan for his expertise in combat mobility, to Master Sergeant Lawrence Gilman for his thoughts on the Army in Alaska, to Lieutenant General Richard "Tex" Brown for giving my column a chance in his newspaper, to the men and women of the 354th Fighter Wing "Iceman Team" for reading that column, and to Lieutenant Colonel James Rice and all the "Roughnecks" from Alpha Company, 1st Battalion, 69th Infantry Regiment, for supporting me while I completed this project. I couldn't have written this book without any of you.

Special thanks to Martin Lueck and Günta for their hospitality, to Joel Wieden, Patrick Price, Kate Lee, and Richard Abate for making this book a reality, to Sean Desmond for making this book a story, and to my true friend Curtis Smith for educating me about Alaska then and reminding me about it now.

Finally, I could never have undertaken, let alone completed, this project without the support of my family, especially my wife Lori Ann. Thank you.